CONTEMPORARY MORAL THEOLOGY

Volume I

QUESTIONS IN FUNDAMENTAL MORAL THEOLOGY

Contemporary
Moral Theology

Volume I

QUESTIONS IN FUNDAMENTAL MORAL THEOLOGY

by

John C. Ford, S.J. *and* Gerald Kelly, S.J.

THE MERCIER PRESS LTD.
Cork

First published, June 1958
Second printing, November 1958
Third printing, August 1959
Fourth printing, October 1960

Imprimi potest: WILLIAM S. BOWDERN, S.J.
Vice Provincial, Missouri Province
September 26, 1957

Nihil obstat: EDWARD A. CERNY, S.S., D.D.
Censor Librorum

Imprimatur: ✠ FRANCIS P. KEOUGH, D.D.
Archbishop of Baltimore
March 21, 1958

Foreword

FROM 1941 TO 1954, the present writers were responsible for notes on current moral theology published in *Theological Studies*. These annual (now semiannual) surveys are so comprehensive that the treatment of any given topic must necessarily be rather brief. For this reason, our friends often suggested that we select the main problems of contemporary moral theology and give each problem a more thorough treatment. It seemed to us that by following this suggestion we might not only synthesize our most important efforts but also put them on a more permanent basis and thus make a contribution to the moral theology of our time. But, in carrying out this plan, we discovered that a mere selection from our previously published "Notes on Moral Theology" would not suffice. The selected topics had to be reorganized, greatly expanded, and developed anew. The result is the present volume.

This is the beginning of a projected series on contemporary moral theology, each volume of which will deal with special questions pertaining to one part of moral theology. In this first volume of the series we include the questions in fundamental moral theology that we consider to be especially interesting or difficult. The material is partly a survey of contemporary theological literature and partly our own thought on the various topics.

In referring to other theological literature, we have not limited ourselves to the years when we wrote the annual surveys of moral theology for *Theological Studies*. Some of our material greatly antedates those surveys, and we have made liberal use of the "Notes on Moral Theology" written after 1953 by John R. Connery, S.J.; Joseph J. Farraher, S.J.; and John J. Lynch, S.J. Moreover, we tried to keep abreast of current publications up to the time when we composed this volume. We are deeply conscious, however, of the fact that many of the questions in this book are still being discussed and that much valuable material has been published since we completed our own manuscript and gave it to the publisher. We should like to include references to all these more recent writings; but that is obviously impossible. There must necessarily be a considerable gap between our latest references and the date of publication.

It would be impossible for us to mention here all those who have helped us complete this work. It would be less than just, however, if we did not express our thanks publicly to John R. Connery, S.J., professor of moral theology at West Baden College; Joseph S. Duhamel, S.J., professor of moral theology at Woodstock College; and John J. Lynch, S.J., professor of moral theology at Weston College, each of whom read our entire manuscript and made helpful suggestions.

THE AUTHORS

Contents

[vii]

Contents

CONTEMPORARY MORAL THEOLOGY

Volume I

QUESTIONS IN FUNDAMENTAL MORAL THEOLOGY

1

The Church and the Moral Law

B ASIC TO THE discussions which will follow is the distinction between ethics and moral theology. Ethics is the
science of morality based on reason; it considers man in the
natural order, possessed of a natural destiny. Moral theology
includes ethics and goes beyond it—absorbs it, so to speak.
Moral theology studies man in the supernatural order, possessed of a supernatural destiny; it is a science based not
only on reason—nor principally on reason—but especially on
revelation and on the teaching of the Church. Reason is the
supreme argument in ethics; authority is the sovereign
guide of the theologian.

The foregoing summary, though perhaps trite, is essential
to a proper understanding of subsequent discussions. And,
with this distinction in mind, we shall now follow a procedure which to the unbeliever may seem to be a vicious circle:
we shall ask certain questions about the need and extent of
the authority of the Church in moral matters, and we shall

answer these questions principally on the basis of that same authority. To the theologian this is a logical method; to the unbeliever, and even to the devout Protestant, this poses the problem: "The Catholic Church asserts that it does not make the laws of God; but it claims to be the only authentic interpreter of them. In other words, the laws mean what the Church says they mean. That seems to be tantamount to making the laws." No doubt, this is a real problem for non-Catholics. The only answer to it, however, is to be found in a treatise on apologetics. For us, the problem is already solved; and we shall proceed from the general premise as stated: the Church has authority to teach the laws of God. With this general premise in mind, we shall examine more minutely into some of the questions pertinent to a complete understanding of it.

In the present chapter we shall consider the necessity of revelation and of an authentic interpreter of revelation in moral matters, particularly with reference to the natural law. The two following chapters will treat specifically of papal and episcopal teaching.

NECESSITY OF REVELATION

The Vatican Council clearly taught that, although supernatural revelation is not an absolute requisite for knowing the natural truths of religion, yet it is a moral, or practical, necessity for knowing such truths with ease, with certitude, and without any admixture of error.[1] The Vatican Council did not expressly mention the natural law as a part of the truths of natural religion. The following paragraphs from

[1] Cf. DB, 1786.

[4]

the introductory section of the encyclical *Humani generis*,[2] however, clearly refer to the natural law:

Truth to tell, it is not surprising that discord and error should always have existed outside the fold of Christ. For though, absolutely speaking, human reason can, by its natural powers and light, arrive at a true and certain knowledge of the one personal God whose providence watches over and governs the world, and also of the natural law which the Creator has written in our hearts, still not a few obstacles prevent reason from using its natural ability effectively and profitably. For the truths that have to do with God and the relations between God and men transcend completely the sensible order and, where there is question of their practical application and realization, call for self-surrender and self-abnegation. In the acquisition of such truths the human intellect is hampered not only by the impulses of the senses and the imagination, but also by evil passions stemming from original sin. As a result, men readily persuade themselves in such matters that what they do not wish to be true is false or at least doubtful.

It is for this reason that divine revelation must be called morally necessary, so that those religious and moral truths which are not of their nature beyond the reach of reason may, also in the present condition of the human race, be known by all with ease, with unwavering certitude, and without any admixture of error.[3]

NECESSITY OF THE MAGISTERIUM

Implicit in this papal statement is the necessity, not only

---

[2] Aug. 12, 1950; *AAS*, 42 (1950), 561–78.

[3] Cf. *Ibid.*, pp. 561–62. The translation used here is that of A. C. Cotter, S.J., *The Encyclical "Humani Generis"* (Weston, Mass.: Weston College Press, 1951), pp. 3–5. This book contains the original Latin text of the encyclical, with an English translation on opposite pages, and an excellent commentary.

of revelation itself, but also of the teaching of the Church, because the pope speaks of those outside the fold of Christ. This point was later made explicit in his radio message on the Christian conscience as an object of education.[4] Here the pope said:

But where can both the educator and the one to be educated find the Christian moral law with ease and certitude? In the law of the Creator, engraved in the heart of every man [cf. Rom. 2:14–16], and in revelation, that is, in all the truths and precepts that the divine Master taught. Both of these—the natural law written in the heart and the truths and precepts of supernatural revelation—Jesus, our Redeemer gave to His Church as the moral treasure of humanity in order that she might preach them to all creatures, explain them, and hand them on intact and safeguarded from all contamination and error from one generation to another.[5]

In his commentary on the *Humani generis*, A. C. Cotter, S.J., compares the teaching of Pope Pius XII on the obstacles to a correct knowledge of the natural truths of religion with that of St. Thomas in the *Summa contra gentiles* [6] and makes an apt observation. According to the pope the obstacles are: the truths themselves lie beyond the range of the senses; their practical application calls for severe self-control; and man's evil inclinations tend to interfere with right judgment. St. Thomas, on the other hand, enumerates lack of leisure for serious study, lack of interest,

---

[4] Mar. 23, 1952; AAS, 44 (1952), 270–78.

[5] Cf. *Ibid.*, p. 272. English translation based on *Catholic Documents*, 8 (July, 1952), 2.

[6] Cf. ch. 4. A readable translation of the *Summa contra gentiles* is given by Anton C. Pegis in the Image Book edition entitled *On the Truth of the Catholic Faith*. Image Books are published by Doubleday & Company, Inc., Garden City, N.Y., at prices well within the range of the ordinary income.

and lack of mental equipment, as the reasons for the moral necessity of revelation.

"The difference in the reasons assigned," says Father Cotter, "seems to lie in this that the encyclical speaks of non-Catholic theologians or scholars whereas St. Thomas had in mind the generality of the human race." [7] In a word, it is not only the common man, but also the intellectual, who needs revelation and the guidance of the Church in order to have an adequate knowledge of the natural law. Our daily experience, as well as the testimony of history, confirms this; and a few examples from the literature of the last two decades or so will serve to illustrate it.

ERRORS OF INTELLECTUALS

To state all the basic errors of unguided intellectuals, even of our own times, would require volumes. For the purpose of illustration, however, it may help to cite a few that seem to merit (if that is the word) special mention. There is for instance, Oliver Wendell Holmes, Jr., who until recently has been the idol of lawyers and legislators of the United States. Natural law, as we conceive it, was an absurdity to Holmes. According to him, the essence of law is physical force: in a word, might makes right. [8]

Another influential writer was Professor Earnest A. Hooton of Harvard University, an outright exponent of extreme

[7] *Op. cit.*, p. 57.
[8] For an analysis of Holmes' juristic philosophy and its effect on American legal thought, see John C. Ford, S.J., "The Fundamentals of Holmes' Juristic Philosophy," *Proceedings of the Jesuit Philosophical Association*, 18th Convention, 1941, pp. 49–81, reprinted by Weston College Press, Weston, Massachusetts. And for a well-drawn portrait of Holmes' attitude on religion, see John E. Coogan, S. J., "The Religious Ultimates of Justice Holmes," *American Ecclesiastical Review*, 132 (1955), 73–83.

philosophical determinism. In his *Crime and the Man*,[9] it is assumed that along with the physical organism, the entire mental, volitional and emotional qualities of the character are inherited, and that conduct, social behavior, and cultural adjustment are completely determined. Obviously, in such a philosophy there is no place for natural law.

In holding that the end of law is the progressive unfolding of the human powers, the former Dean of the Harvard Law School, Roscoe Pound, went a long way against the biological determinists. Nevertheless, though one of the profoundest thinkers on law and right outside the Church, the Dean never reached the real truth about law. He simply handed over the law to a new absolute, society. For him, the one moral measure of law was the will of society.[10] This is nothing else but the fundamental principle of the totalitarianism that has crucified our twentieth-century civilization.

It is hardly necessary to mention here the philosophical and religious errors of Freud which have had such devastating effects on moral thinking and conduct. Some of these errors will be referred to later. But we think that, before concluding our brief list of erring intellectuals, something should be said about Albert Schweitzer and his thesis on

[9] Cambridge, Mass.: Harvard University Press, 1939.

[10] Cf. Karl Kreilkamp, "Dean Pound and the End of Law," *Fordham Law Review*, 9 (1940), 196–232. Our material about Professor Hooton and Dean Pound is taken from "Recent Canon Law and Moral Theology: Some Important Items," *Theological Studies*, 1 (1940), 412–43. This article, which was published anonymously, was the first of the surveys of moral theology which have appeared annually (and recently semiannually) in *Theological Studies*. This first survey was prepared by the editor, William J. McGarry, S.J., and some collaborators. The subsequent surveys were all signed. It is hardly out of place here to say a word of praise for Father McGarry, whose premature death was a real loss for American theological thought. It was mainly through his genius and hard work that *Theological Studies* was successfully begun.

"The Ethics of Reverence for Life," [11] because excerpts from this beautifully sounding thesis are often cited with approval even by Catholic writers. Whatever may be said of the genius and personal heroism of Dr. Schweitzer, his concepts of life and ethics are morally unsound. His thesis of reverence for life applies to all forms of life; he recognizes no essential distinction between the various forms. Moreover, besides seeing no essential difference between animal and human life as *objects* of ethics, he says that "any instance of creatures giving aid to one another" reveals them as *subjects* of ethics. This last is illustrated by moving stories of wild geese, monkeys, and sparrows.

In a word, Dr. Schweitzer's thesis on reverence for life is simply sugar-coated moral poison. He wishes to avoid destroying any life, even the lowest; but he sadly realizes that some such destruction is "necessary." And when it is "necessary" it is permitted. The logical conclusion of this supposedly magnificent thesis (a conclusion that Dr. Schweitzer himself might want to repudiate) is that even innocent human life may be directly destroyed when this is "necessary."

WIDESPREAD IGNORANCE

The foregoing are but a few prominent examples of the modern intellectuals who, lacking the guidance of the Church, err in very fundamental moral matters. If we add to these few the rationalists of our time and the Protestant theologians, the number of erring intellectuals would indeed be legion. But the problem of ignorance of the natural law concerns not only the philosophical and theological elite; it extends to men in general, and therefore includes

[11] *Christendom*, 1 (1936), 225–39.

professional men, such as lawyers and doctors, and the common people. This problem is generally discussed by moralists when they consider the possibility of invincible ignorance of the natural law. On this point, special reference should be made here to the dissertation by Stanley Bertke.[12]

After giving the principles and the various distinctions and subdistinctions commonly known, Father Bertke applies these points to some of the very practical moral problems of our age (and perhaps of any age), with special reference to conditions as they exist in the United States. These problems are, for example: birth control, mercy killing, abortion, masturbation, fornication, adultery, and divorce. Among non-Catholics, Father Bertke admits a rather widespread *de facto* ignorance of the absoluteness of the natural law in some of these matters; and he thinks that this ignorance is to a great extent inculpable. He also admits —but with greater reservation, of course—the existence of much apparently inculpable ignorance among Catholics who are not well instructed. One point in the dissertation seems to us to be particularly well expressed and we think it should be quoted here in full. After noting how even the most eminent Protestant leaders err regarding contraception and even campaign for it, he readily concludes that vast numbers of ordinary non-Catholics may be invincibly ignorant on this point. But he adds that the Catholic *rudes* may also be victims of this error; and he explains this possibility as follows:

Purely from the standpoint of the natural law, which is to say, from the standpoint of reason as uninformed by faith, the

12 *The Possibility of Invincible Ignorance of the Natural Law* (Washington: Catholic University of America Press, 1941).

perception of the evil of Birth Control requires the ability to make rather fine distinctions. It is certainly not among the immediate and evident deductions from first principles and it has been seen that even acute minds are capable of erring concerning remote conclusions. The mind must evade such intellectual shoals as, "Birth Control is only the harnessing and controlling of nature and man is made for that purpose," or, "The use of food for pleasure alone generally does not exceed a venial sin, and food concerns a primary inclination to the preservation of individual being." The comparative obscurity of the doctrine itself from the point of view of the natural law, together with the whole weight of environment and the inclinations of the lower appetites involved, would tend to produce error in these matters. This error is a judgment made not in the armchair of abstract thought but in the noisy traffic of daily life. The issue may be presented as a choice between two evils in which the apparent good of the wife or family is at stake. The power of these influences together with the force of public opinion may combine to so obscure the issue that the final miserable error is inculpable. The writer believes this to be true in some instances. This is not to say the condition is to be condoned in Catholics. The solemn duty of pastors and others who have care of souls is clear. Not even the suspicion that the Church may condone these errors may be tolerated. The full truth must be taught.[13]

AMBIT OF MORAL LAW

The preceding explanations and quotations make it clear enough that men in general, including philosophers and

[13] *Ibid.,* p. 99. Perhaps we should stress the point that Father Bertke thinks that genuine invincible ignorance is only rarely verified among Catholics. Even the Catholic rudes are usually well instructed about the authority of the Church to teach in moral matters; and, when this is the case, their failure to conform themselves to the teaching of the Church is not invincible ignorance, but rather culpable disobedience or the result of a process of rationalization. In this last case (rationalization), it is difficult to appraise the formal guilt.

professional men, need some authoritative guidance in order to have an adequate knowledge of the moral law. Yet one is naturally prone to ask just what this means in terms of the concrete situations of daily life. Regarding the teaching itself—that is, how the Church fulfills its mission of giving moral guidance—we shall speak later. But it seems that, before concluding the present chapter, we should try to make more definite the meaning of the moral law, not by means of abstract definitions, but by outlining the various spheres of life in which duties and rights—and therefore morality—are of primary, and not merely incidental, concern. We can hardly do this better than by quoting from the address given by Pope Pius XII on November 2, 1954, to the cardinals, archbishops, and bishops who had gathered in Rome for the ceremonies in honor of our Lady.[14] On this occasion the Holy Father said:

And first, there are some noticeable attitudes and tendencies of mind which presume to check and set limits to the power of the bishops (the Roman pontiff not excepted), as being strictly the shepherds of the flock entrusted to them. They fix their authority, office, and watchfulness within certain bounds which concern strictly religious matters, the statement of the truths of the faith, the regulation of devotional practices, administration of the sacraments of the Church, and the carrying out of liturgical ceremonies. They wish to restrain the Church from all undertakings and business which concern life as it is really conducted—"the realities of life," as they say. In short, this way of

[14] AAS, 46 (1954), 666–77. This address was intended as a complement to the Si diligis, given May 31, 1954 (ibid., pp. 313–17). In the Si diligis, the pope professedly discussed the teaching authority of the Church, whereas the later address (Magnificate Dominum) was expressly concerned with the powers of orders and jurisdiction. As is evident from the quotation given in our text, however, the Magnificate Dominum contained much about teaching authority.

thinking in the official statements of some lay Catholics, even those in high positions, is sometimes shown when they say: "We are perfectly willing to see, to listen to, and to approach bishops and priests in their churches, and regarding matters within their authority; but in places of official and public business, where matters of this life are dealt with and decided, we have no wish to see them or to listen to what they say. For there, it is we laymen, and not the clergy—no matter of what rank or qualification—who are the legitimate judges."

We must take an open and firm stand against errors of this kind. The power of the Church is not bound by the limits of "matters strictly religious," as they say, but the whole matter of the natural law, its foundation, its interpretation, its application, so far as their moral aspects extend, are within the Church's power. For the keeping of the natural law, by God's appointment, has reference to the road by which man has to approach his supernatural end. But, on this road, the Church is man's guide and guardian in what concerns his supreme end. The apostles observed this in times past, and afterwards, from the earliest centuries, the Church has kept to this manner of acting, and keeps to it today, not indeed like some private guide or adviser, but by virtue of the Lord's command and authority. Therefore, when it is a question of instructions and propositions which the properly constituted shepherds (i.e., the Roman pontiff for the whole Church and the bishops for the faithful entrusted to them) publish on matters within the natural law, the faithful must not invoke that saying (which is wont to be employed with respect to opinions of individuals): "the strength of the authority is no more than the strength of the arguments."

Hence, even though some individual may think that certain declarations of the Church are not proved by the arguments put forward, his obligation to obey still remains. This was the mind, and these are the words, of St. Pius X in his encyclical *Singulari* quadam of September 24, 1912 [AAS, vol. 4, 1912, p. 658]: "Whatever a Christian man may do, even in affairs of this world, he may not ignore the supernatural, nay, he must direct all to the highest good as to his last end, in accordance with the dictates of Christian wisdom; but all his actions, insofar as they are morally good or evil, that is, agree with, or are in opposition to, divine and natural law, are subject to the judgment and authority of the Church." And he immediately transfers this principle to the social sphere: "The social question and the controversies underlying that question . . . are not merely of an economic nature, and consequently such as can be settled while the Church's authority is ignored, since, on the contrary, it is most certain that it [the social question] is primarily a moral and religious one, and on that account must be settled chiefly in accordance with the moral law and judgment based on religion" [ibid., pp. 658, 659].

Many and serious are the problems in the social field. Whether they be merely social or socio-political, they pertain to the moral order, are of concern to conscience and the salvation of men; thus they cannot be declared outside the authority and care of the Church. Indeed, there are problems outside the social field, not strictly "religious," political problems, of concern either to individual nations, or to all nations, which belong to the moral order, weigh on the conscience, and can, and very often do, hinder the attainment of man's last end. Such are: the purpose and limits of temporal authority; the relations between the individual and society; the so-called "totalitarian state," whatever be the principle it is based on; the "complete laicization of the state" and of public life; the complete laicization of the schools; war, its morality, licitness or illicitness when waged as it is today, and whether a conscientious person may give or withhold his cooperation in it; the moral relationships which bind and rule the various nations.

Common sense, and truth as well, are contradicted by whoever asserts that these and like problems are outside the field of morals, and hence are, or at least can be, beyond the influence of that authority established by God to see to a just order and to direct the consciences and actions of men along the path to their true and final destiny. This she is certainly to do not only "in secret," within the walls of the Church and sacristy, but also in the open, crying "from the rooftops" (to use the Lord's words [Matt. 10, 27]), in the front line, in the midst of the struggle that rages between truth and error, virtue and vice, between the "world" and the kingdom of God, between the prince of this world and Christ its Saviour.[15]

A cursory reading of this lengthy quotation is apt to give one the impression that the Church claims authority over the whole of life, that nothing is left to the judgment of civil authorities or to professional societies or to the individual man. This, of course, is not true. The pope is simply stating—in very strong words, it is true—that the Church has authority to speak on all aspects of life *insofar* as they involve morality and religion. The pope does not deny, therefore, that the state is a perfect society, with supreme authority in civic matters. To deny this would really be to contradict Christ's words, "Render to Caesar the things that are Caesar's," as well as the long-standing Catholic tradition of the state's authority in purely temporal matters. Nor does the pope say that ecclesiastical authorities have the unqualified right to tell Catholics how to vote. This is true only in those rare instances when the issues of an election are really moral or religious issues: for example, when one party professes atheistic communism. In reminding the faithful of their moral obligation to vote

[15] *Ibid.*, pp. 671–73. For the English translation, cf. *Catholic Mind*, 53 (May, 1955), 315–17.

against such a party, ecclesiastical authorities are not meddling in purely political affairs. Finally, the pope certainly did not mean that the Church has the last word in stating the laws of science, art, economics, and so forth. As a matter of fact, both he and his predecessors have unequivocally stated that such things do not come within the competence of the Church.

It is obvious, however, that these various spheres of life —art, economics, politics, the various sciences—are not isolated from the rest of human life. They belong to the ordered universe, with its hierarchy of values; and, because of this hierarchy of values, the various arts and sciences are not completely controlled by their own laws, but are subordinated to the higher principles of morality and religion. Regarding these higher principles, not merely in the abstract, but as they actually affect the activity of human beings, the Church is certainly competent to judge and speak.[16]

---

[16] As a good example of the papal teaching concerning the competence and the noncompetence of the Church, we might cite the social question. Pius XII succinctly summarized his own and his precedessors' teaching in the following words from the radio message, *La solennità della Pentecoste*:

"It was in the profound conviction that the Church has not only the right but even the duty to make an authoritative pronouncement on the social quesion, that Leo XIII addressed his message to the world. He had no intention of laying down guiding principles on the purely practical, we might say technical side of the social structure; for he was well aware of the fact—as Our immediate predecessor of saintly memory Pius XI pointed out ten years ago in his commemorative Encyclical, *Quadragesimo anno*— that the Church does not claim such a mission. In the general framework of labour, to stimulate the sane and responsible development of all the energies physical and spiritual of individuals and their free organisation, there opens up a wide field of action where the public authority comes in with its integrating and coordinating activity exercised first through the local and professional corporations, and finally in the activity of the State itself, whose higher moderating social authority has the important duty of forestalling the dislocations of economic balance arising from plurality and divergence of clashing interests individual and collective.

"It is, on the other hand, the indisputable competence of the Church,

This question of the hierarchy of values, of the dependence of art, science, politics, economics and so forth, on the higher values of morality and religion, has been a very prominent theme in the addresses of Pius XII; and it seems advisable to outline here some of his statements. Since this is merely for the purpose of illustration, we shall limit ourselves to addresses to members of the medical profession.

In his address to the Italian Guild of St. Luke (perhaps the most comprehensive of all his statements on medical morality)[17] he spoke of those men who repudiated the idea of a "Christian medical science." According to these men, the exact and experimental sciences are completely outside the scope of religion and morality; such sciences are governed solely by their own laws. The pope pointed out that this is an unrealistic concept of life and of the divine plan of the universe. The various sciences are not isolated from one another nor from the ultimate finality of the universe itself. Rather, the sciences are themselves interdependent and all of them are subordinated to the higher values directly concerned with man's eternal destiny.

---

on that side of the social order where it meets and enters into contact with the moral order, to decide whether the bases of a given social system are in accord with the unchangeable order which God our Creator and Redeemer has shown us through the Natural Law and Revelation, that two-fold manifestation to which Leo XIII appeals in his Encyclical. And with reason: for the dictates of the Natural Law and the truths of Revelation spring forth in a different manner, like two streams of water that do not flow against one another but together, from the same divine source; and the Church, guardian of the supernatural Christian order in which nature and grace converge, must form the consciences even of those who are called upon to find solutions for the problems and the duties imposed by social life."

The papal message was given in Italian. When the pope had concluded, translations in eight other languages were broadcast over the Vatican radio. The original and all these translations are published in *AAS*, 33 (1941), 195–293. Our quotation is taken from p. 218.

[17] Nov. 12, 1944. For text see *Pio XII: Discorsi ai medici* (Rome: Orrizonte Medico, 1954), pp. 7–21.

This same theme was developed at greater length in his celebrated address on the moral limits of medical research and experimentation,[18] when he warned his audience that science itself is not the highest value and that it must be "inserted into the order of values." Moral values, he insisted, are higher; and experimentation or research cannot be justified merely on the score that it will help advance science; it must also take account of these higher values: for example, of the rights and duties of the patients and others who might be the subjects of experimentation. Similarly, in his later address to psychotherapists,[19] he insisted that man must be considered in all his relationships and that the justification of psychotherapy in its various forms must always include a consideration of the moral law.

These are but a few examples of Pius XII's insistence on the hierarchy of values in the universe. Why the insistence? One reason doubtlessly, was to show that the moral law reaches down into every phase of human activity. Another reason—a logical inference from the first—was to explain that the Church is not going beyond its God-given commission of teaching and protecting revealed truth when it pronounces judgment on the moral aspects of art, science, politics, economics and so forth.[20]

To summarize this chapter briefly: men need authoritative guidance concerning the moral law and its application to the various spheres of human activity; and it was Christ's will that His Church should give this guidance. The methods by which this teaching office of the Church is exercised will be discussed in the next two chapters.

[18] Sept. 13, 1952; AAS, 44 (1952), 779–89.
[19] Apr. 13, 1953; AAS, 44 (1953), 278–86.
[20] Another aspect of the tendency to divorce the various spheres of life from morality and religion will be discussed in chapter 7, on situation ethics.

2

Doctrinal Value and Interpretation
of Papal Teaching

A T THE ANNUAL meeting of the Catholic Theological Society of America in 1949, a paper read by Eugene M.
Burke, C.S.P.,[1] devoted considerable space to the methods
of teaching used by the magisterium, especially by the
Roman pontiff, and to the doctrinal value of these methods.
At the meeting of the same society in 1951, the entire paper
read by Edmond D. Benard concerned the doctrinal value
of the ordinary teaching of the Holy Father.[2] The discus-

[1] Cf. "The Scientific Teaching of Theology in the Seminary," *Proceedings of the Fourth Annual Convention* of The Catholic Theological Society
of America, pp. 129–73.

[2] "The Doctrinal Value of the Ordinary Teaching of the Holy Father
in View of *Humani Generis*," *Proceedings of the Sixth Annual Convention,*
CTSA, pp. 78–107. Father Benard (*ibid.*, pp. 84–85) gives the following
explanation of the terms *ordinary* and *extraordinary magisterium.*
"(1) *The Pope employs his Extraordinary Magisterium when he speaks ex*
cathedra. *This Extraordinary Magisterium is de se, always, and necessarily*
infallible. . . . (2) The Pope employs his Ordinary Magisterium when he
speaks to the faithful, indeed as their supreme Pastor and Teacher, but in
order to expound, explain, present Catholic teaching, or to admonish, persuade, enlighten, warn, and encourage the faithful; without calling upon
the supreme exercise of his Apostolic Authority, and without, in the strict
sense, defining a doctrine. *In this case he does not speak ex* cathedra *and the*

sion evoked by both papers showed that the topics were of speculative interest and practical moment. This response was not surprising. Problems relative to the doctrinal value of ecclesiastical pronouncements have always been of special interest to theologians; and it is safe to say that this interest has never been more intense, nor of more immediate practicality, than during the reign of Pope Pius XII.

MORAL TEACHING OF PIUS XII

An earnest student of papal pronouncements, Vincent A. Yzermans, estimated that during the first fifteen years of his pontificate Pius XII gave almost one thousand public addresses and radio messages.[3] If we add to these the apos-

---

Ordinary Magisterium *is hence not de se infallible.* (3) However, the Pope *may, if he chooses, employ a usual organ or vehicle of the Ordinary Magisterium as the medium of an ex cathedra pronouncement. In this case, an Encyclical Letter, for example—certainly a type of document usually associated with the Ordinary Magisterium—may be used as the vehicle of the Extraordinary Magisterium, and hence as the vehicle of an infallible pronouncement. . . ."*

[3] Cf. *The Catholic Mind*, 53 (1955), 252. Father Yzermans wrote originally in *Columbia*, for January, 1955. The complete quotation given in *The Catholic Mind* is interesting:

"Some five years ago I began to dream of an American work that would record all the addresses of His Holiness, Pope Pius XII. So I set to work in search of the sources. Little did I dream I would be so quickly disillusioned! To my utter dismay I discovered that our Holy Father has spoken so often that the mere recording of his words would be a super-human task. It would entail, first of all, the collection of all the addresses from an innumerable variety of sources. During the first fifteen years of his pontificate, from March 2, 1939 to March 2, 1954, the Supreme Pontiff delivered almost 1,000 public addresses, allocutions and radio messages. Over and above the mere recording of these addresses there would be the added task of translating them from the various languages in which they were delivered. Of the total number of addresses only a little more than a third have been translated into English."

A recent advertisement for *The Pope Speaks* carries this information: "In the course of a year, the Holy Father delivers 80 to 100 public messages—encyclicals, allocutions, radio messages, letters, addresses to audiences from all over the world." And the autumn, 1956, number of the same publication, begins with the following paragraph:

tolic constitutions, the encyclicals, and so forth, during that same period of fifteen years, and add furthermore all the papal statements during the subsequent years, we have well over a thousand papal documents. It is true, of course, that many of these were not concerned with faith or morals; yet certainly a very large percentage, if not the vast majority, were concerned with either faith or morality. The moralist in particular has only to think of the stream of pronouncements on international peace, on labor relations, on family morality, on medicine and so forth, to realize that his own work is profoundly affected.

Merely from the point of view of volume, therefore, one can readily appreciate that it was not mere facetiousness that led a theologian to remark that, even if the Holy See were now to remain silent for ten years, the theologians would have plenty to do in classifying and evaluating the theological significance of Pius XII's public statements. And it may be added that the theologians' problem is created not merely by the number and variety of the papal statements, but also by the fact that many of them are in modern languages rather than in the traditional Latin, and that they were given in a more or less oratorical setting. We mention these as added problems because, whatever be the disadvantages of Latin, it has the theological advantage of an "established terminology"; and oratory, though perhaps more pleasing than the cut-and-dried theological statement,

---

"The Holy Father has temporarily overwhelmed our hopes of printing translations of all his important and interesting messages in a given quarter. In the second three months of this year (the period covered in this issue), Pope Pius XII addressed over *sixty* messages to various groups or to the world at large. And this includes only those which appeared in the *Acta* or *Osservatore Romano*. These messages range in length from the booklet-sized encyclical on devotion to the Sacred Heart (printed in this issue) to several one-page letters (just mentioned in this issue)."

forces the theologian to dig for the theological core of a statement.

Among these numerous pronouncements of Pope Pius XII, one (*Munificentissimus Deus* [4]) is certainly an ex cathedra definition, and another (*Sacramentum ordinis* [5]) seems to be such. Of these, only the second pertains to moral theology, and that more or less indirectly. In general, the teaching of the Holy Father on moral matters has been given in encyclicals, radio messages, and allocutions—which are normally the media of his authentic, but not infallible, teaching. This is not to say that such media could not contain ex cathedra pronouncements; but usually they do not, and there seems to be no reason for saying that during the reign of Pius XII these media have contained any infallible *definitions* concerning morality. By this we do not mean, however, that none of the moral teaching of Pius XII could be characterized as infallible. It is hardly conceivable that the papal teaching on such things as divorce, contraception, the direct killing of the innocent, and the possibility of observing continence with the grace of God is anything short of infallible. However, aside from such cases, we may safely assume that the moral teaching of Pius XII need not be characterized as infallible but rather belongs to the authentic, though not infallible, magisterium of the Church. Regarding this noninfallible teaching, questions of special interest concern (1) its doctinal value, and (2) the function of theologians in their use of such teaching.

DOCTRINAL VALUE

Since the noninfallible moral teaching of Pius XII has

[4] Nov. 1, 1950; *AAS*, 42 (1950), 753–71.
[5] Nov. 30, 1947; *AAS*, 40 (1948), 5–7.

been given through the medium of encyclicals, radio messages, and allocutions (as well as through papally approved decrees and instructions of the Roman congregations), something should be said here about the doctrinal value of these various media. Obviously, lest we turn this chapter into a book, we must be carefully selective in this matter. On the basis of such selectivity, the principal place must be given to the pope's own statement in *Humani generis*, which is concerned primarily, but not exclusively with encyclicals. After criticizing the exponents of "the new theology" for their lack of appreciation of the ordinary magisterium (perhaps this expression is an understatement), the pope adds the following now celebrated paragraph:

Nor must it be thought that what is contained in encyclical letters does not of itself demand assent, on the pretext that the popes do not exercise in them the supreme power of their teaching authority. Rather, such teachings belong to the ordinary magisterium, of which it is true to say: "He who heareth you, heareth me"; very often, too, what is expounded and inculcated in encyclical letters already appertains to Catholic doctrine for other reasons. But if the supreme pontiffs in their official documents purposely pass judgment on a matter debated until then, it is obvious to all that the matter, according to the mind and will of the same pontiffs, cannot be considered any longer a question open for discussion among theologians.[6]

There have been many excellent commentaries on the *Humani generis* in general and on this paragraph in particular. Typical among these and especially notable, we think, for its simplicity and clarity, is the explanation given by Father Cotter under the heading, "Authentic Teaching of the Magisterium." We quote this in full:

[6] *AAS*, 42 (1950), 568; for translation, cf. Cotter, *op. cit.*, pp. 21-23.

[23]

The Pope has no doubt that those Catholic theologians whom he has in mind throughout the encyclical are willing to abide by the definitive decisions of the magisterium, those handed down, "*solemni iudicio.*" They are neither heretics nor schismatics. But he complains that they ignore papal pronouncements that come to them with less authority, such as encyclicals. If reputable theologians have disagreed in the past, they assume that nothing less than a solemn definition can settle the matter; and as long as none such is forthcoming, everyone is presumed free to construe papal documents according to his own interpretation of Tradition (27).

In reply, the Pope reminds them that encyclicals, besides often containing matters of dogma, may intend to settle points hitherto disputed, and that such decisions demand of themselves a positive assent on the part of the faithful, theologians included. In issuing them the popes exercise what is technically known as the ordinary or authentic magisterium, of which it is true to say: "He who heareth you, heareth me." The reason for all this is that to the living magisterium alone has God entrusted the official interpretation of the deposit of faith (21, 23).

According to theologians, the doctrinal decrees of the Holy Office and the responses of the Biblical Commission belong in the same category because of the close connection of these two Roman congregations with the Pope. Also their decisions demand per se the positive assent of the faithful (Denzinger 2113).

This is technically known as "religious assent." It is a true internal assent, not a mere *silentium obsequiosum* such as the Jansenists were willing to give the papal decrees issued against them. Yet it is not the assent of either divine or ecclesiastical faith; its motive is not the authority of God speaking nor the infallibility of the magisterium, but the official position of the living magisterium in the Church assigned to it by Christ.

Complaints have been raised against this doctrine as if it were putting shackles on the Catholic theologian (18). Yes and no. First of all, there are any number of problems in Catholic theology on which the magisterium has said nothing so far either definitely or authentically; witness the numerous probable theses or assertions in our manuals and the questions freely disputed in our reviews. Secondly, the authentic decisions of the magisterium, when examined closely, are generally seen to leave the door open for further study of the problem; witness especially the responses of the Biblical Commission. And if a reputable scholar should arrive at a different solution, theologians advise him to communicate his findings to the respective Roman congregation, but not to broadcast them, in defiance, as it were, of the magisterium. Thirdly, even when the decision is definitive, progress is still possible and desirable (21), and that means, partly at least, further research on the same matter by theologians.[7]

As Father Cotter notes, though the papal statement refers primarily to encyclicals, it is not restricted to these. Rather, it covers the whole range of what is called the "ordinary magisterium" of the Holy Father. Everything that has been said, therefore, could apply to the papal radio messages and allocutions; yet, since these have played such

[7] *Ibid.*, pp. 75–77. The numbers Father Cotter has in parenthesis refer to the paragraph numbers of the encyclical as given in his book. The question of the "assensus religiosus" that must be given to noninfallible teaching is an intriguing one. Closely connected with this, of course, is the problem of divine assistance for the magisterium in this kind of teaching. Dogmatic theologians give different explanations. For more about this, see the paper given by Father Benard (*supra*, footnote 2); also Charles Journet, *The Church of the Word Incarnate: I. The Apostolic Hierarchy* (New York: Sheed and Ward, 1955), esp. pp. 351–53; and Wernz-Vidal, as cited *infra*, chapter 3, footnote 6. And for the replies of the Biblical Commission in particular, see the remarks of E. A. Sutcliffe, S.J., in *A Catholic Commentary on Holy Scripture* (New York: Thomas Nelson and Sons, 1953), pp. 67–68. Father Sutcliffe's explanation is very complete and it shows that in some questions the submission required of the Catholic exegete may consist only "in not opposing by word or writing the decisions of the Biblical Commission."

a prominent part in the moral teaching of Pope Pius XII, they merit some special attention.

On at least one occasion, the pope himself made it strikingly clear that his discourses, even when given to small groups, can contain authoritative teaching for the whole Church. Thus, in his radio message on the education of the Christian conscience, he said:

Mindful, however, of the right and duty of the Apostolic See to intervene authoritatively, when need arises, in moral questions, in the address of 29th October last we set out to enlighten men's consciences on the problems of married life. With the self-same authority we declare today to educators and to young people also that the divine commandment of purity of soul and body still holds without any lesser obligation for the youth of today.[8]

At the conclusion of a commentary on this radio message and the subsequent allocution on the "new morality" (situation ethics),[9] F. X. Hürth, S.J., made a brief analysis of the doctrinal value of such pronouncements.[10] His conclusion was that, in general, they have about the same doctrinal value as encyclicals: they are an integral part of the ordinary teaching of the pope; and, as such, though not infallible, they require both internal and external acceptance. An

[8] *AAS*, 44 (1952), 275; English translation based on *Catholic Documents*, 8 (July, 1952), 5. The address of October 29, 1951, to which the pope refers in this quotation, was given to the Italian Society of Obstetrical Nurses, and it was certainly one of the most important moral pronouncements of his reign. Cf. *AAS*, 43 (1951), 835–54. It is often referred to as the allocution to the "midwives"; but it seems that the Italian is better translated by "obstetrical nurses," or perhaps "obstetrical social workers."

[9] For a more detailed consideration of these papal statements, as well as the subsequent instruction of the Holy Office on situation ethics, cf. chapters 7 and 8.

[10] Cf. *Periodica*, 41 (1952), 245–49. See also Father Hürth's brief remarks about the doctrinal value of decrees of the Holy Office, *ibid.*, 45 (1956), 141; cf. *supra*, footnote 7.

analysis of their *content,* said Father Hürth, shows that they consist largely of matters of faith or morals or of natural truths in their relation to faith and morals. The *audience* varies from the whole world (as in some of the radio messages) to a small professional group (as in an allocution to doctors); but even in the latter case the message assumes a universal character when, by command of the supreme pontiff, it is published in the *Acta apostolicæ sedis.* As for the *speaker,* though the pope may, if he wishes, speak as a private person, Father Hürth thinks it obvious that such is not his intention when he professedly speaks on matters pertaining to faith and morals in these various public messages.

Joseph Creusen, S.J., who, like Father Hürth, was a consultor of the Holy Office, offers the following observations to help determine when, and to what extent, papal discourses should be considered authoritative teaching:

What is important to us here is the character of the allocution: has the pope the intention of teaching, and in what measure does he invoke his authority? Apart from an express declaration, his intention can be manifested by the quality and number of the persons to whom he speaks, and by the subject-matter of the discourse.

If the Holy Father, in an audience granted to a sports association, praises the physical and moral effects of sport, everyone remains quite at liberty not to share this or that opinion of the Holy Father in the matter. His praise will often be the delicate expression of an invitation to seek in the use of sports, or of any other human activity, progress in moral values, in nobility of soul, in the duties of one's state well done. But the more the number of members of a congress increases, the greater the importance of their profession, of their responsibilities, and of their influence, the more we see the Holy Father select the subject-matter of his discourse and inculcate the duty of conforming oneself to his teaching and directives.[11]

Furthermore, Father Creusen tells us in another place, it would not make sense to restrict the obligation of assent and obedience merely to those who are present at the papal discourse:

In our case [the allocution on conjugal morality] there is no doubt that the obligation of internal submission cannot be restricted to those whom the pope addressed. An obligation of this kind cannot be defined by the distance one happens to be from the pope during his discourse. But perhaps someone will say: we are not obliged to read the allocutions of the pope! Certainly, but we are all obliged to know our duties, especially those of our profession.

The "how" is not relevant, whether we come to know them by means of sermons, reading good books, lectures, or conversations with learned and reputable men.[12]

NORMS OF INTERPRETATION

The foregoing seems to be sufficient discussion of our first point: the doctrinal value of the various media of the ordinary teaching of the Holy Father. As for the second point—the function of theologians in their use of this teaching—we must first observe that the theologians have the same duty as the faithful in general to give the religious

[11] *Bulletin social des industriels,* 24 (1952), 153. P. DeLetter, S.J., summarizes the teaching of Father Creusen and Father Hürth, in *Clergy Monthly,* 17 (1953), 181–83.

[12] Cf. *Problemi di vita coniugale* (Rome: S.A.L.E.S., 1955), p. 31. It should be noted that Father Creusen is referring to the duties discussed in the allocutions on conjugal morality. These duties are obviously of universal application. But in some cases the practical applications of papal directives are not universal. Thus, Father Creusen himself later notes that such applications "can be obligatory in one country and not in another; they are also subject to change in accordance with changing circumstances" (*ibid.,* p. 32).

assent required by the papal teaching, as was stated by Pope Pius XII and explained by Father Cotter.

But the distinctive function of the theologian goes much beyond this acceptance of the papal teaching; as a theologian he must study the papal pronouncements and incorporate them into his teaching and his writing. One writer has deplored the tendency of theologians to "interpret" the papal statements; according to him the theologians' function is to explain the papal teaching, not to interpret it. In practice, this is a distinction without a difference. To fulfill his acknowledged duty of explaining the papal teaching, a theologian must in some measure interpret it; and all that can be reasonably demanded of him is that he follow sound theological norms of interpretation. Unfortunately, we do not have an official set of norms for interpreting pronouncements on the moral law such as we have, for example, regarding canon law; nevertheless, there seem to be at least three basic norms of interpretation that are in conformity with the mind and practice of the Holy See.

One such norm concerns the verbal formulas used in the moral pronouncements. These formulas are very important and should be carefully studied by theologians. Nevertheless, the words themselves are not the ultimate criterion of the true sense of the papal pronouncement; they can be obscure and admit of reformulation. This can be illustrated by the *acta* of both Pius XI and Pius XII relative to punitive sterilization, as well as by the tenor of canon law and by the reactions of eminent theologians to certain aspects of significant moral pronouncements.

In the originally published text of *Casti connubii*, the words of Pius XI at least strongly implied that he was condemning punitive sterilization; but a *notandum* in the next fascicle of the *Acta apostolicæ sedis* contained a rewording of the passage which showed that the pope did not intend to commit himself on the controversy among theologians about the licitness of punitive sterilization.[13] Ten years later the Holy Office, with the approval of Pius XII, condemned direct sterilization, without qualification, as being contrary to the natural law.[14] That was in 1940. But in 1951, and again in 1953, Pope Pius XII, when referring to this condemnation, restricted it to the direct sterilization of the innocent.[15] In both these instances, the popes apparently realized that, though perfectly apt for condemning the errors at which they were aimed, the formulas were broader than their own intention.

The very fact that popes themselves have gone out of their way to clarify or restrict their moral pronouncements indicates that a theologian is not necessarily irreverent or disloyal in supposing that other such statements may need clarification or restriction or rephrasing. This is confirmed, it seems to us, by the rules for the interpretation of canon law, as well as by theologians' reactions to some recent and very important papal pronouncements on the social order. In canon law, the Church explicitly admits that the meaning of some laws may be dubious or obscure. The reason for this is surely not that the legislator wanted to be obscure but rather that he failed to make his own intention clear when framing the law. It is true, of course, that this concerns canon law, not pronouncements regarding moral law. But we do not think this affects the point we are stressing: namely, that the words themselves may fail to express the

---

[13] Cf. *AAS*, 22 (1930), 565, 604.
[14] *Ibid.*, 32 (1940), 73.
[15] Cf. *Ibid.*, 43 (1951), 844; 45 (1953), 606.

mind of the Holy See. That this has actually been the case concerning some important moral pronouncements seems evident from the controversies among eminent and unquestionably orthodox moralists regarding the meaning of social justice, the title to a family wage and so forth. In these cases, as in the framing of ecclesiastical laws, the popes were certainly not intentionally obscure. They must have had something definite in mind, but this was not expressed with sufficient clarity—otherwise, how explain the controversies among learned commentators?

From the foregoing it follows that the words alone do not always give us the sense, the true meaning, of a papal pronouncement. To get to the true sense, the theologian must study not only the words, but their context and the papal intention in making the pronouncement. By the context we mean not so much the verbal context as the historical setting, because it is there particularly that we are apt to find the true meaning of the statement. For example, if the pope is settling a controversy, his words should be taken in conjunction with the controversy; if he is condemning an error, the words should be interpreted with reference to the error and so forth.[16]

In the *Humani generis*, Pope Pius XII made it clear that

[16] What is said in this paragraph seems to be in keeping with the spirit of the Church as manifested in canon 18, which prescribes that words are to be taken according to their proper meaning as indicated by text and context, and that in case of doubt one should consider the purpose and circumstances of a law and the mind of the legislator. As for verbal formulas alone, one might note the following quotation from the *Quamquam pluries* of Leo XIII: "*Certe matris Dei tam in excelso dignitas est, ut nihil fieri maius queat. Sed tamen quia intercessit Josepho cum Virgine beatissima maritale vinculum, ad illam praestantissimam dignitatem, qua naturis creatis omnibus longissime Deipara antecellit, non est dubium quin accesserit ipse, ut nemo magis.*" Cf. *ASS*, 22 (1889–90), 66. The pope's meaning is obvious; yet a stickler for the primacy of verbal formulas would have no little difficulty with the expressions we have italicized.

even a noninfallible pronouncement can close a controversy among theologians. We feel sure, however, that the pope himself would agree that this decisive character of the pronouncement must be evident. That is in accord with canon 1323, § 3, which states that nothing is to be understood as dogmatically declared or defined unless this is clearly manifested. The canon refers to infallible teachings; yet the same norm seems to apply with at least equal force to the binding character of noninfallible teaching, especially when there is question of pronouncements that would close a controversy.

To summarize briefly the main points of this section: A theologian must study and use and, to some extent, interpret papal pronouncements. In interpreting them, he should have regard not only for verbal formulas but also—and, it seems to us, especially—for the papal intention as manifested in the historical context of the pronouncement. When there is question of official teaching that would end legitimate controversy, this decisive character should be evident.

3

Episcopal Teaching

O N MAY 31, 1954, Pope Pius XII spoke to the bishops who had assembled in Rome for the canonization of St. Pius X. The general topic of this allocution (*Si diligis*) was the teaching authority of the Church. In the course of the allocution, the pope said:

Christ our Lord entrusted the truth which He had brought from heaven to the apostles, and through them to their successors; and, as He Himself had been sent by the Father, so He sent the apostles to teach all peoples all the truths they had learned from the Lord. The apostles are, therefore, by divine right true doctors and teachers in the Church. Besides the lawful successors of the apostles, namely, the Roman pontiff for the universal Church and the bishops for the faithful entrusted to their care, there are no other teachers divinely constituted in the Church of Christ.[1]

Later, in the *Magnificate Dominum*, which was really a continuation of the *Si diligis*, Pius XII made it very clear

[1] *AAS*, 46 (1954), 314.

that a part of this truth brought from heaven by Christ and entrusted to the Church is the moral law. Having pointed out the tendency of some moderns to exclude the teaching authority of the Church from many, if not all, of the practical spheres of life, he said:

. . . When there is question of instructions and propositions which the properly constituted shepherds (i.e., the Roman pontiff for the whole Church and the bishops for the faithful entrusted to them) publish on matters within the natural law, the faithful must not invoke that saying (which is wont to be employed with respect to opinions of individuals): "the strength of the authority is no more than the strength of the arguments." [2]

These papal statements touch on a matter of vital concern to the faithful in general and to theologians in particular: the teaching authority of bishops. In the ordinary providence of God, the faithful usually learn the Church's teaching on matters of faith and morals, not directly from the Holy See, but rather through their own bishops and those delegated by the bishops.[3] As for theologians, they can hardly write or teach adequately on any currently discussed topic without taking account of such things as pastoral letters, the various statements of provincial or national hierarchies and so forth. Our preliminary chapters,

[2] *Ibid.*, p. 672. The *Magnificate Dominum* was given November 2, 1954. A more lengthy quotation from this allocution is given *supra*, chapter 1, pp. 12–15.

[3] This was especially true before the progress of science made it so easy to publicize papal statements throughout the world. Obviously, this ready communication with Rome has been productive of many benefits; but not without unpleasant by-products: for example, the garbled statements in the press, and the apparently growing tendency of the faithful to expect all questions to be explained by the Holy See rather than by their own bishops. Furthermore, in recent years many important and profound papal messages have reached the people before the bishops and theologians have had the opportunity to read and digest them.

therefore, would hardly be complete without a brief word about the doctrinal value of episcopal teaching.

On some points, the question of the bishops' teaching authority is clearly stated in the documents of the Church and is rather thoroughly explained by canonists and theologians. United with the Roman pontiff, the bishops enjoy the prerogative of infallibility both in the solemn declarations of ecumenical councils and in the ordinary and universal magisterium of the Church. Moreover, considered collectively and united with the pope, the bishops also have the prerogative of authentic, noninfallible teaching which was discussed in the last chapter. Also, even the decrees on faith and morals made by individual bishops and by provincial and plenary councils have the authority of papal teaching when they are approved *in forma specifica* by the Holy See. Finally, it is evident from the documents of the Church and from the traditional explanations of the subject of infallibility that individual bishops are not and cannot be infallible.

There may be difficulties at times in the application of some of the foregoing points; but at least the theory is clear and sufficiently explained by authors. A further question, however, and one which is of greater practical significance than any of the foregoing, concerns the doctrinal authority of individual bishops as authentic teachers in their own dioceses.[4] What is said on this topic by standard authors can be summed up in two points: (1) the authentic magisterium of a bishop is limited to teaching and safeguarding Catholic doctrine—that is, truths concerning faith and

----

[4] Cf. canon 1326: "Although they do not enjoy the prerogative of infallibility of teaching, either singly or even when assembled in particular councils, bishops are also true doctors or teachers, under the authority of the Roman pontiff, of the faithful committed to their care."

morals that have already been defined or declared by the universal magisterium; and (2) individual bishops have not the authority to settle theological controversies. These two points are stated with exceptional clarity and simplicity by Van Noort:

The *teaching power* of the individual bishop is not infallible. Obviously a bishop's doctrinal decision, by the very fact of stemming from a subordinate pastor, can be retracted and corrected by the supreme pastor. It would, then, be contradictory to say that some decision is by its very nature simultaneously reformable and irreformable, or, fallible and infallible. Because of this subordination it follows that a bishop's magisterium (besides being limited to a definite locality) does not extend to a decision in controverted matters; rather, it extends to the handing down, safeguarding, and defense of those matters which are already established either by an explicit definition, or by the universal consent of the Church.

Be careful, however, not to conclude from the restrictions laid down that when a bishop is teaching in his official capacity he carries practically no more weight than any other learned man. The opinion of any private doctor can be rejected by anyone without injuring the duty of religious obedience. Indeed, common prudence itself usually dictates that one should carefully weigh his arguments. But the case is entirely different when a bishop is officially exercising his magisterium in his own diocese. For the bishop in virtue of his very office, that is, not because of his renown for learning, and not because of the power of the arguments he may adduce, but because of the very public authority he possesses in the Church, should out of religious obedience be heeded by his subjects in such fashion that they feel obliged to accept his teaching as the true doctrine of Christ, unless there be special reasons to prove the contrary. This is what theologians mean by saying that the bishop possesses for his own diocese a *magisterium* which is not indeed infallible, but which is *authentic,* i.e., authoritative.[5]

OBJECT OF AUTHENTIC TEACHING

With regard to the first point, it seems clear that when a bishop (or group of bishops) makes a public pronouncement or issues a pastoral letter with the express purpose of giving the teaching of the Church on some moral doctrine —e.g., on divorce or contraception—he intends to use his magisterial power; and that in such a case his subjects are to receive his teaching, as Van Noort puts it, "as the true doctrine of Christ, unless there be special reasons to prove the contrary." [6] But in actual life we have not only these general pronouncements, but also interpretations and applications of the Church's moral teaching. For example, there may be

[5] G. Van Noort, *Tractatus de ecclesia Christi* (Bussum, the Netherlands: Paulus Brand, 1931), n. 198, and footnote; English translation: *Christ's Church,* revised and adapted by John J. Castelot, S.S. and William R. Murphy, S.S. (Westminster, Md.: The Newman Press, 1957), pp. 321–22. Cardinal Franzelin states the same points, under the aspect of the *providentia particularis* which belongs to bishops in their teaching office and in some way to others, such as spiritual directors, who must direct the consciences of the faithful. Cf. Franzelin, *Tractatus de divina traditione et scriptura* (2nd ed.; Rome, 1875), pp. 153–54. For a very complete discussion of episcopal power see Gerald A. Ryan, *Principles of Episcopal Jurisdiction* (Washington: The Catholic University of America Press, 1939). Cf. especially pp. 125–32 for Father Ryan's discussion of the points given in our text.

[6] Wernz-Vidal put the limitation of religious assent somewhat differently. Speaking of the assent required by authentic, but not infallible, teaching, whether of the Holy See or of bishops, they say: ". . . nihilominus assensus præscriptus aliquid habet de provisorio et fundatur in præsumptione, quod authenticus doctrinæ magister non erret *nisi de contrario adsit vehemens suspicio* ideoque ipsi docenti debetur obedientia intellectus, sicut superiori legitime præcipienti debetur obedientia voluntatis, *nisi adsit vehemens suspicio ipsum inhonesta præcipere.*" The words we have italicized help to clarify Van Noort's expression, "unless there be special reasons to prove the contrary—nisi in contrarium militet specialis ratio." Cf. Wernz-Vidal, *Ius canonicum,* IV (Rome: Gregorian University, 1935), n. 617, p. 10.

an episcopal judgment that the moral teaching in a certain book is incompatible with the teaching of the Church; an episcopal decision that some action, such as swallowing a piece of paper, is a superstitious practice; a diocesan ruling that participation in a beauty contest would be scandalous; or a prohibition to attend a certain motion picture which might be an occasion of sin; and so forth. Obviously, since many such rulings may depend on local conditions, and since they may differ from diocese to diocese, they cannot be direct expressions of universal doctrine.

But the ever-inquiring mind of the theologian is prone to ask whether these particular judgments, decisions, and statements, are really doctrinal in the strict sense, or rather legislative enactments or official exhortations. The standard authors apparently have little to say on this interesting problem. As for ourselves, we would offer the following suggestions. First, an individual pronouncement of a bishop might involve all three elements—authentic teaching, legislation, and exhortation; and the main question might be which of the three is *primarily* involved. Secondly, when it is clear that an episcopal pronouncement which is made with a view to existing conditions in his diocese is concerned with an *obligation*, it should be presumed that the bishop is using his legislative, rather than his doctrinal authority, unless it is evident that he intends to use his power of authoritative teaching. Thirdly, in the absence of a clear indication that strict obligations are involved, the pronouncement should be interpreted as an official exhortation.

These suggestions have a distinct practical advantage for the consciences of the faithful and for those who guide them. Even eminent theologians seem to have no little difficulty in explaining the so-called "religious assent" that must be given to authentic teaching; and the difficulty increases when one tries to explain this duty of interior submission in terms of grades of obligation. On the other hand, both the use and the interpretation of legislative enactments are so clearly delineated by the Church and by theologians and canonists, that pastors, confessors, and spiritual directors can readily know them or at least find clear explanations of them. Thus the direction of consciences is rendered much more easy and secure—something which is of the greatest importance. And it might be recalled here that the divine assistance promised to bishops is not limited to their teaching authority; it extends in proportionate degrees to all the exercises of their pastoral office—that is, to teaching, governing, and guiding their respective flocks.[7]

CONTROVERTED QUESTIONS

The limitation of episcopal power regarding legitimately controverted questions was thoroughly discussed by Cardinal Lambertini (later Benedict XIV) in his celebrated *De synodo diœcesana.*[8] Authors who have written since the time of Lambertini have usually been content with merely stating the fact that individual bishops have not the power to settle theological controversies, while referring to *De synodo* for the explanation. The doctrinal reasons for this limitation of episcopal power are, first, that by reason of the controversies, these matters do not yet pertain to formally established doctrine; and, secondly, since the Holy See at least implicitly permits these controversies, an episcopal prohibition would constitute interference with the higher

[7] Regarding this divine assistance, see our brief remarks at the conclusion of this chapter.
[8] Cf. book 7; *passim.*

power.[9] A practical reason for the limitation is that it would be confusing to the faithful and harmful to theology to have one of these theological opinions forbidden in one diocese and permitted or perhaps even imposed in another.

This matter of freedom in controverted questions is of special concern to moral theologians because their controversies so often involve very practical matters: for example, the meaning of a proximate occasion of sin; some aspects of the use of rhythm; not a few problems of medical morality; administration of the sacraments to unconscious dying persons; and so forth. As regards these and many other questions, it is well to note that the mere fact that an opinion is a minority view is not sufficient to remove it from the sphere of legitimate controversy. An opinion of this kind is legitimately defensible, and therefore beyond the proscriptive power of individual bishops, as long as it retains genuine solid probability, either intrinsic or extrinsic. This follows logically from the fact that the Holy See permits the controversy over moral systems (probabilism, equiprobabilism, etc.).

DIVINE ASSISTANCE

Earlier in this chapter we mentioned the divine assistance which is given to bishops. A guarantee of such assistance is implicit in the divine institution of their office. But, in what does this guarantee consist? It cannot be a guarantee of infallibility; nor can it, as history testifies, be an assurance that

[9] In his article, "Bishop," in *The Catholic Encyclopedia*, II, A. Van Hove adds a reasonable qualification. He writes: "He [the bishop] has not, it is true, the right to define, outside an œcumenical council, controverted questions with regard to faith and morals, but when a heated discussion arises in his diocese, he can impose silence upon the parties concerned while awaiting a decision from the Holy See" (p. 586).

each individual episcopal decision, whether doctrinal or legislative, will be prudent. But it seems to be, as Charles Journet explains it, a guarantee of the prudence of the general orientation of these particular judgments; "and whatever ignorances, errors and faults may be found in this domain—and they are inevitable—we shall nevertheless be able to hold these decrees to be beneficial on the whole, and in most cases. We may think here of the multitudinous pronouncements made from time to time by provincial councils or by bishops, with a view to the proper regulation of the lives of clergy and laity." [10]

---

[10] Cf. Charles Journet, *The Church of the Word Incarnate, I. The Apostolic Hierarchy* (New York: Sheed and Ward, 1955), 333–34.

4

Modern Criticisms of Moral Theology

A FEELING OF uneasiness about moral theology has been in the air for some years. It is a feeling which cannot be brushed aside as mere murmuring by malcontents. It is shared by thoughtful critics who obviously have at heart only the good of souls and the ideals of our Lord. The feeling that something is wrong strikes anyone who reflects on the attitudes often displayed by priests and seminarians.

What is the first thought that comes to the mind of the seminarian when the moral theology course is mentioned? Is it the practice of virtue and the pursuit of Christian perfection? Or is it, perhaps, "Thou shalt not commit adultery"? Is it the preaching of the good news of the Christian way of life? Or is it the sad news that there are sinners, Christians, legions of them, waiting to have their confessions heard, waiting to be absolved from mortal sin?

The word "moralist" to the general public—certainly to the general public outside the Church—connotes most often the censorious critic who spoils the fun. But the word "moralist" to the priest and seminarian is more likely to connote quite the opposite. "Consult so-and-so. He will get you out of it if anyone can." Too often the moralist has come to be looked on as a sort of criminal lawyer engaged by the defense. Or the seminary joke attributes to him the familiar judgment on a peccadillo: "Licet—sed sub levi."

GENERAL CONSPECTUS OF CRITICISMS

When critics try to pinpoint what is wrong and what it is that gives rise to this widespread feeling of uneasy dissatisfaction, they make a great variety of charges against various aspects of moral teaching.

Some say that charity, the all-embracing heart of Christian life, no longer vivifies moral doctrine and teaching. Some say that the practice of virtue is passed over quickly to make room for the distinction of sins. Or that the scriptural sources and patristic writings are neglected. Or that moral, to its detriment, has been divorced from dogma. Or that social obligations are not emphasized, while man's egocentric, individualistic leanings are too much indulged. It is said that moralists are still talking about a "man" who does not exist, because they have not rewritten the treatise *De actibus humanis* in accordance with the findings of psychoanalytical psychology. Or that moralists continue to talk in abstract terms of universal absolutes, using a language and a way of thinking that repel the modern mind.

Some even say that we have lost sight of the person of Christ, the revelation of God in Man, who is the way, the truth, and the life. Instead, the emphasis is all on casuistry, on legalism, on sinful deviation. How far can one go without crossing the line of mortal sin? The moral theology

[43]

books have become manuals of spiritual pathology—"peccatometers," someone has called them.

HISTORICAL BACKGROUND

It will not lead us astray to indicate very briefly here a little of the history which will help us to understand how it came about that moral theology has arrived at its present status and has its present scope, and why it is that such complaints, well- or ill-founded, could come to be made.[1]

As a separate science, having a scope in some sense distinct from other theological studies, moral theology dates only from the fifteenth century. Before that time the matters now treated in moral theology were found partly in the general treatises of the theologians, partly in the works of the canonists. The theoretical part of moral, with philosophical development of the system of the virtues and a large influence by Aristotle, was joined with the exposition of dogma. The *Summa* of St. Thomas was the crowning example of such a systematic, theoretical synthesis. Still earlier, in the writings of the fathers of the Church, the emphasis was on preaching the moral doctrines of Christ, rather than on the scientific elaboration of them.

The casuistic side of moral, destined for the use of confessors, originated in the old *Libri pœnitentiales*, many of them written by the monks of Ireland and Scotland in the ninth century, and then disseminated widely through France, Germany, Spain and Italy by the missionaries. In the beginning these books were little more than lists of sins with an appropriate penance assigned for each. They had

[1] Cf. Ivo Zeiger, S.J. "De conditione theologiæ moralis moderna," *Periodica de re morali, canonica, liturgica*, 28 (1939), 177–89 at 179 sq.; Ph. Delhaye, "La théologie morale d'hier et d'aujourd'hui," *Revue des sciences religieuses*, 27 (1953), 112–30 at 112 sq.

no theory of moral imputability, and the practical solutions were often reflections of the external standards of Celtic and Germanic law—such and such a penance for a voluntary act; a lesser one, but still severe, for an involuntary transgression, etc. In the eleventh and twelfth centuries the *Libri pœnitentiales* were incorporated into various canonical collections. The canonists corrected and refined the cruder efforts of the original penitentials, but it is not at all surprising that they did so by means of juridical principles and juridical criteria. Thus, almost from the beginning the casuistic part of moral was developed under the aegis of canon lawyers. Furthermore, when the newer type of *Libri pœnitentiales*, the *Summæ confessariorum* of the thirteenth and fourteenth centuries, came into existence, their authors were usually canonists. The *Summa* of Raymond of Peñafort is the classical example. It is clear then, that the juridical point of view exercised an immense influence on the development of the casuistic side of moral theology.

This state of affairs, with theoretical moral joined to dogma, and casuistic moral joined to canon law, came to an end in the fifteenth century. For reasons of a practical kind, moral theology was dissociated from dogma and canon law and began to emerge as a separate discipline. The changed moral atmosphere of the Renascence, the changing political institutions, the changing economic institutions, would all exert their influence. The Roman law would make its deep impression on the classical treatises *De jure et justitia*. The Jansenist heresy lay ahead. The enervating storms of probabilistic controversy—with the discussion carried on for the most part on a juridical and rational plane—had to be weathered before modern moral would take shape.

We have inherited, therefore, says Ivo Zeiger, S.J.,[2] a moral theology in which these three elements are the most prominent: the *casuistic,* to serve the practical necessities of confessors; the *philosophical,* based on the Aristotelian-Scholastic system; and the *juridical,* stemming both from canon and civil law.

But to return to the criticisms, what has become of the revealed sources? What has become of the inspiring moral appeals of the fathers? Where does one find the spiritual food with which to nourish the practical lives of the faithful? In fact, where does one look to find the spirit of the Sermon on the Mount, the specific charter of Christian morality? Where is it translated into terms of modern life and proposed to the faithful as the dynamic and controlling force in their lives? These are the questions asked by the modern critics of moral theology. They say that they look in vain for all this in a modern manual of moral theology—or else when they look they find it with difficulty, because the emphasis is all on casuistry, on legal distinctions, and on the human reasonings of philosophy.

Having noted the general criticisms and the historical background, it will be useful for us to consider the remarks and suggestions of some of the more prominent critics.

G. THILS

G. Thils, after making an investigation of the attitudes of professional moralists, came to these conclusions in 1940.[3] The most urgent need was to make our Lord the very cen-

[2] *Loc. cit.,* p. 182.
[3] G. Thils, *Tendances actuelles en théologie morale,* Gembloux, 1940. Cf. Marcelino Zalba, S.J., "Exposición de la moral cristiana," *Estudios eclesiasticos,* 29 (1955), 65–80 at 72; *idem,* "Inquietudes metodológicas en teologia moral," *Arbor* (Madrid), 3 (Mar., 1955), 1–19 at 1 sq.

ter of morality. Abstract norms, theoretical analyses, and duties incumbent on men in general should be replaced by the concrete, living reality of Jesus Christ, the model of our conduct and the life of our souls. He called for a more personalist moral, in which the Christian conscience would be a more important norm of action than external laws and customs, a norm which would operate not merely in the negative way of restraint and renunciation in the face of prohibitions, nor in an anatomical dissection of sins, but in a vital, enthusiastic, all-conquering impulse of the interior life of the Christian. To this end the creaking vocabulary of moral theology should be accommodated to modern taste, eliminating expressions that no longer have meaning, and adapting the conceptions themselves to the style of the age—an age which is repelled by abstract reasoning and attracted by the concrete fact and the dynamic reality. Jesus Christ, His life, His ideals are that concrete and dynamic reality. To present Him as He is, to inspire contact with Christ psychologically through the emotions, and sacramentally through grace, would give life to a teaching that is dead.

PH. DELHAYE

Among the sharper critics of moral theology as it is today, and of the manuals which are used to teach it, is Ph. Delhaye. Writing in 1953 he had some severe strictures to make.

The manuals which serve as a basis for the teaching of moral carry in vain the date of a recent edition; one feels that they are antiquated. Almost entire treatises, like that on the virtue of religion, are nothing but a series of traps and question marks.

The definition of this virtue is called into question. No one knows any longer what are the servile works forbidden on Sunday. What professor would dare to teach without a smile what is printed today on superstition, and to evoke the devil to account for phenomena which are explainable quite simply in terms of psychology and parapsychology? In recent treatises charity occupies an unaccustomed place, which contrasts strikingly with the importance given it by the sources of revelation. In reality charity should inspire us in all things and animate each of the virtues. But this leaves little room for casuistry which imposes its sway everywhere. To top it all, the few pages which one devotes to it are run through with this leitmotif: *caritas non obligat cum tanto incommodo,* charity does not oblige with so great an inconvenience. It is true, perhaps, in certain cases, and this allows one to gauge responsibilities or faults. But really did our Saviour see things from that angle? Did He not rather enjoin us to give our life for our brother?—which is, after all, a certain inconvenience. . . .[4]

Delhaye called for a more positive science of moral based on Scripture and tradition, with less of the philosophy of unbelievers and more of the Scriptures, both Old and New Testaments, more of the fathers and of the great encyclicals. He charged that moral had neglected the interests of layfolk, had held salaried labor in disrepute, had been too reserved in treating of sexual life, had tended to devalue marriage—and he blamed these defects in part on the fact that moral was written and taught by priests and monks. Moral should be kerygmatic. But it is an abuse of casuistry to teach people from the pulpit just how late one can come to Mass without committing a mortal sin, or just how many ounces one may take as a collation on a fast day. Abstract formulations do not serve to inculcate Christian principles

[4] Art. cit., p. 121 sq.

[48]

in the faithful. When we talk to them we should propose once more the profound and sublime simplicity of Christ and His message. He recalled the famous saying of St. Ambrose: "Non placuit Deo in dialectica salvum facere populum suum."

R. GARRIGOU-LAGRANGE

Altogether removed from Father Delhaye's views, but similarly critical of the overemphasis on casuistry, is R. Garrigou-Lagrange, O.P. His work *Beatitude*, which is a commentary on the first fifty-four questions of the *Prima Secundæ*, was intended by the author as a textbook of moral theology. Far from shunning abstractions, his work is frankly scholastic in method. He defends the view that moral is not a specifically different science from dogma, and he follows the plan of St. Thomas in which the two, though distinct, are not separated. He writes:

The distinction of moral and dogma became distinct in the *Summa*. But some later theologians, Vasquez, for example, maintained that moral and dogma are not two parts of one science, but two distinct sciences. In line with this tendency, moral theology, ignoring dogmatic questions (e.g. grace, merit, the nature of infused virtue), often became a casuistic treatise. In our view, casuistry is but an inferior exemplification, just as asceticism and mysticism are superior exemplifications, of moral theology. . . .

To consider dogma and moral as two sciences is to ignore the sublimity and simplicity of moral theology. Separated from dogma, reduced to casuistry, under a kind of materialistic and statistic tendency, moral theology loses its native elevation and dignity. . . .

Casuistic theology solves questions of conscience and distinguishes degrees of obligation. Its tendency is negative, the avoidance of sin, rather than positive, the cultivation of virtue. It is not really distinguished from prudence, since prudence is the source of a correct and secure conscience. . . .

The two centuries from 1650 to 1850 were devoted to casuistry. Many authors in this period omit all doctrinal questions. Many deal almost exclusively with practical questions; the law, conscience, probable conscience, cases of conscience, the limits of obligation. Moral theology is the science rather of avoiding sin than of cultivating virtue. This casuistic method, inefficacious in urging men to lead good lives, tends to laxism. Asceticism and mysticism lack foundation. Many treatises, ascetic and mystic, have simply no doctrinal value. . . .

When Leo XIII had, we might say, raised Thomism to life, many authors followed St. Thomas. But textbooks generally still labor under the defects of casuistry. They omit important doctrinal questions on human acts, on the passions, on habits.

When asked for treatises on grace, infused virtue, and the gifts, they send you to classes of dogma. But the question returns: How can moral, if it refuses to dwell on the nature of virtue and merit, proceed to a scientific explanation of human acts as the road to a supernatural goal? Science rests on sources and causes. Now the sources of salvific human acts are the infused virtues. Look at the divisions in many moral textbooks. You will find the following general division: on the last end, on human acts, on laws, on conscience, on sins, on virtues in general. Further, you will find a treatise on special moral, which deals indeed with virtues, theological and cardinal, but does not determine their nature, dwells, but all too briefly, on their necessity, while it emphasizes the sins to be avoided. At the end you find a treatise on the sacraments. The moral theology of St. Thomas, it is clear, has not yet found a home in our schools.[5]

[5] R. Garrigou-Lagrange, O.P., *Beatitude:* A Commentary on St. Thomas' Theological Summa, Iᵃ IIᵃᵉ, qq. 1–54. Translated by Patrick Cummins, O.S.B. (St. Louis: B. Herder Book Co., 1956), pp. 4–14.

The author goes on to explain why St. Thomas preferred to treat morality according to the order of the virtues rather than according to the order of the precepts. The reasons given are both theoretical and practical. It would seem that to Father Garrigou-Lagrange the source of the present difficulty in moral theology and the solution of it are both clear. The source was a departure from St. Thomas' method. The solution is a return to it.

J. LECLERCQ

The most important and the most controversial of all the authors who have criticized moral theology is Canon Jacques Leclercq of Louvain.[6] His book, *L'enseignement de la morale chrétienne*, which appeared in 1949 and has been translated into Italian and Spanish, contains most of the criticisms listed at the beginning of this chapter, explaining and developing some of them at great length. He outlines the present-day problems of moral theology as follows (pp. 8–9):

Problems of morality: I see at least four of them. To begin with, what exactly is the teaching of Christ, the essential and the accessory, the specific object of His teaching and the elements which are common to it and to other moral systems. Next, how to teach His morality, the method of teaching; where to start from, and where to continue. In the third place, how to put to good use all the work of human reflection which has developed around the morality of Christ, and to sort the gold from the dross. Finally, how to adapt Christian morality to the world of today. And that is not all; I recognize also a fifth problem: how to lead Christians to follow this morality of Christ.

[6] Jacques Leclercq, *L'enseignement de la morale chrétienne*, Paris: Éditions du Vitrail, 1950.

In developing these questions he begins with an explanation of what he calls the extremely grave crisis in the teaching of Christian morality. Fervent and saintly Catholics are dissatisfied with a negative kind of moral teaching. When Canon Leclercq speaks of a morality of joyous growth unbelievers say: that is all very beautiful, but it is not the morality of the Church; strictly speaking one might call it Christian but not Catholic morality (p. 11). And they hint that he is running the risk of having his views condemned. He continues:

One must have the courage to acknowledge that this morality of enthusiastic Christians contrasts with the official teaching. The morality which is reflected in the seminary courses of moral theology, in religion courses for which the catechism serves as a basis, is hardly dynamic, hardly inspiring, does not appear to be a morality of enthusiasm and victory, but of control and restraint. The same thing is true of the official preaching—which is done from the high pulpit in the parishes and in the public churches. And that morality really seems to be the official morality of the Church. The same thing is true also even of the spiritual literature which speaks of humility, poverty, chastity, modesty, renouncement, obedience—nothing of enthusiasm, nor of victory. The young generation will not put up with the spiritual writings which only a half century ago were the delight of pious souls. *The Practice of Christian Perfection*, by Rodriguez, *Christian Life and Virtues*, by Msgr. Gay, seem to them impossible to assimilate. These authors speak a foreign language, with no relation to the aspirations of today. But then, if all that is really the official teaching of the Church, the authentic tradition, is it not true that one is in search of a new morality—and can a new morality be the Christian morality?

Having outlined the problems and the difficulties, the

canon devotes a chapter to a consideration of morality and Christianity. His conclusion (p. 35) is:

It is not possible for Christian morality to be only the simple morality of the upright man, reinforced by some religious or liturgical practices. It must be transforming: and we all know that it is, but we have to say how. To express that *how*, we must work out a synthesis which presents perhaps a certain appearance of novelty with reference to certain plans of teaching; and in order to utilize the contributions of the centuries we have to see how to integrate them in this synthesis. In order to put each notion in its place, the order of the explanation is vital.

To explain Christianity and Christian morality in proper relief it is essential to start with the person of Christ (pp. 37 ff.). Only so, will one learn what is specifically Christian and what it means to be a Christian. Developing this idea still further, the canon expounds the fundamental themes of the moral teaching of our Lord, beginning with the paternity of God, the mystery of failure, human misery, the doing of penance, the personal character of the Christian vocation, purity and detachment of heart, the spirit of the Kingdom and the love of the neighbor (pp. 57 ff.).

The relation between Christian morality and moral philosophy is the subject of a lengthy chapter (pp. 131–68). The author seems to be very sympathetic with the feelings and aspirations of those outside the Church, or those within, who disdain the religious practices and the mediocre virtues of the bourgeoisie. He seems to dislike the idea of linking the state of grace to regularity in one's daily moral life, prescinding from the values of enthusiasm, victory, and the outpouring of self (p. 148). The "returns" to the sacraments, of which missionaries make so much, do not awaken his enthusiasm. Forty years ago he read an account by Father Willie Doyle of a man who returned to the sacraments after thirty years (pp. 148–49). It was easy, said Father Doyle, because his estrangement from religious practice had all been due simply to a misunderstanding, and the man had nothing to correct in his life. From that time on Canon Leclercq has asked himself: "If religious practice does not change anything in one's life, of what importance is it?" (p. 149). He poses the following problem: "Is it conceivable that a Christian remains in the state of grace by leading a life of average uprightness, self-centered, enjoying himself, avoiding only certain excesses which many non-Christians also avoid, adding only some practices of piety to what the non-Christians do? Or rather should his charity shine before men?" (p. 153).

In another long chapter (pp. 169–216), he studies the great central themes of contemporary morality, such as the grandeur and perfectibility of human personality, the love of mankind, and the search for God. He confronts Christian morality with these themes that have aroused the enthusiasm of modern man, finding in them anew the fundamental positions of our Lord. The challenge to the Church today, as always, is to present its sublime and eternal moral doctrine in a manner adapted to the conditions and mentality of the age.

The chapter on moral theology as a morality of sin (pp. 217–85) contains some of the canon's most trenchant criticisms. The moral theology books, he says, open up lines of thought altogether different from those that he has been describing. Moral books do not sound like the gospel (p. 251). Even Vermeersch, one of the great names, exemplifies the fact that moral theology today is a morality of sin (p. 226). It is a morality of acts rather than tendencies and dispositions, and the acts that receive the most attention are the sinful acts (pp. 226 ff.; 284). One can have a thousand bad tendencies and still be in the state of grace, as long as there is no sin (p. 227). The student looks in vain in *general* moral for treatment of the general conditions requisite for the development of Christian virtue (p. 229). Nowhere in moral theology, or in fact in any other discipline, does one find an over-all view of the specifically Christian way of life (pp. 278, 280; cf. also pp. 14, 57).

"The first moral duty is . . . to reflect and . . . to form one's personality" (p. 280). Therefore, moral teaching should not be occupied primarily with acts, much less with acts of sin (p. 284). The general precepts and virtues, which permeate all moral activity, have been neglected or treated as if they were acquired habits (pp. 235, 242 ff.). The ordinary Christian, if he had been properly oriented and formed in the cardinal virtues, would easily solve most of his moral problems himself, without running to the confessor—who, in turn, runs to the professional moralist—for solutions (pp. 245, 276–77). The penitent himself should make the final decision in a great many cases, because the abstract norms and even the well-elaborated casuistry of the moralists cannot possibly be adequate to the infinite complexities of actual life (pp. 281–83).

Outside critics (not named by the author) say that instead of morality we have moralists; that morality is no longer the problem of life which confronts each individual, responsible to himself, but rather a domain reserved to a closed corporation, the moralists, who decide everything without being responsible to anyone. Priests and faithful have but to be docile; one does not ask them to reflect.

All this is caricature, he says, but it remains true that theologians, including moral theologians, form a corporation to which the Church gives official recognition. When the theologians are in agreement on a case their opinion is authoritative. People act "as if agreement among moralists manifested the action of the Holy Spirit" (pp. 276–77).

He defends casuistry and says it has its proper place, but a subordinate one (p. 281). He insists that the object of morality is to do good, not merely to avoid evil. Avoiding evil is merely a condition of doing good (p. 284). But moral theology does not leave that impression on priests and people. They are accustomed to the idea that morality means not sinning. "Is it debatable? Could one even defend that to avoid sin is not the whole of morality? If a man has not committed any sin will he not go straight to heaven? To be in the state of grace—one has it by baptism—and then not sin, what more do you want?" (p. 225).

Canon Leclercq's final chapters are on the morality of perfection and on social morality (pp. 287 ff.). With many others he underlines the individualistic tendencies of the moral books. The special problem of the Catholic moralist, who must be faithful to Christian tradition (which from the beginning up to the twentieth century was individualistic) is this: In the social spirit of our times, what is legitimate, what is deficient, and how are we to integrate the sound contributions into the Christian tradition?

The foregoing is by no means a complete or systematic description of the thought contained in this book of about three hundred and fifty large pages. It is merely a sampling, which cannot possibly do justice to the sustained and subtle thought of the author. We were able only to touch on what E. Guerrero, S.J., called "the magnificent chapters" on the central themes of the gospel and the central themes of contemporary moral thought. But enough has been said, it is hoped, to indicate the trend and the flavor, and to hint at the causes of the disquietude which has apparently preoccupied the canon for many years. Perhaps enough has been said, too, to make the reader himself a little uneasy about some of the "perspectives" opened up by this critic.

"L'OSSERVATORE ROMANO" ON LECLERCQ

The early reviews of Canon Leclercq's book were, in general, very favorable, although even then some serious defects were pointed out.[7] But *L'Osservatore Romano*, February 2, 1956, published a sweeping repudiation of the book in an unsigned article entitled, "Constructive Criticisms and Destructive Criticisms."[8] Although the reviewer admits that some of the canon's observations are "opportune and even acute," he considers that the general effect of the work is that of "implacable demolition by a battering ram." The book, he says, "frankly passes all limits to attack substantial aspects of Catholic doctrine, morality, and worship."

Some of the points singled out for animadversion are these. One of the fundamental theses of the book, says the writer, is that in the course of the development of moral doctrine there has been a notable deviation from the original teaching of Christ, with the consequence that we must now discover the morality really taught by the Master, and

[7] See for example, E. Guerrero, S.J., *Razón y Fe*, 148 (July–Aug., 1953), 84, who found faults in the book, but spoke of some of its chapters as "magnificent"; R. Carpentier, S.J., "Vers une morale de la charité," *Gregorianum*, 34 (1953), 33 sq. and 40 sq., finds serious flaws in the book but refers to it as "ce grand ouvrage."

[8] *L'Osservatore Romano*, Feb. 2, 1956, p. 1.

purify our teaching of the accretions of the centuries which have been superimposed on it like alluvial deposits. The book is accused of having a Modernistic savor. In it Catholic morality is set forth as being abstract, antiquated, casuistic, marred by juridical obligationism and by asocial individualism—even in the ascetical literature. It leaves one with the impression that almost everything written so far has been wide of the mark and a continual alteration of the teaching of the divine Master. And so the author does not safeguard sufficiently the role of the infallible magisterium.

Canon Leclercq is too ready to leave to the faithful themselves the final judgment on their cases of conscience. He underlines too much subjective values, at the expense of the meaning of the law, and of universal principles. He seems to minimize the importance of the sacraments in moral life. Pius XII's warnings are recalled, indicating the dangers of a personalistic morality which rejects traditional norms as being too abstract to be adapted to the exigencies of the concrete man.

The reviewer confesses that in giving such a negative opinion on the book he had taken note of numerous phrases like "One says" or "One has the impression" which recur in the book and behind which Canon Leclercq appears to "eclipse himself." But then, "where to find the thought of the author?" It looks as though all his labor has been "to compile an 'anthology' of maledictions on Catholic morality." Before concluding, the reviewer makes the following remark—especially significant, it seems, since it appears in *L'Osservatore Romano*: "It is no wonder that the higher authorities—as we understand from authoritative sources—

have ordered the withdrawal from commerce of the book and of its translations." [9]

Our own evaluation of some of the criticisms made by Canon Leclercq and others mentioned in this chapter will be given later. At present we might merely mention that the total picture presented by the canon's book is one of almost mystifying contrast. On the positive side, his delineation of Christian ideals and of the role of the Church reaches heights of awe-inspiring grandeur; yet, on the negative side, his criticisms of traditional moral teaching and Catholic practices have a certain resemblance to the tenets of the new morality which has come to be known as situation ethics. [10]

[9] Alfredo Boschi, S.J., "La così detta 'Morale nuova,'" *La Scuola Cattolica*, 84 (Sept.–Oct., 1956, n. 5), 337, note 6, mentions that the book was withdrawn from commerce by ecclesiastical authority.

[10] Cf. *infra*, chapters 7 and 8. Perhaps it was not mere coincidence that the article in *L'Osservatore Romano* appeared on the same day that the Holy Office published its official warning against situation ethics. But if the strictures of the writer in *L'Osservatore Romano* are well founded, especially that in which he says that the book "attacks substantial aspects of Catholic doctrine, morality and worship," it is hard to see why it was not put on the Index, instead of merely being withdrawn from commerce.

5

New Approaches to Moral Theology

THE NEW APPROACHES to moral theology which have been discussed for the last twenty years and brought to a sharp focus during the last five or six are not entirely new. In 1817, J. M. Seiler published a *Handbook of Christian Morality*,[1] the principal merit of which according to F. Tillmann, was that the author refused to become involved in a welter of opinions, or in the acrobatics of casuistry. He made moral theology a science of virtue and a way of Christian perfection.[2] About twenty years later J. B. Hirscher published a work (at Tübingen, 1835–1836), with the significant title: *Christian Morality as the Doctrine of the Realization of the Kingdom of God in Mankind*.[3] But it cannot be said that the nineteenth century produced works by moralists who were keenly conscious of the type

---

[1] J. M. Seiler, *Handbuch der Christlichen Moral*, Munich, 1817.

[2] Cf. Marcelino Zalba, S.J., "Inquietudes metodológicas en teologia moral," *Arbor* (Madrid), 3 (Mar., 1955), 1–19 at 3.

[3] John Baptist Hirscher, *Die Christliche Moral als Lehre von der Verwirklichung des göttlichen Reiches in der Menschheit*, Tübingen, 1835–

of criticism we have been discussing. Many of the works of that century are the very ones under attack.

ARTHUR VERMEERSCH, S.J.

When Arthur Vermeersch, S.J., published his four-volume work on moral theology more than thirty years ago (the first edition was in 1922), he called it: *Theologiæ moralis principia, responsa, consilia.*[4] *Principia*, because he wanted to meet the complaint that moralists were not giving the intrinsic reasons for their solutions; *responsa*, because it contained the practical solutions of cases ordinarily met by confessors; *consilia*, because it was his purpose not merely to investigate sins to be avoided, but to explain and inculcate the positive side of Christian justice and the pursuit of the greater good. It was for the same reason that he chose to follow in his exposition the order of the virtues rather than that of the commandments. Vermeersch was a man of God who had written inspiringly on the spiritual life of the Christian, and who himself had taken a vow, on Christmas Day, 1891, of perpetual and total self-abnegation.[5] "Voveo . . . perpetuam et totalem abnegationem mei, juxta litteram et sensum ab eo qui me dirigit in spiritu approbatum et scripto consignatum." The force of the vow, which was found among his papers after his death, was such that if he were to hesitate between two alternatives, not knowing which represented the more perfect choice, he would be obliged to choose that which entailed greater renouncement, that is, the side which the world would not choose. It is not surprising, then, that he would be pecul-

[4] Arthur Vermeersch, S.J., *Theologiæ moralis principia, responsa, consilia* (3rd ed.), Rome: Gregorian University, 1947.
[5] J. Creusen, S.J., "Le 'Voeu d'Abnégation' du R.P. Vermeersch, S.J., (1858–1936)," *Gregorianum*, 21 (1940), 607.

iarly sensitive to the charge of minimalism made against moralists, and that he would become, as it were, a spokesman for those who even then were looking for higher things from moral theology.

Thomas Slater, S.J., writing in 1923 on "The Confessor's Standard of Morality," insisted that that standard was the one

laid down by Jesus Christ in the Sermon on the Mount; it is the standard of Christian perfection according to which Jesus Christ Himself lived. . . . Principally on this account we welcome the new course of Moral Theology inaugurated by Father A. Vermeersch, S.J., the Professor of Moral Theology at the Gregorian University. . . . He regards Moral Theology as the science not only of right and wrong, but as the science of Christian perfection and beatitude. He looks forward with confidence to a new golden age of Moral Theology, but to realize this hope he is conscious that much remains to be done by modern writers on the subject. They must in the first place make a more thorough study of the rational basis of that portion of moral doctrine which is not above natural reason. In the next place they must give a more honorable place to the treatment of the principles of Christian perfection. . . .[6]

But Vermeersch's efforts and Slater's approval were not unanimously acclaimed. In 1924 a certain "Episcopus" writing in the *American Ecclesiastical Review*, protested rather strongly, in a communication entitled (by the editor, presumably): "Disinfecting Moral Theology," against the mixing of ascetical ideals into the moral theology course.[7]

[6] T. Slater, S.J., "The Confessor's Standard of Morality," *American Ecclesiastical Review*, 68 (1923), 38–43 at 40.

[7] "Episcopus," "Disinfecting Moral Theology," *American Ecclesiastical Review*, 70 (1924), 187–89. Cf. also "Theologus," reviewing Vermeersch's work in *American Ecclesiastical Review*, 70 (1924), 327–28; and James T.

He quoted with approval the famous Abbé Hogan, Sulpician Rector of St. John's Seminary in Boston. Dr. Hogan, distinguishing between moralist and moral theologian, had written many years previously:

As found in St. Liguori, and as taught in the schools, the main object of Moral Theology is in no wise to establish an ideal, but simply to determine a minimum of duty. The moralist holds up ideals to which a man and a Christian may and, in some sense, should aspire; the moral theologian, or the casuist, as he is often called, considers only to what a man is strictly bound. His whole concern is to establish the *scientia liciti et illiciti*. He is in morals what the writer on criminal law is in jurisprudence. The latter may be the most noble-minded and best of men; but, as a criminalist, he has to deal, not with high aims and generous actions, but with crimes, trespasses, and misdemeanors.

"Episcopus" is forthright in accepting this view of moral theology and in making his own application of it to Vermeersch's work:

There is a widespread demand for the teaching of civics, or the ideals of citizenship, in the schools. If a lawyer attempted to meet this demand by compiling an elementary book on criminal law, augmented by appropriate reflections on the ideals of citizenship, the teachers of the country would certainly reject his production as unsuitable for school work. Similarly, the attempt by Father Vermeersch to meet the demand for a text book on the ideals of the Christian by incorporating ascetic considerations in his book of Moral Theology should be rejected as unsuitable.

Cotter, "Teaching Moral Theology," *ibid.*, 413–15. Both the latter authors reject the views of "Episcopus."

Questions in Fundamental Moral Theology

Let the name Moral Theology be retained unchanged in meaning. It denotes a science needed for the guidance of priests in judging cases submitted to them. It has acquired this technical meaning in the usage of centuries. It might have been appropriately adopted to mean something very different; but the historical fact is that it has been appropriated to express the *scientia liciti et illiciti*, for use in the confessional. There has been a corresponding development of moral science for use in the pulpit and for personal guidance; but this has not been formally taught as a class-room subject in seminaries until recently. It was confined to meditation books, spiritual reading, retreats, religious instruction, etc. Now there is a demand for regular class-room teaching of the ideals of the Christian life in scientific form. This demand cannot be met by any change in Moral Theology. . . . It is a different science and requires different treatment by a different professor with a different text book.

Possibly "Episcopus" was anxious to guard against any tendency towards rigorism which would result from confusing counsels with commandments. Or perhaps, on the contrary, his real fear was not so much that moral theology would lose its specific "criminal" character if touched by asceticism, but that the teaching of asceticism would be contaminated and soon be in need of disinfection itself if it once got into the hands of the moralists.

At any rate, a year later, in 1925, it was the ascetical element which was singled out for special commendation when Cardinal Gasparri conveyed to Vermeersch the congratulations of Pope Pius XI on the *Principia, responsa, consilia*. He placed special emphasis on the fact that Vermeersch had joined to the treatment of the precepts and obligations a part of moral "too often neglected in similar

[64]

scientific treatises, the part of the counsels and of Christian perfection." [8]

Subsequently, Pius XI himself spoke publicly of moral theology as the school of Christian love:

Just as dogmatic theology can be called the school of the Truth of Christ, so Moral Theology can, in a certain way, be said to be the school of the Charity of Christ, or that Queen Charity to which everything is raised up and ennobled, while seeking from her light for the field of action. [9]

Vermeersch saw very clearly the task that lay before moral theology. In 1929, writing a general conspectus of the previous sixty years of moral theology, after indicating the principal work confronting the moralist, he concluded as follows:

The role, the great task of contemporary moral is to supernaturalize the aspirations of men; unto the cross, and thence unto heaven. But on the cross there is not merely suffering; there is above all the love that has accepted, desired the suffering: the twofold love of God and of man because of God. Through the personal love of Jesus Christ it is toward this twofold love that all true moral theology should be oriented: that of the manuals, that of the more profound treatises, that of oral preaching as that of written exhortation. . . . The enthusiasm of the mystic is directed toward love: it confirms our final conclusion: moral theology should bring about the love of good; however not an abstract good, but that good which is identified with the divine Person of Jesus Christ. [10]

[8] Arthur Vermeersch, S.J., Theologiæ moralis principia, responsa, consilia (3rd ed.; Rome: Gregorian University, 1947), I, v.

[9] Pius XI, Ex Sermone post disputationem Theologiæ Moralis coram SS^{mo}, Pontificia Universitate Gregoriana habitam, 20 Mar. 1926 in Enchiridion Clericorum (Rome: Vatican Polyglot Press, 1938), n. 1451.

[10] Arthur Vermeersch, S.J., "Soixante ans de théologie morale," Nouvelle revue théologique, 56 (1929), 880.

All this has been noted here, because sometimes one gets the impression from the writings of recent years that nothing was ever thought or done about this problem until now. Vermeersch would be the first to concede that his was only a contribution to the task which confronted moral theology. But his influence has been far-reaching. A whole generation of moralists has grown up since his work appeared and, thanks to him, has grown up acutely aware of the dangers of legalism and of moral minimalism. Much of the present writing on the subject, then, must be considered the product of a ferment which considerably antedates the somewhat impatient thrusts of later and less constructive critics.

O. SCHILLING AND F. TILLMANN

In 1928, six years after Vermeersch's work appeared, O. Schilling was publishing the first edition of his Moral Theology in which he set forth briefly the fundamental proposition that charity is the leading principle of moral theology.[11] Schilling derives this principle from the end of Christian morality, which is assimilation and union with God. This end can be achieved only through charity, hence charity must be considered the first principle of moral theology. It is not his thought, however, that charity is the formal or exemplary cause of the other virtues such as justice. It is rather that he considers justice to be the minimum of charity. Inasmuch as charity commands this minimum, and is, as it were, its efficient cause, justice becomes

[11] O. Schilling, *Handbuch der Moraltheologie*, Stuttgart, 1952. The first edition appeared in 1928. See Joseph Fuchs, S.J., "Die Liebe als Aufbauprinzip der Moraltheologie," *Scholastik*, 29 (1954), 79–87 at 80.

a means to union with God and a principle of supernatural merit. Schilling does not believe any definition of moral theology can be adequate which does not make explicit mention of charity, for charity is the unique means of leading us to union with God, our last end.

Six years later, in 1934, Fritz Tillmann published his moral opus on the following of Christ. He stands out as one of the first and greatest of our modern contributors to a more Christocentric moral theology.[12] His work is based on the fundamental proposition that the moral perfection of a Christian is the progressive realization of the ideal of "a Son of God." Our Lord has been revealed to us as both God and man, and with the help of grace we are destined to become other Christs, as far as sinful creatures can. The imitation of Christ thus becomes not a mere external copying but an attempt to be assimilated to the very thoughts and desires of our Lord. This sort of imitation is the heart of Christian morality. Tillmann's exposition of moral follows this guiding principle. Sin is treated at the end of the general section, as something beside the mark, something which is in partial or total opposition to the great duty of following Christ. In the treatment of the virtues and the means of grace the material is not presented as a system of laws with the emphasis on legal norms of conduct. The Christian's obligations are conceived rather as necessary developments from two fundamental facts, his need of actuating and realizing his own perfection as a human person, and the fact that in the present order of

---

[12] Fritz Tillmann, Vol. III, *Die Idee der Nachfolge Christi*, Düsseldorf, 1934; Vol. IV, 1 and 2, *Die Verwirklichung der Nachfolge Christi*, Düsseldorf, 1935–1936.

[67]

divine providence the ideal proposed to him is the imitation of Jesus Christ, the divine model of all humanity.[13]

Tillmann was a New Testament exegete before he took up the field of moral; hence, he was specially well qualified to paint our Lord's moral character in brilliant colors as a model for imitation. His method is to develop the precepts of the New Law from our Lord's own words, not making sharp distinctions between what is of counsel and what is of obligation, and thus to inspire generous souls to follow our Lord's call: "I am the light of the world. He who follows me does not walk in the darkness, but will have the light of life." [14]

His is a work, therefore, of kerygmatic theology, by which is understood "that method of treating theological materials which is directly and immediately suitable for kerygma, i.e. the preparation and promotion of the *preaching* of sacred truths." [15] The title of Tillmann's shorter work on morals for the layman is in itself indicative of the kerygmatic scope of his teaching: *The Master Calls: A Layfolk's Moral Theology for Believing Christians.*[16] Tillmann's work, too, pointed out by anticipation one way of meeting the demands of later critics; but it is well to note at the outset that to meet all these demands and at the same time provide a suitable instrument for the training of confessors is a goal yet to be achieved.

[13] See Marcelino Zalba, S.J., "Inquietudes metodológicas en teologia moral," *Arbor* (Madrid), 3 (Mar., 1955), 1–19 at 11, 12.

[14] John 8:12. Cf. Ivo Zeiger, S.J., "De conditione theologiæ moralis moderna," *Periodica*, 28 (1939), 176–89 at 186.

[15] *Ibid.*, p. 185.

[16] Fritz Tillmann, *Der Meister Ruft. Eine Laienmoral für gläubige Christen*, published first in 1937 at Düsseldorf, with a new edition in 1948.

New Approaches to Moral Theology

ÉMILE MERSCH, S.J.

While Tillmann was writing his moral theology based on the following of Christ, Émile Mersch, S.J. was publishing the articles which later, in 1937, became his famous work *Morality and the Mystical Body.*[17] The complaint has been frequently made, as we have seen, that the moral theology of the manuals is too individualistic, that it has neglected social considerations. The morality of the Mystical Body is more than Christocentric; it is pre-eminently social, because it starts with the dogmatic presuppositions of the doctrine of the Mystical Body. Incidentally, it was not until six years after Mersch's first edition that the great encyclical *Mystici Corporis* was issued.

Every Christian, by baptism, is incorporated into the spiritual society which is the Church, and is made a member of the Mystical Body of Christ. He no longer stands alone but is bound to others by supernatural social bonds. Accordingly his moral life would not correspond to the supernatural realities if he were to act with purely individualistic principles, unaware of, or indifferent to, the implications of that mystical incorporation.

In the introduction to the book, Mersch explains the scope of his work:

It is an entire Moral Science which we would like to have constructed, a Moral Science specifically Christian and theological, a Moral Science whose principles would be the great Christian dogmas of the Trinity, the Incarnation and of the Incorporation through Grace in the Incarnate Word, a Moral

17 Émile Mersch, S.J., *Morale et Corps Mystique* (3rd ed., enlarged), Paris: Desclée, de Brouwer, 1949 (1st ed., 1937); English translation (from second French edition) by Daniel F. Ryan, S.J., New York: P.J. Kenedy and Sons, 1939.

Science which would address itself to the members of Christ inasmuch as they are members of Christ and to the children of adoption inasmuch as they are children of adoption. . . . Our desire is to suggest at least the spirit of supernatural ethics, the spirit of the precept of Charity.

The unifying idea is that the Christian law is essentially positive, even and especially in its demands of sacrifice and of mortification: its purpose is that the divine seed may increase at whatever cost. Optimism then, but optimism which, far from denying suffering, illumines it, the optimism of redeemed and risen men.

Just as incorporation in Christ and union with the entire Trinity through Christ are the most magnificent gift which man could receive in the order of being, so the power and the blessed obligation of detaching oneself from oneself in order to act as a member of Christ and as God's son of adoption is the most splendid grace which could fall to man in the order of his will.[18]

In summing up the fundamentals from which he would derive the morality of all Christian life, Mersch speaks as follows:

To sum up this entire article in a few words, we would say that a spiritual doctrine, like the Christian doctrine in general, is not in the first place a declaration of war, but a formula of union.

The fundamental truth is that God has created everything, that Christ has redeemed all of us, and that, in Him, human nature forms only one person with the divine nature.

Union with God, union with Christ, union with all men in Christ and in God, that is the essential, and in a certain sense, the whole thing.

[18] *Op. cit.,* Introd., p. vii sq.

The first, the unique precept even, is to love God and the neighbor.

And also, since God is not accessible except through the humanity of Christ, and since the humanity of Christ is no longer visible here below except in men, the centre of all spiritual doctrine and the great means of sanctification is the love of the neighbor, zeal for souls.

To contribute, in ourselves and in others, to this mystical prolongation of the Incarnation, which is the divinisation of the human race, is our entire duty, and it should constantly preoccupy us.[19]

There is no doubt that if moral obligations and moral aspirations were approached from these sublime heights a quite different emphasis would attach to a problem like that of social justice, to mention but one example, and a quite different setting and tone to all our morality. Even the more individual actions involved in the profession of faith, or the public denial of faith, cooperation with the sins of another, or scandal, fidelity to promises, veracity, obedience —all these would receive new light if viewed as the acts of a member of the Mystical Body. In the first edition of his work, Mersch made some practical applications of his moral doctrine to questions of Christian poverty, love, marriage, chastity, authority, obedience—the obedience of children, of citizens, and of religious. In the third French edition, published after his death, the editors added some further essays of his on the theological virtues of faith, hope, and charity.

The whole tone and spirit in which he makes these applications is magnificent and inspiring, and it can best be conveyed, perhaps, in a concluding citation in his own

19 *Ibid.*, p. 95.

words;—but again it must be remarked that, lofty as the teaching is, it was not thought of by its author as being in itself adequate for the professional formation of confessors.

A Christian is a member of Christ: that is the résumé of Christianity.

A Christian should act as a member of Christ: that is the résumé of Christian asceticism and the code of all sanctity.

But, to be a member of Christ implies two aspects, two attachments. In the first place, the attachment to Christ, for the member ought to adhere to the head. Then, the attachment to all Christians, for the member ought to adhere to the entire body. These two attachments, in fact, constitute only one: for a member, adherence to the chief or adherence to the other members is the same attachment, the one which gives life to the member. *Multi unum corpus in Christo, singuli autem alter alterius membra.* (Rom. 12: 5; I Cor. 12: 14.)

Christian sanctity, in consequence, since it consists in acting as a member of Christ, consists in acting with the same double attachment. Attachment to Christ in the first place: all our virtues can be only a flowing, an influx coming from the Head. Then attachment to the members: all our virtues can be only an element, a part, a member in some sort in the only sanctity which is total, the sanctity of the entire Mystical Body of Christ.[20]

The new approaches to moral theology which we have just briefly described (Vermeersch, Schilling, Tillmann, and Mersch) were formulated in the twenties and thirties, and were summarized by Zeiger in 1939.[21] These were the fore-

[20] *Ibid.,* p. 97. Cf. also Constantin Noppel, S.J., *Ædificatio Corporis Christi. Aufriss der Pastoral* (2nd ed.), Freiburg: Herder, 1949 (1st ed., 1936); and F. Jurgenmeier, *Der mystische Leib Christi als Grundprinzip der Aszetik* (7th ed.), Paderborn, 1938 (1st ed., 1933).

[21] *Art. cit.* (note 13 *supra*) *passim.*

runners of present attempts to rejuvenate moral theology. It is not easy to estimate the extent to which these earlier writers influenced the work being done today, and it would be a mistake to discount other influences from modern systems of thought, but it is safe to say that the influence of these forerunners has been large and strong.

As examples of more recent efforts let us now look at the suggestions of Ermecke and the imposing work of Gilleman.

GUSTAV ERMECKE

In 1951, Gustav Ermecke, Rector of the University of Paderborn and professor of moral theology there, outlined briefly a plan for the structure of the moral theology course.[22] Preliminary to this plan he made some observations on method and on the concept of Christian activity.

It is his belief that only by combining five different methods will our knowledge of moral become complete: the *positive* method, which expounds the teachings of Scripture, tradition, and the magisterium; the *metaphysical* method, which uses scholastic philosophy and theology to explore the secrets of nature and grace; the *mystical* method, based on man's new oneness of being and oneness of life in Christ, and deriving the laws of moral activity from this new being; the *casuistical* method, which is the application of the general principles taught by the Church to the manifold situations and occasions of everyday life; and the *ascetical* method, which examines the nature of Christian perfection and determines the means which are of precept or of counsel in tending toward this goal.

[22] Gustav Ermecke, "Die katholische Moraltheologie heute," *Theologie und Glaube*, 41 (1951, n. 2), 127–42. Cf. *Theology Digest*, 2 (Winter, 1954, n. 1), 19–22.

The concept of Christian activity is closely related to the mystical method. We develop only by activity. The one who develops by activity is the new man in Christ, and his end is Godlikeness or the imitation of Christ. Moral theology, then, should study more deeply the nature of specifically Christian activity. The author has four propositions concerning activity: First, to act is and should be the development of a being. (Here the being is the new supernatural man in Christ.) Second, activity is the proclamation of a truth. (Our supernatural activity proclaims Christ to the world.) Third, activity is the realization of a value. (If an action gives me more supernatural being it is good; if it lessens it, it is bad. If it destroys my living supernatural actuality, it is seriously sinful.) Fourth, activity is the fulfillment of a norm. (Every creature should strive to be its best self within the framework of God's universal order of creation and redemption. In this way it fulfills God's norm, His will in its regard, and becomes perfect.)

Christ our Lord is infinite being, supreme truth, unlimited perfection, and God's law perfectly fulfilled; and in Him is the fulfillment of all our activity. Moral theology, then, has the task of studying more closely the nature of this unique activity of the new creature supernaturalized in Christ.

In general moral, Father Ermecke would treat such preliminary questions as the relationship between ethics and moral, and certain key ideas of his system. These key ideas are three: (1) *The new life* in Christ. Under this heading would be treated: Christ as the goal, and imitation of Him as the means to the goal, supernatural life, the danger of sin, and beatitude. (2) *The new love* would be explained as supernatural Christian charity, vitalizing and elevating all our merely natural virtues and acts. (We shall see in a moment Father Gilleman's development of this theme.) (3) *The new law,* brought to us by our Lord. This new law is promulgated to us first of all by the Church, not by conscience, and in working out the individual applications of Christ's command to follow Him the casuistical method is brought into play.

In special moral, the author would depart from traditional divisions according to commandments or virtues and use as a unifying principle in the Christian formation of life the threefold degree of sacramental likeness to Christ. Part I of special moral would treat the Christian moral doctrine of the states of life, and treat them according to the increasingly intimate sacramental likeness to Christ of the baptized, of the confirmed, and of the ordained. Part II would treat the Christian moral doctrine of obligations to God, to the Church, to individual fellow men, and to the different social communities—all based on the new being and life in Christ. Part III would treat the psychological, pedagogical, ascetical, and sociological means to help the Christian lead his new life.

This is only the briefest outline of how a Christologically constructed moral theology would look. For Father Ermecke, Christians really have one great task—to make their own lives, the visible Church, and the world more like Christ. Applied to the moral act this means that the Christian should develop his likeness to Christ by living the new life in Christ under the influence of grace. In this way he will put the idea of Christ into effect and will contribute to the efficacious Christianizing of the world.

Questions in Fundamental Moral Theology

GÉRARD GILLEMAN, S.J.

The widely acclaimed work of Gérard Gilleman, S.J.; *The Primacy of Charity in Moral Theology*, was substantially completed in 1947, but was not published until 1952.[23] Our manuals today, says Father Gilleman, do not sufficiently express the central theme of the Christian dispensation, as we find it in the gospels, epistles and fathers. In the course of its development, moral theology has had to incorporate natural morality and law; because of methodological problems, it has become more and more divorced from dogma; and, because of the necessity of instructing with a view to integrity of confession, there has been a tendency to overemphasize sin. Father Gilleman would like to re-establish the connection with dogma and to give moral theology a dynamic unity under its distinctively Christian aspect, charity.[24]

It is the law of charity given to us by Christ as his "new commandment" which is specifically Christian in moral theology. Charity means to love God, and to love the neighbor for the sake of God, as Christ loves him. "On these two commandments depend the whole law and the Prophets." [25] Christianity has always been keenly aware of the primacy of charity in the life of Christians. It would be natural to

[23] Gérard Gilleman, S.J., *Le primat de la charité en théologie morale*, Paris: Desclée, de Brouwer, 1952.

[24] A writer in the *Revue diocésaine de Namur*, 7 (May–July, 1953), 190–91, finds it "astounding, not to say scandalous" that after twenty centuries of Christianity a work like Gilleman's should be necessary to counteract the casuistical, legalistic attitudes of moralists, to whom it has to be proved "in due form" that love is the soul of Christian morality. But Gilleman himself does not take quite this view. There is no need, he rightly says, to prove the primacy of charity; what is needed is to see how the method of moral theology can make that primacy explicit and evident throughout the science.

[25] Matt. 22:40.

expect that textbooks of moral theology would make this the cardinal point of their whole treatment, in order to point up the all-pervading presence of charity in the activity of the children of God.

But many manuals give insufficient space to the theological virtue of charity. It is not presented as the first principle from which all applications are derived; it is not made the soul which gives life and meaning to moral theology. Rather it is often treated merely as a virtue *alongside* other virtues. Its vital role in every phase of Christian life is neglected. Father Gilleman sets out

. . . to investigate in a theological way how to apply to the whole organization of moral theology the universal principle enunciated by St. Thomas, *Caritas forma virtutum:* to establish, therefore, the principles of a method which would explicitly assign to charity, in the organization of moral theology, the same vital function that it exercises in actual living and in the revelation of Christ: not a role that it would play parallel to other moral realities, but the role of soul, of *animating,* which is exercised on a level that is deeper than that of any act or any definite virtue.[26]

The first part of his work is devoted to a study of St. Thomas, with emphasis on the primacy of charity. He notes at the conclusion of this section (p. 65) that the sincere modern mind, trying to formulate moral values, tends to desert the objective world and enter the domain of the subjective, the psychological; to forsake abstract formulations for an existential description of conscience. He believes that his interpretation of *caritas forma virtutum* will give due emphasis to the subjective and the concrete in our moral

[26] *Op. cit.,* p. 13.

[77]

activity, thus satisfying the yearnings of the modern mind, without sacrificing, but rather enhancing the objective data of our moral science.

The second part studies the moral act as an expression of love in the natural order and of charity in the supernatural order. Our supernatural virtuous acts are "mediators" of charity. By means of them man is put in actual contact with the marvelous treasures of charity. Our moral life, product of our liberty, is creative of our spiritual personalities. It incarnates, as it were, Christian charity because it exteriorizes the Christian's love and enables it to extend itself in space and time. At the end of this section, too, the author (p. 181) is careful to note that his work offers the hope of a *rapprochement* with contemporary existentialist thought (of the orthodox variety) and especially with the contemporary philosophy of value.

The third part of the work is a practical illustration of how his thesis might be applied in teaching moral theology. Under general moral he speaks of the relations of moral to spiritual and pastoral theology, of obligation, of law and love, of charity and sin, and of charity and the moral virtues. The practical applications to special moral are headed: Religion and Charity; Fraternal Charity; Body, Suffering, and Charity; Chastity and Charity; Charity and Justice.

It is not Father Gilleman's intent to make additions to the already large subject matter to be taught in moral theology, but to infuse into the teaching a new atmosphere. He believes that despite some new terminology the content of his work is, in its totality, traditional. And he modestly concludes by calling it a mere commentary "in the spirit of the Church [to which he submits his effort] on that law which is the first of all and in the last analysis the only one: 'Thou shalt love'." [27]

---

[27] An article by Servais Pinckærs, O.P., "The Revival of Moral Theology," *Cross Currents*, 7 (Winter, 1957), 56–67, gives an account of the new approaches to moral theology. See also Bernhard Häring, C.SS.R., *Das Gesetz Christi* (Freiburg: Wewel, 1954), pp. 71–84.

6

Reflections on the Criticisms
and New Approaches

WE BELIEVE THAT moralists ought to welcome the modern criticisms of, and new approaches to, moral theology and frankly admit that there is need of change. There is need for new emphasis, and need for a more positive approach to the moral life of a Christian in Christ. At the same time, however, the welcome we extend to critics should itself be a critical one.

The first thing one notices in reading the extensive literature critical of moral theology—and the somewhat less extensive writing which makes constructive contributions—is that here we are not generally dealing with petty carping or foolish fantasies. Of course there is bound to be some of this. Someone picks out a weak point remembered from his own moral theology class and harps on it for the rest of his life. Ridicule is an easy weapon, always ready to hand.[1] Then there are always some whose nostalgia for the sim-

[1] E. Ranwez, "Pour ou contre une spiritualité du devoir," *Revue diocésaine de Namur*, 8, nn. 1–3 (Jan.–June, 1953), 43–58 at 43, cites a conference which was printed in *Évangéliser* (Jan., 1952), pp. 340–355. Ranwez

plicity of primitive Christianity will make them impatient of things as they are, no matter what they are, in this workaday world. The realities of the human developments in the Mystical Body of Christ, the complexities of ecclesiastical organization are too much for them to adjust to, and they would prefer to escape to the imagined sweet simplicity of the past.

We have quoted enough to show that the criticisms are not of this insignificant variety. In fact, there is something at stake here much bigger than a mere criticism of the methods and the content of the seminary course in moral theology. Actually much of the criticism is an attempt to change the atmosphere and raise the tone of our whole approach to Christian life and spirituality. The criticisms may be considered under the following headings: first, there is impatience with medocrity in the moral life of a Christian; secondly, there is impatience with the restrictive effects of "obligationism" in the life of a Christian; thirdly, there is impatience with the moral theology course as it is taught in seminaries.

IMPATIENCE WITH MEDIOCRITY

It is a good thing to be impatient with spiritual mediocrity—especially in one's own life. And it is a good thing to be impatient with it in the lives of others, if this impatience is the burning zeal which animated the saints and urged them on to inspire others to spiritual heroism like their own. But it would not be a good thing if it consigned to outer darkness the millions of mediocre men, the millions

says of this conference: "It would be difficult, we think, to explain with more verve and less accuracy what it is proper to admit or to deny apropos of obligation and supererogation."

upon millions of ordinary Christians, who follow Christ, as it were, from afar. No matter what method of teaching or preaching we use, no matter what aspect of Christianity we stress, whether it be the fear of sin, the love of virtue, or the perfect love of God through Christ, it will always remain true that the vast majority of Christians will not be spiritual heroes. To demand of them that they strive for perfection just as the saints have done, insisting on the gravity of this obligation, and even denying the state of grace to those who fail so to strive, would be a type of rigorism not unknown in the history of the Church and lethal in its effects.

The authors who call for a more dynamic morality, a more inspiring morality, a morality of *élan*, enthusiasm, personal creativity, and the outpouring of self; for the victorious flowering of the spirit of Christ and for the whole-hearted fervor and dedication of the early Christians—these authors are obviously impatient with the mediocrity they see all about them. And this is all to the good. When they look for a remedy and find it in the great doctrine of love, the first and greatest commandment given to us by our Lord, and demand that this law of love receive the attention it deserves and the place which is really its own in the Christian scheme of things—this also is all to the good. And when it is said that practically and ultimately the obligation of true Christian charity and the obligation to seek Christian perfection coincide, this can be understood properly without any difficulty. But if the obligation of seeking perfection is then explained in a way that in practice would exclude the objective distinction between precepts and counsels, and would make of every "ought" an obligation as unlimited as that of love itself, then we are in danger of distorting the law of charity, and of defeating the whole purpose of the effort to revitalize morality.

Father Joseph Fuchs, S.J. makes a relevant comment:

Love as a basis of morality is bound up, as history shows, with certain dangers. We are acquainted with the interpretation which situation ethics puts on Augustine's *ama et fac quod vis*; with the Quietistic significance given to the commandment of love by Fénelon; and with the rigoristic meaning attached to it in Protestantism. By this we mean the doctrine that primarily and properly speaking God does not demand from men definite good deeds, but rather his entire love; but since sinful man never fully renders it, he constantly sins.[2]

Everyone agrees, then, with the authors who say that charity is the soul of moral theology, and everyone would wish to bring this truth home to priests and people, confessors and penitents alike. But the difficulty is in finding a way of inculcating this doctrine which will avoid dangerous doctrinal shoals.

We should not allow our impatience with mediocrity to lead us to forget some simple fundamentals of Catholic doctrine. Something less than "perfect charity" will suffice for justification when joined with the reception of the sacraments. In order to stay in the state of grace it is not essential to be free of venial sins and imperfections. Saints have recognized three degrees of humility, all of which imply substantial friendship with God and therefore that minimum of love which is necessary to supernatural life. The first degree excludes mortal sin, the second venial sin, and the third strives for complete conformity with the will of God. The Church itself insists that love motivated by fear

[2] Joseph Fuchs, S.J., "Die Liebe als Aufbauprinzip der Moraltheologie," *Scholastik*, 29 (1954), 79–87 at 86.

can be supernatural, and the distinction between *amor simpliciter servilis* and *amor serviliter servilis* is part of our theology.

The question of love, therefore, as the basis of morality, must be treated with circumspection if we are to avoid errors and distortions which so easily occur in this slippery terrain.[3] The Quietistic distortion would make all particular obligations of little account as long as one loves. The rigoristic distortion would make even the counsels of perfection obligatory. R. Carpentier, S.J., finds in the work of Canon Leclercq statements which do not sufficiently guard against misinterpretation in both of these directions. For instance we find in Leclercq the statement:

[Spiritual writers] show that . . . the only means of not sinning is to be perfect. Consequently the only way of not being responsible for the sins one does commit is to do everything that one can to attain perfection. . . . One who of deliberate purpose refuses to seek perfection, accepts by that fact not only all the sins he will commit, but those he could commit. . . .[4]

There is an implication here, probably not intended, but due to the inadequacy of the phrasing, that a Christian is not responsible for the individual acts of sin he commits (or which "escape his weakness") as long as his general

[3] Pierre Pourrat, S.S., *Christian Spirituality*, Vol. IV, Westminster, Maryland: The Newman Press, 1955, devotes hundreds of pages to Jansenism and Quietism. It is instructive to notice how persistently through these pages disputes about love are fundamental issues. The Jansenists made perfect contrition a prerequisite for absolution. The Quietists defended a species of pure love of God so disinterested that it was compatible with an absolute sacrifice of one's eternal happiness to God. Because distortions of the doctrine of supernatural charity have led to so many errors in the past we call this a slippery terrain.

[4] Jacques Leclercq, *L'enseignement de la morale chrétienne* (Paris: éditions du Vitrail, 1950), p. 294. See R. Carpentier, S.J., "Vers une morale de la charité," *Gregorianum*, 34 (1953), 32–55 at 40 sq.

orientation is toward perfection; and that he is responsible even for all the sins he could but does not commit if his orientation is not toward perfection. Leclercq more than once expresses his dissatisfaction with a morality which is based so exclusively on individual acts and so little on the moral tendencies and general dispositions of the Christian. He seems shocked by the idea that one can have a thousand bad tendencies and still be in the state of grace as long as there is no act of sin. One does not accuse him of holding the principle *ama et fac quod vis* in a Quietistic sense, or in a situationist sense; but one calls attention to a tendency of his phrases which might easily be misinterpreted.

On the other hand, he continues the above passage with an example which illustrates the opposite, rigoristic tendency:

. . . Every counsel which becomes an indispensable means of perfection for me, becomes also obligatory for me. If in order to tend toward perfection it is necessary for me to get up at five o'clock in the morning, I incur the obligation of getting up at five o'clock in the morning. For to say that getting up at five o'clock in the morning is for me a necessary condition of perfection or of seeking perfection, is to say that getting up later is an occasion of sin.[5]

And it would appear that in this matter he is thinking in terms of grave sin, because, according to him, the obligation of perfection is a grave obligation. Another example of his, taken from another part of his work, illustrates this last point:

The Christian who is fully conscious of the bearing of his acts, who would deliberately refuse to assist at Mass and receive

[5] Leclercq, *op. cit.*, p. 295.

Communion, even if he encountered no difficulty—let us imagine the case of a boarding school where the pupils are taken to Mass fasting, no breakfast being served until afterwards—can one conceive that this Christian does not commit a grave sin by thus resisting the divine love with complete knowledge and in a fully deliberate manner? [6]

This example is in surprising contrast to the universal teaching of Catholic morality, which distinguishes clearly between obligations imposed under pain of mortal sin or of venial sin, and those works of supererogation which are not of precept but of counsel. It is part of our well-established tradition to appeal to objective norms for determining sinfulness and to recognize that a Christian can refuse a divine invitation to higher things, and even deliberately commit a venial sin, without losing his substantial friendship with God: that is, the essential bond of minimum love which is the supernatural life of the soul.

Moralists are keenly aware of the damage done to consciences when obligations under pain of sin are not clearly distinguished from works of supererogation. They are also aware of the theoretical difficulties concerning the nature of venial sin, the sinfulness of deliberate imperfections in the concrete, the need of explicit reference of good works to God as the last end, and the whole question of the concept of obligation itself when used of gravely obligatory, venially obligatory and—if one may use the expression—ascetically obligatory acts. But a vague use of the word "obligation" in practical instructions to the faithful does not make for well-formed consciences and can easily lead to serious troubles of conscience.

Father Carpentier, therefore, does a distinct service when

[6] *Ibid.*, p. 248.

he insists on minimum objective norms of love, and of perfection, and of obligation under pain of sin, and when he
reiterates the distinction between precept and counsel.[7]
After all it is a distinction introduced by our Lord Himself,
and taught by the Church throughout the centuries. It
would appear that Canon Leclercq's explanation of love as
the leading principle of morality, while adhering verbally
to the distinction, actually departs from it, and does not
sufficiently guard against the dangers we have mentioned.
Father Carpentier believes, on the other hand, that Gilleman's work, *The Primacy of Love in Moral Theology,*[8] has
established this principle in a way which is theologically
satisfying and which avoids the Scylla and Charybdis of
laxism and rigorism. It is impatient, indeed, with spiritual
mediocrity, but does not exclude from the Kingdom the
legions of the mediocre.

IMPATIENCE WITH "OBLIGATIONISM"

A second characteristic of certain modern critics is impatience with what they call "obligationism." The French
can now write about a "*mystique* of the nonobligatory."
People can speak beautifully of the law of love casting out
fear. But sometimes it leaves one with the uneasy feeling
that they are casting out the restraints of objective morality
along with the fear—somewhat like those who insist on
worshipping "the God of their own understanding." It is
remarkable at times what this God allows them to do without any qualms of conscience.

We are not quarrelling here, in fact we sympathize, with

[7] Carpentier, *art. cit.,* pp. 40–48.
[8] Gérard Gilleman, S.J., *Le primat de la charité en théologie morale,*
Paris: Desclée, de Brouwer, 1952.

those critics who complain of the multiplicity of detailed obligations imposed on the faithful nowadays—provided they are not speaking of obligations imposed by the authoritative teaching of the Church. The application of moral principles to particular situations by private teachers, be they lay or cleric, be they professional moralists or not, is another matter entirely. The Catholic press abounds in expressions of opinion that this is a mortal sin or that is a mortal sin, and even the devout Catholic becomes confused when he picks up a Catholic publication and reads of a new mortal sin he had never heard of before. The source of the difficulty seems to be that the personal opinions of moralists giving individual, practical solutions of their own are often reported as if they were authoritative teaching, binding on all Catholics. The authors of such opinions, and the editors who publish them, have the obvious duty of making it clear whether the statements in question are made as representing the teaching of the Church or as purporting to be only a private opinion, based on the learning of the author. Competent moralists are slow to invoke "the common teaching of theologians" on a given case unless it is perfectly clear that the theologians actually offer a consensus on that very case. For in practice, the common consent of theologians in moral matters is a practical source of obligation, and obligations are not to be presumed or lightly imposed. They are to be proved.

This is not to imply that every individual Christian is competent to make his own application of moral principles to his own individual case, or that he is justified in neglecting the advice of those who, in God's providence, are qualified to give him advice, or of refusing to submit to the judgment of those who are empowered to speak authoritatively. Pius XII has commented on the attitude of those who are thus impatient of external authority and of obligations imposed from without:

Let the Church—they do not hesitate to say—propose her doctrine, pass her laws as norms of our actions. Still, when there is question of practical application to each individual's life, the Church must not interfere; she should let each one of the faithful follow his own conscience and judgment. They declare this is all the more necessary because the Church and her ministers are unaware of certain sets of circumstances either personal or extrinsic to individuals; in them each person has been placed, and must take his own counsel and decide what he must do. Such people, moreover, are unwilling in their final personal decisions to have any intermediary or intercessor placed between themselves and God, no matter what his rank or title.[9]

In this passage the Holy Father is defending the right of authorized teachers in the Church to apply the moral law to individual lives. But he is not saying that the private opinions of moralists or confessors, no matter how learned the men may be, are binding on the faithful—especially when other moralists and confessors legitimately hold other opinions.[10]

However, it is not this brand of "obligationism"—the unwarranted assumption of authority by private persons—

---

[9] Pius XII, *Magnificate Dominum*, *ASS*, 46 (1954), 666–77 at 674.
[10] Since every individual case of conscience has something unique about it, there is a pretext for disparaging universal laws and general moral principles on the ground that each case is in some sense a law unto itself. When an ecclesiastical judge applies the law of the Church to an individual case, it is clear that he does it authoritatively. But when a confessor applies the moral law to an individual case which really is of new occurrence and cannot be clearly subsumed under the common opinions of moralists or the authoritative decisions of the Church, one cannot speak of his judgment as being authentic or binding. Another confessor may reasonably disagree with it. There is an interesting problem here which we have not seen discussed.

which modern critics, especially in France, decry. Their objections have much deeper philosophical and theological roots and are concerned with an alleged incompatibility between the ethics of love and the ethics of obligation, the palm being awarded, of course, to the ethics of love.[11]

Thus the axiom from St. Augustine mentioned above, *Ama et fac quod vis*, "Love and do what you will," is given interpretations which range from an orthodox, truly Augustinian meaning all the way to situationism and Quietism. Situationism, in the sense that one's personal, loving confrontation with Almighty God may convince one that it is according to His will to forsake the objective standards of the moral law in some particular and difficult situation. Quietism, in the sense that one who truly loves God and has a general disposition of wholehearted love for Him will not be responsible for particular deviations from the law.

The actual words of St. Augustine, differ slightly from those usually attributed to him, and the context excludes the above misinterpretations. He said: *"Dilige et quod vis, fac,"* not *"Ama et fac quod vis."* The complete passage in which these words occur reads as follows:

Once and for all, therefore, this brief law is laid down unto you: Love and do what you will. Whether you keep silence, keep silence with love; whether you cry out, cry out with love; whether you chastise, chastise with love; whether you forbear, forbear with love. Let love be the interior source; from that source nothing but good can arise.[12]

---

[11] Cf. G. Bortolaso, S.J., "Etica dell' amore ed etica dell' obbligazione," *La Civiltà Cattolica*, 103 (1952, n. 2), 368–79; and A. Boschi, S.J., "La così detta "Morale Nuova'," *La Scuola Cattolica*, 34 (Sept.–Oct., 1956, n. 5), 336–50. These two articles take up and refute certain propositions of Yves de Montcheuil, S.J., *Mélanges théologiques*, Paris, 1946.

[12] St. Augustine, *In Epist. Joan.* vii. 4. 8; ML 35:2033.

It is to be noted that the examples given by Augustine are all examples of indifferent actions, which might be performed for good motives or for bad motives. Is it not clear that according to Augustine such actions, when they proceed from supernatural charity, become good and meritorious actions, and that it would be entirely foreign to his thought to conclude that bad actions become good, or at least are not imputed as sins, as long as the doer of them loves?

Another phase of anti-obligationism is its frequent carping at the legalism of moral theology. By legalism is meant principally casuistry.[13] This is not the place to defend the legitimate and indispensable uses of casuistry, especially in the preparation of confessors, or to point out once more the errors and excesses in which casuistry has been involved in the history of the Church. But it is surprising that this characteristically Protestant repudiation of "legalism" in morals should be so common in the countries where Anglo-Saxon law holds sway. We live by case-law in these countries, and law students learn their profession by the case-system, which is casuistry pure and simple. But the phrases "case-law" and "judicial precedent" have a very acceptable and respectable ring to them, while "casuistry," which is the same thing, has a very bad name indeed, and is brushed off like a disreputable relation.

Law is law, whether it is the law of God, or the law of the

---

[13] Another aspect of the criticism of legalism hits at the externalism or extrinsicism, or even Pharisaism to which the teaching of moral can lead when it is based on the Commandments. The sources of this type of criticism are partly psychoanalytical. Cf. Albert Plé, O.P., "Thou Shalt Love," *Cross and Crown*, 4 (Dec., 1952, n. 4), 466–72. Father Plé speaking of "a moral teaching based upon the Commandments, not to say practically limited to them" considers that "This legalization of morality constitutes a regression, as it were, from the Gospel to the Old Testament."

land, or the law of a correctly-formed conscience. The essential unity of this threefold law has been lost sight of in modern times, owing largely to the Kantian divorce of the moral from the juridical order. The critics of legalism in morality are at times, apparently, taken in unwittingly by this philosophical error. Catholics who complain that generations of juristic theologians have made of morality a mere province of the law may need to be reminded that legal obligations are ultimately and *per se* moral obligations, and that conversely, moral obligations are legal obligations, that is, have their source in divine law, whether it be the eternal law of nature, or the law of God's revelation in the Old Testament, or the law of the gospel.

The law of the gospel contains commandments which are of obligation, and counsels which are not. To abolish the counsels is one extreme, to belittle the commandments is the other. And while a morality of precepts without counsels is conceivable, a morality of counsels without precepts is not. It is a dangerous thing, therefore, to decry a morality of duty, of law, and of obligation, because in the last analysis there is no other.

A peculiar incidental of anti-obligationism is the notion that sanctity begins where obligation leaves off. One would think that obedience to the obligations of the law of God is somehow incompatible with generosity, liberty, joy, and the flowering of one's spiritual personality. E. Ranwez is quite critical, and rightly so, of those Catholic authors (writing for young people, which makes it worse) who speak as if obedience were somehow an irrational abdication of the self, as if authority were somehow the enemy of one's personal liberty and perfection; and who caricature duty and obligation in such fantastic and exaggerated terms as to make them odious concepts.[14] Such writers, unintentionally of course, are calumniators of the law.

Father Ranwez invites us to ponder again some very simple fundamentals of the morality of Christ. Love and obligation are not enemies but friends. "If you love me, keep my commandments," [15] says our Lord. "Whoever does the will of God, he is my brother and sister and mother." [16] The Holy Father has inculcated this same basic truth. He reminds us that our Lord "has established as the touchstone and distinctive mark of love towards Him, the Christ, the observance of the commandments." [17] Spiritual writers have taught unanimously that obedience is the final and highest criterion of sanctity. The greatest generosity is to give the greatest gift, the sacrifice of one's own will, the denial of one's own self. "There is greater merit of charity in a meal under obedience than in a fast undertaken of one's own choice." [18] "It is more perfect to welcome the trials which God has in store for us than to choose ones to our taste." [19]

St. Ignatius in his "Rules for Thinking with the Church" says that we should speak well of vows,[20] because he lived in an age when heretics were saying that it was better to do a good deed freely and spontaneously than to do it under the obligation of a vow. Do we not hear it argued today that it would be a better thing to go to Mass on Sunday freely,

[14] *Art. cit., passim.*
[15] John 14:15.
[16] Mark 3:35.
[17] Pius XII, "On the Right Formation of Christian Conscience in Youths," *AAS,* 44 (1952), 270–78 at 274.
[18] "Majoris est meriti caritatis injuncta refectio jejunio propria deliberatione suscepta." Attributed to Gregory the Great, *In Regum Expositione* 1. 2, 4. 12; ML 79: 9–467.
[19] The venerable Libermann, cited by Ranwez, *art. cit.,* p. 55.
[20] *The Spiritual Exercises of St. Ignatius,* translated by Louis J. Puhl, S.J. (Westminster, Md.: The Newman Press, 1951), n. 357.

that is, without any obligation, than to do so when the law imposes a grave obligation to go?

There is here an equivocation in the use of the word "freely." Naturally it is better to do something by choice rather than by physical coaction. In fact, if one is physically forced to act there is no human act and no moral value at all. But there is no absolute value or special spiritual merit in choosing to do a good thing precisely because one is not morally forced, that is, not morally obliged, to do it. Father Vermeersch's practice of self-abnegation did not become less perfect from the time he bound himself by vow to the practice. When one obeys the law of God and fulfills a moral obligation acting as a human being, one is physically free to do the opposite. It is this free choice, made with God's help, that has merit in His eyes and is the means of our perfection. In the process of conforming ourselves to His will in our actions, our free choice may fall on an obligatory work or on one of supererogation. But the obligatory work will not be less valuable in His sight or less perfect in itself merely because it is obligatory.

To act under moral necessity, under the mysterious and imperative ought of moral obligation which leaves liberty intact, is to embrace the will of God by one's own free choice. To make such a free choice not merely of a good which *is* obligatory, but even to choose it precisely *inasmuch* as it is obligatory, can be just as perfect as, or more perfect than, the spontaneous choice of a work of supererogation. Moral obligation is not to be thought of as a barrier between God and man, or as a hindrance to the perfection and flowering of human personality. Moral obligation is a unique kind of necessity which binds man to God and unites him with his last end, beatitude. The law of God is our truest good, and conformity to His will is our highest perfection. There is no surer way of finding that good and embracing that will than the way of God's commandments.

The objectors have apparently confused the idea of acting under grave obligation with the idea of acting through fear of punishment. This is quite a different question, the question of motivation. Obviously it is more perfect to act from love of God than from fear of punishment. It is more perfect to act from *amor benevolentiæ Dei* than from *amor simpliciter servilis*. But let us not disparage this lowest form of love. It, too, is compatible with God's friendship and with substantial sanctity. Let us lead Christians to the higher motives, but not forget that fear of punishment and a perfect love of God, as motives, are not mutually exclusive, but can exist simultaneously in the same person. One does not necessarily contradict the other. It is the Church which teaches the faithful to say the familiar act of contrition: "I detest all my sins because I dread the loss of heaven and the pains of hell, but most of all because they offend Thee, my God, who art all good and deserving of all my love." We can love God and also fear Him. But the closer we are to God the more His commandments become the very things which we spontaneously and joyously embrace.

To connect the observance of the commandments with mediocrity in virtue and to speak as though the obligations imposed by God's law were a drawback to the perfection of His love, does not reflect a Christian philosophy but some alien one, and betrays an unreal view of God, of His creatures and of their spiritual life. We all know something of the beauty of a single human soul in which the divine likeness is unblemished by sin. What if all souls were like that?

What if all men at all times and in all places observed the commandments of God? The combined interior beauty of those souls would be indescribable; and exteriorly also the world would be a paradise. If *only* the commandments were observed, the one true God would be worshipped everywhere according to His will; His holy name would be sounded only in reverence; all authority, as it comes from Him, would be pledged to Him and exercised only according to His wise laws; parents would be devoted to their children, and children to their parents; human life and property and honor would be sacred; purity and marital fidelity would be everywhere esteemed. No idolatry, no persecutions, no blasphemies, no murder, no thefts, no unjust wages, no obscenity, no back-biting or slander, no wars, no class conflicts! We could close our jails, divorce courts, reform schools; we could do away with burglar alarms and safes. There would be no armaments to consume our capital, no death weapons to slay our youth.

A picture such as this reminds one of the Garden of Eden. Of course, when we view the moral turmoil that actually exists, we must label such a picture another fantasy. Yet it is well for us to contemplate it, unreal though it happens to be, when we are tempted to associate devotion to duty and the obligations of the commandments with mediocrity. For it shows us what beauty, what harmony and what perfection, both interior and exterior, the commandments are supposed to produce. It would keep us from slipping into the fallacy that sanctity begins where obligation leaves off.

IMPATIENCE WITH THE SEMINARY COURSE

The open-minded moralist will have to admit that a

great deal of the criticism of the seminary course is justifiable. When the moral theology class is associated with low ideals in the minds of the students, and when the moral professor is looked upon as a lawyer for the defence who gets people out of things— "qui tollit peccata mundi," as the facetious and not altogether reverent saying puts it— then there is definite need for change.

It seems to us, therefore, that the views of "Episcopus," recorded in the previous chapter, need careful qualification. It is true that the moral theologian must clearly distinguish precept from counsel, the licit from the illicit, and the venially sinful from the mortally sinful. But we cannot agree that the moral theology course should be strictly confined to the *scientia liciti et illiciti.*

It is true that the course as taught in most seminaries today is aimed principally at the formation of confessors; true also that the confessional is for sinners first of all, and for the remission of serious sins most of all. Both the historical evolution of the science and the principal goal to which it is directed explain to some extent the necessary emphasis on sin and the limits of mortal sin. Francis Clark, S.J., has explained this point well:

As to the charge of "moral minimalism," it is one that the Catholic moralist must in one sense admit, and about which he can offer little satisfaction to his critics. The chief aim of the science of moral theology as it exists in the Church today is the formation and guidance of confessors whom the Church can officially approve for the ministry of the Sacrament of Penance, and she must have some sure criteria by which to judge that they possess the required knowledge and judgment. The confessor is without doubt also a guide and a teacher of perfection, but the primary work of the sacramental tribunal which Christ

[97]

instituted is the remission of sins. So moral theology has to deal with sins, and has to determine their limits, their species and their distinction in unambiguous terms. And so it cannot escape from the duty of considering at every turn the moral minimum and what it is that binds under pain of sin. It belongs to the Church's power of the keys that her ministers should know clearly what human acts separate man from God, should mark out plainly the edge of the abyss beyond which lies death for the soul.[21]

Father Clark wisely notes that the confessor is "also a guide and teacher of perfection." Today, by reason of the frequency of confessions of devotion, the priest encounters many generous souls who are hungry to advance in the truly Christian way of life, and whose only opportunity for personal spiritual guidance is often in the confessional. This need and this emphasis have now been made abundantly clear in Pius XII's encyclical on the Mystical Body of Christ.

As you well know, Venerable Brethren, it is true that venial sins may be expiated in many ways which are to be highly commended. But to ensure more rapid progress day by day in the path of virtue, We will that the pious practice of frequent confession, which was introduced into the Church by the inspiration of the Holy Spirit, should be earnestly advocated. By it genuine self-knowledge is increased, Christian humility grows, bad habits are corrected, spiritual neglect and tepidity are resisted, the conscience is purified, the will strengthened, a salutary self-control is attained, and grace is increased in virtue of the Sacrament itself. Let those, therefore, among the younger clergy who make light of or lessen esteem for frequent confes-

[21] Francis Clark, S.J., "The Challenge to Moral Theology," *Clergy Review*, 38 (Apr., 1953), 214–23 at 222–23.

sion realize that what they are doing is alien to the Spirit of Christ and disastrous for the Mystical Body of our Saviour.[22]

In other words, according to the Holy Father, the work of educating Christian consciences, of bringing them to true spiritual maturity and guiding them in the way of perfection is *an apostolate of the confessional.* General moral principles plus an orientation toward God are not enough for the vast multitude of Christians. To ask *oneself:* "What would Christ have done in these circumstances?" is a woefully inadequate guide even for the mature Christian. The advice and guidance of a confessor who knows both the traditional teaching of the Church and the needs of the modern mentality is a safeguard against subjectivism, and against a rash independence of authority. Perhaps one reason why modern intellectual Catholics are tempted to be too independent and self-reliant, and are taken in by spiritual novelties, is that they have sought solid, understanding, spiritual help in the confessional and have failed to find it there. Catholic spirituality has stood the test of long centuries in adapting itself to human nature in divers times and places and cultures. It is not outmoded now. But perhaps some of its purveyors are.

That seminarians be prepared for such confessional work they need a great deal more than the *scientia liciti et illiciti.* They need, among other things, training in ascetical theology. But to demand that they receive some of this training in the moral course itself does not imply that the course in ascetics be abolished. It implies rather that both textbook and professor pay heed to the ascetical implications of the conduct of Titius and Sempronius, and not

[22] *Mystici Corporis, AAS,* 35 (1943), 235.

merely their moral guilt. It demands a more integral view of the Christian life of Bertha and Sempronia than these ladies have become accustomed to. The reason why it is important to do this in the moral course and not leave it all to the professor of ascetics is that the moral course is the big course, in the minds of the students and in the time devoted to it. It has an academic prestige, very influential in the formation of young minds, which the course in ascetics has not, and will not have unless the entire seminary curriculum is to undergo radical revision.

Just as one cannot incorporate the whole science of ascetics into the moral course, much less can one incorporate the dogma. Those who deplore the separation of moral from dogma are a bit unrealistic. St. Thomas separated them into different parts of his *Summa*, and even the universities which adhere rigidly to the *Summa* in their classroom teaching have separate professors for the dogmatic and the moral parts of that great synthesis. What difference does it make, really, whether grace and merit are taught in the dogma class or in the moral class? There are advantages and disadvantages no matter which way it is done. "One cannot study everything in connection with everything," [23] as E. Guerrero, S.J., remarked in reviewing Leclercq's work. In teaching theology one must necessarily partition it. Dogma is taught treatise by treatise, but there is scarcely a treatise that can stand by itself. It is the same with moral, ascetical, pastoral, and canon law. The professor must pause to remind his hearers that this point or that will be treated later, or elsewhere, or has already been treated. This limitation is inherent in theological doctrine

[23] E. Guerrero, S.J., *Razón y Fe*, 148 (July–Aug., 1953), 84.

itself. It is so vast that it must be taken piece by piece. And if the professor takes advantage of this situation to evade his responsibility of teaching what is difficult or unpleasant, this is an abuse which should be blamed on the professor and not on the course.

At present we seem to be in a period of transition in the development of the moral theology course. The valuable elements contained in modern approaches to the subject are being sifted out from what is not worthwhile for practice, and from what is dangerous in tendency, or even false. It remains to be seen, for instance, to what extent the primacy of charity, as magnificently conceived by Gilleman and systematized by him, can be incorporated into the ordinary seminary course of moral theology. It is actually being attempted, we understand, in more than one seminary. Seminary professors will be eager to know with what success such a system will prepare confessors for their task. Certainly no widespread adoption of such a new method can be hoped for until textbooks are available for classroom use. For even though Father Gilleman declares that it is the atmosphere and the emphasis rather than the content of the course which needs to be changed, the changes will not take place without a textbook which has the new atmosphere and the new emphasis.

In the meantime the all-important element is the personal attitude of the professor of moral. It is up to him to create the atmosphere (perhaps under difficulties) and to supply the emphasis. Nothing will take the place of his personal *viva voce* indoctrination of his students with true Christian perspectives in moral theology. If his approach is the negative one of the minimalist, the students will learn to hear confessions with an ear cocked for mortal sin and for nothing else. Confessors have to be trained, of course, to be constantly aware of the clear-cut distinctions of mortal sins, but they should keep them in the back of the mind, not in the forefront, while actually hearing confessions. The positive approach of the professor to the discussion of cases in class and his emphasis on the total requirements of the Christian way of life, as well as on the dividing line of sin, are the best antidote to minimalism and legalism. It is his responsibility also to repair the damage done by fragmentation, to integrate the contents of the course with the other parts of theology, with dogma and ascetics, with Holy Scripture, canon law and pastoral, and with ecclesiastical history. Nowadays he has the additional heavy burden of keeping abreast of the enormous papal documentation in matters of morals and of integrating all this material into the course as well. He may well ask his students not to add impatience with the professor to all the other impatiences we have been discussing.

CONCLUSION

In these three chapters we have been considering criticisms of moral, and new approaches, which have been suggested by orthodox Catholic writers, and which for the most part have stayed within the bounds of orthodoxy. It must be confessed, however, that sometimes, in some of these writings, there are exhibited tendencies which savor of the "new morality" condemned by the present Holy Father. It is easy for dissatisfaction with obligationism to boil over into dissatisfaction with obligation; for irritation with legalism to become irritation with law; for affection for the concrete, the personally creative, and the subjectively satisfying to verge on disparagement of the abstract, universal, and objective values of Christian morality. In the following chapters we shall take up some of these deviations from Catholic teaching.

7

The Holy See and Situation Ethics

THE NEW MORALITY which has been developing *pari passu* with the more recent criticisms of moral theology (and is in some things strikingly similar to them) has been designated by various names: "ethical existentialism," "ethical actualism," "ethical individualism," "morality according to situations," and finally—perhaps the most common of all the expressions—"situation ethics." An instruction of the Holy Office, dated February 2, 1956, contained a condemnation of this new morality.[1] The text of this instruction will be given at the close of the present chapter. As a background for the proper understanding of the instruction, however, various statements of Pope Pius XII should be considered first.

PAPAL STATEMENTS BEFORE 1952

Situation ethics, as is now well known, is a product of existentialism. Pius XII's first explicit reference to this new

[1] Cf. *AAS*, 48 (1956), 144–45.

philosophy—as far as we have been able to discover—was in his brief address to delegates to the International Congress of Philosophy, November 21, 1946.[2] At that time he spoke of existentialism as a philosophy of despair and stressed the necessity of a solid intellectual basis of Catholic philosophy to guard against it. "What else but despair," he asked, "is left to a philosophy which does not find its answers in God, in eternity, in personal immortality?"

The same philosophical system was mentioned three times in the encyclical, *Humani generis.*[3] In the early part of the encyclical, when dealing with philosophical errors of those "outside the fold," the pope described existentialism as one of the natural offshoots of the error of crass evolution:

The fictitious tenets of evolution, which repudiate all that is absolute, firm, and immutable, have paved the way for the new erroneous philosophy which, a rival of idealism, immanentism, and pragmatism, has come to be called existentialism because, forgetful of the immutable essences of things, it concerns itself only with individual existence.[4]

The next mention of existentialism in the encyclical was with reference to critics of scholastic philosophy. These critics—and apparently some Catholics were included among them—objected that a philosophy of immutable essences is not suited to the contemporary mind. They wanted to re-formulate our doctrines in terms of contemporary philosophies. The pope roundly scored this criticism in the following paragraph:

[2] *Ibid.*, 38 (1946), 426–30; see especially pp. 428–29.
[3] Aug. 12, 1950; *ibid.*, 42 (1950), 561–78. Translations used in this chapter are taken from Cotter, *op. cit.* (cf. *supra,* chapter 1, footnote 3).
[4] *AAS,* 42 (1950), 563.

How deplorable it is then that this philosophy, received and honored by the Church, is scorned by some who are impudent enough to call it outmoded in form and rationalistic, as they say, in its thought. They keep repeating that this our philosophy wrongly maintains the possibility of a metaphysic that is absolutely true; whereas, they say, reality, especially transcendent reality, cannot be expressed better than by disparate propositions which complete one another, even though they are almost contradictory. They concede that the philosophy taught in our schools, with its clear exposition of questions and their solution, with its accurate definitions of terms and clearcut distinctions, can be useful as a preparation for scholastic theology, and that it was marvelously adapted to the medieval mentality; but they deny that it offers a method of philosophizing suited to the needs of our modern culture. They object also that our *philosophia perennis* is only a philosophy of immutable essences, whereas the contemporary mind must be interested in the existence of individuals and in the incessant flux of life. And while despising our philosophy, they extol others, ancient or modern, oriental or occidental, by which they seem to imply that any kind of philosophy or theory can, with a few additions or corrections if necessary, be harmonized with a Catholic dogma. But this is absolutely false, especially where there is question of those fictitious theories which go by the name of immanentism or idealism or materialism, whether historic or dialectic, or also existentialism, whether atheistic or the type that denies at least the validity of metaphysical reasoning. No Catholic can have the least doubt on that score.[5]

Up to this time no explicit reference was made to existentialism with regard to morality. Before dropping the discussion of the new philosophical theories, however, the

[5] *Ibid.*, p. 573.

pope briefly hinted at their disastrous effects on sound ethics. Thus, he said:

It is not surprising that these new theories endanger two philosophical departments which by their nature are closely connected with faith, that is, theodicy and ethics. According to the new views, their function is not to prove with certitude anything about God or any other transcendent being, but rather to show that truths which faith teaches about a personal God and about His precepts, correspond perfectly to the necessities of life, and are therefore to be accepted by all in order to avoid despair and to attain eternal salvation. All of which is evidently contrary to the documents of our predecessors, Leo XIII and Pius X, nor can it be reconciled with the decrees of the Vatican Council. It would indeed be unnecessary to deplore these aberrations from truth if all, even in the domain of philosophy, showed proper reverence for and paid attention to the magisterium of the Church which has the divinely given mission not only to guard and interpret the deposit of divinely revealed truth, but also to watch over the philosophical sciences lest erroneous theories harm Catholic dogma.[6]

Even this passage, though mentioning the disastrous effects of existentialism on ethics, makes no reference to moral conduct itself. A few months later the pope came to closer grips with this problem when he said:

It was not mere chance that brought about in our day the rise and elaboration of the philosophy known as existentialism. The men of our time, when confronted by events which bring up difficult metaphysical and religious problems to be solved, gladly, without a thought of higher principles, persuade them-

[6] *Ibid.*, pp. 574–75.

selves that it is enough to act as the exigencies of the moment demand.[7]

Surprisingly enough, these words were used in the pope's address to the Congress of Religious Men, in Rome, December 8, 1950.[8] And—what is still more surprising—the pope asserted that, despite repeated warnings, many ecclesiastics, including religious, had been deeply infected by the contagion of the new philosophy. He added, however, that this crisis seemed to have been overcome.

Perhaps it had been overcome for ecclesiastics and religious; or perhaps this was only a hope that the pope was voicing. At any rate, that he believed the new morality continued to influence men in general and Catholics in particular is evident from the fact that in early 1952 he devoted a radio message and an allocution to it. Since these addresses are explicitly concerned with existentialist morality, they merit a somewhat detailed consideration.

ON THE EDUCATION OF THE CHRISTIAN CONSCIENCE

The radio message on the Christian conscience as an object of education was given on March 23, 1952,[9] at the conclusion of a "family day" promoted throughout Italy by Catholic Action groups. The pope's general approach was in terms of canon 1113, which refers to the duties of parents to provide religious and moral education for their children. Many of these duties, he said, were already ex-

---

[7] *Ibid.*, 43 (1951), 32.

[8] The complete text is given in *AAS*, 43 (1951), 26–36. There is a very readable English version in T. L. Bouscaren, S.J., *Canon Law Digest*, 3 (Milwaukee: Bruce Publishing Co., 1954), 119–31.

[9] *AAS*, 44 (1952), 270–78. The translation on which our quotations are based is in *Catholic Documents*, 8 (July, 1952), 1–7.

plained in papal messages. For the present discourse he was choosing the education of the child's conscience because "certain currents of modern thought are beginning to change the concept of conscience, and to attack its value." He then proceeded to explain positively the meaning of a true Christian conscience and to state the general norms for educating conscience.

The true Christian conscience, he insisted, is a faithful reflection of the word and the will of Christ. Understood in this sense, conscience is certainly the ultimate and deciding norm for personal action. It follows from this that the education of conscience must consist in enlightening the child as to what Christ said and what Christ wants; and in this, of course, the Church is indispensable because it was to the Church that Christ left the moral treasure of mankind—including both natural and divine positive law—and it was Christ's will that the Church should preserve this treasure uncontaminated and hand it on from generation to generation of the faithful.

To put it briefly: the function of parents and teachers in educating the child's conscience is to inform him of the meaning of these divine laws, as interpreted by the Church, and to inspire and encourage the child, inasmuch as this is possible, to want to observe them.

Having stated the positive doctrine, the pope went on to consider various objections advanced by the proponents of a new morality. Their general aim, he said, was "to make a radical revision of Catholic moral law, in order to arrive at a new appraisal of its value." In this, they were much like the would-be revisers of the Church's dogmatic teaching, already condemned in *Humani generis*. To accomplish this aim, they would first free man's conscience from the "oppressive overseeing by the authority of the Church," and thus return to the primitive simplicity of early Christianity. The "sophistic subtleties of the casuistic method" had destroyed this simplicity. A second step—or perhaps it would more aptly be called a second criticism, not necessarily involving a progressive series of changes—was to encourage the law of human freedom and love, insisting on this as the driving force of moral life. In moral precepts, as now expounded by the Church, there is too much insistence on the rigor of the law, which is manifested by the frequent recourse to such phrases as "you must," and "you may not." As an example of how this harshness affected the private lives of individuals, the new moralists had apparently cited the problems of continence in marriage and of purity during adolescence. According to them, Catholic teaching in these matters demands the impossible.

Finally, as regards public life, the new morality offered the "autonomy of art, science, politics, etc." This means that each of these spheres of public life has its own laws and that conduct within each sphere would be judged merely on the basis of its own laws. These things do not pertain to either morality or religion and must not, therefore, be judged according to moral or religious norms.

The foregoing are some of the tenets of the new morality as given in the radio message of March 23, 1952. In each of them, there is a criticism of traditional Catholic morality. The pope answered each criticism.

The suggestion that the moral law be brought back to its original simplicity might mean a recognition of some objective norms of conduct, at least of those enunciated in Scripture. But the pope saw in the suggestion much more than this. It really meant the doing away with objective ethical criteria so that the conscience of the individual would be absolute master of his own decisions. There would be no ulterior norm for measuring the decisions of conscience. The pope called this the "central weakness" of the new morality. It would not merely mean a departure from the plan of Christ; it would also create difficulties of conscience. It was to the Church, and not to individuals, that Christ gave His revelation, "of which moral obligations are an essential part"; and it was to the Church alone that Christ promised the divine aid required for avoiding error. The unstated conclusion of this is obvious: it is only through conformity with the teaching of the Church that the individual conscience can have security from error. The "autonomy of the individual conscience" cannot be reconciled with the plan of Christ and can produce only "poisonous fruits."

The second criticism: the Church should insist on the law of liberty and love, not on precepts and prohibitions. The pope first admitted the grain of truth in this criticism: the positive riches of the faith should be unfolded to Christians so that they would be drawn to investigate them and live by them. Nevertheless, he added, the Church

. . . cannot refrain from warning the faithful that these riches cannot be acquired or preserved except at the price of definite moral obligations. Any other line of action would mean that a dominant principle was forgotten, and one on which Jesus Christ, her Lord and Master, always insisted. He in fact taught that it was not sufficient to say "Lord, Lord" to enter into the Kingdom of heaven, but rather that the will of the heavenly Father had to be done [Matt. 7:31]. He spoke of the "narrow gate" and of the "strait way" which leads to life [cfr. Matt. 7, 13–14], and added: "Strive to enter by the narrow gate: for

many, I say to you, shall seek to enter and shall not be able"
[Luke 13:24]. He made it clear that to keep the commandments was the touchstone and the distinctive sign of love of
Himself, the Christ [John 14:21–24]. Likewise, to the rich
young man, who questioned Him, He says: "If thou wilt enter
into life, keep the commandments," and to the further question,
"Which?" answers: "Thou shalt do no murder. Thou shalt not
commit adultery. Thou shalt not steal. Thou shalt not bear
false witness. Honor thy father and thy mother." And: "Thou
shalt love thy neighbor as thyself." For everyone who wished to
imitate Him, He laid down the conditions of denying self and
taking up his cross daily [cfr. Luke 9:23]. He demands that
man should be ready to leave for His sake whatever he holds
most dear, such as father, mother, his own children, and, best of
all, his very life [cfr. Matt. 10:37–39]. For He adds: "And I say
to you, my friends: Be not afraid of them who kill the body and
after that have no more that they can do. But I will show you
whom you shall fear: Fear ye him who, after he hath killed,
hath power to cast into hell" [Luke 12:4–5].

Thus spoke Jesus Christ, the divine teacher, who certainly
knows, better than men, how to penetrate souls and draw them
to His love by the infinite perfections of His Heart, which is
full of goodness and of love [Litany of the Sacred Heart of
Jesus].[10]

The third tenet of the new morality—that marital continence and premarital chastity are impossible—seems at
first sight to be more an assertion of subjective weakness
than a denial of a principle. The pope's answer, however,
showed that here, too, a principle is at stake: the principle
that the divine commandments can be observed with the
aid of grace. The answer is important for two reasons: first,
because it shows clearly that both in this radio message as

[10] *AAS*, 44 (1952), 274–75.

well as in his previous allocution to Italian midwives, he intended to teach officially; and secondly, he declared unequivocally that the thesis of "impossibility" is in reality a doctrinal error. We have already quoted a part of the pope's answer in chapter 2 (p. 26). It will be useful, however, to give the complete text here:

> Mindful, however, of the right and duty of the Apostolic See to intervene authoritatively, when need arises, in moral questions, in the address of 29th October last, We set out to enlighten men's consciences on the problems of married life. With the selfsame authority, We declare today to educators and to young people also, that the divine commandment of purity of soul and body still holds without any lesser obligation for the youth of today. They also are morally bound, and, with the help of grace, are able to keep themselves pure. We reject, therefore, as erroneous, the assertion of those who regard lapses as inevitable in adolescence, and therefore as not worthy of serious notice, as though they were not grave faults, because, they add, as a general rule passion destroys the freedom needed for an act to be morally imputable.
>
> On the contrary, it is a wise and proper rule that the educator, while not neglecting to show young people the high worth of purity, so as to win them to love and desire it for its own sake, should nevertheless clearly stress the commandment as it is, in all its gravity and seriousness, namely, as given by God. He will thus persuade young people to avoid proximate occasions, he will strengthen them in their struggles, the difficulty of which he will not hide from them; he will induce them to accept with courage the sacrifices which virtue demands, and he will exhort them to persevere and not to fall into the danger of laying down their arms at the start and yielding, without resistance, to evil habits.[11]

[11] *Ibid.*, pp. 275–76.

The fourth contention of the new morality—the autonomy of science, art, politics, and so forth—has already been discussed.[12] Here it will suffice to stress one point: the pope's insistence that the negation of the hierarchy of values and of the subordination of these various spheres to the higher principles of morality and religion is in reality a "subtle way of withdrawing conscience from the rule of the moral law." It would accomplish two of the purposes of the new morality: first, to free artists, scientists, statesmen, and so forth, from any consideration of the higher principles; and, as a consequence of this, liberate them from the "oppressive overseeing of the authority of the Church." In exposing the falsity and even absurdity, of this attack on the Christian conscience, the pope did not mince words:

Obviously, this is a subtle way of withdrawing conscience from the rule of moral law. In fact, it cannot be denied that such autonomy is just, insofar as it expresses the distinctive methods of each activity and the limits which theoretically separate their different forms; but the separation of method should not mean that the scientist, the artist, the statesman are free from moral anxiety in the exercise of their craft, especially if this has repercussions in the ethical field, as is true of art, politics, and economics. Such a clear-cut theoretical separation is meaningless in life, which is always a synthesis. The unique subject of every kind of activity is man himself, whose free and deliberate acts cannot escape moral evaluation. If we study the problem in a broad, practical manner, sometimes lacking even in philosophers of note, such distinctions and autonomies are used by fallen human nature in order to regard as a law of art, politics, or economics, that which happens to be accommodating to concupiscence, egoism, and greed. Thus the theoretic

12 Cf. *supra*, chapter 1, pp. 15–18.

autonomy in regard to morality becomes in practice a rebellion against morality. Likewise is shattered that inherent harmony of the sciences and arts, of which the philosophers of that school are vividly aware. They regard it as casual, when, instead, it is essential, when considered from the point of view of the subject, which is man, and of his Creator, who is God.

Hence Our predecessors, and We Ourselves, in the confusion of war and in the troubled aftermath of war, did not cease to insist on the principle that the order willed by God embraces life as a whole, not excluding public life, in whatever form. Such insistence was based on the persuasion that this entails no restriction of true freedom, nor any interference in the competence of the State. Rather, it is an insurance against errors and abuses, against which Christian morality, when rightly applied, offers protection. These truths should be taught to young people and impressed upon their consciences by the person, in the family or in the school, who has the obligation of educating them. Thus they would sow the seed of a better future.[13]

THE ALLOCUTION TO YOUNG WOMEN

This allocution was given April 18, 1952, to delegates to the International Congress of the World Federation of Catholic Young Women.[14] The theme of the congress was "The Faith of Youth—Problem of Our Time." Previous to their meeting with the pope, the delegates had given him a printed memorandum, consisting of 32 pages of problems and questions. At the beginning of his address he referred to this memorandum and said that he wished to concentrate on one problem which is mentioned several times and which is thus stated on p. 10 of the memorandum:

[13] *AAS,* 44 (1952), 276–77.
[14] The papal text (French) is in *AAS,* 44 (1952), 413–19. Our quotations are based on the translation given in *Catholic Documents,* 8 (July, 1952), 15–20.

"Confusing Christianity with a code of precepts and prohibitions, young people have the feeling that they are suffocating in this climate of the 'moral imperative,' and it is not a small minority among them who cast off this 'cumbersome baggage'."

The pope chose this particular passage because it was indicative "of a certain phenomenon which is showing itself in some degree everywhere in the life of faith of Catholics, and which, in a manner, affects everyone, but especially youth and its educators." This phenomenon is none other than the new morality, of which he had spoken in the radio message of March 23. He referred to that message, and stated that he now wished to probe more deeply into the new concept of moral life.

To designate the new morality, he used the expressions given at the beginning of this chapter: "ethical existentialism," "ethical actualism," "ethical individualism," "situationsethik," and "morality according to situations." The primary distinctive mark of the new morality is its attitude toward moral laws. It either denies the existence of objective moral laws or at least it subordinates these laws to what it calls personality values. In a word, the moral law, if it exists at all, does not have a universal and absolute character. It cannot cover all the concrete situations of everyday life; these are unique and must ultimately be judged by the individual according to his own conscience. The laws are general guide posts, but they are not a body of premises from which conscience can argue to what is right or wrong in individual cases. The person himself must reach this decision on the basis of his own immediate and direct relationship with God. And God's interest is not in the objective character of the act—that is, its agreement or disagreement with the so-called "moral laws"—but in the "right intention," that is, in the serious-minded response of the individual to the judgment he makes face-to-face with God, so to speak, "without the slightest trace of intervention by any law, any authority, and community, any form of worship or religion."

The pope gave some striking examples of what these serious-minded judgments of conscience might be:

If a seriously trained conscience decided that abandoning the Catholic faith and joining another religion brings it closer to God, then such a step would be "justified." . . . Or again, in the domain of morality, another example is the corporal and spiritual gift of one's self among young people. Here a seriously trained conscience would decide that, because of a sincere mutual inclination, physical and sensual intimacies are in order. . . . In what concerns the rights of married persons, it would be necessary, in case of conflict, to leave to the serious and upright conscience of the parties, according to the demands of concrete situations, the power to frustrate directly the realization of biological values, for the benefit of personality values.[15]

Having thus outlined the claims of existentialist or "situational" morality the pope declared:

From the essential relationships between man and God, between man and man, between husband and wife, between parents and children; from the essential community relationships found in the family, in the Church, and in the State, it follows, among other things, that hatred of God, blasphemy, idolatry, abandoning the true faith, denial of the faith, perjury, murder, bearing false witness, calumny, adultery and fornication, the abuse of marriage, the solitary sin, stealing and robbery, taking away the necessities of life, depriving workers of their

[15] AAS, 44 (1952), 415.

just wage [James v, 4], monopolizing vital foodstuffs and un-justifiably increasing prices, fraudulent bankruptcy, unjust maneuvering in speculation—all this is gravely forbidden by the divine Lawmaker. No examination is necessary. No matter what the situation of the individual may be, there is no other course open to him but to obey.

For the rest, against the "ethics of situations," We set up three considerations, or maxims. The first: We grant that God wants, first and always, a right intention. But this is not enough. He also wants the good work. A second principle is that it is not permitted to do evil in order that good may result (Rom. iii, 8). Now this new ethic, perhaps without being aware of it, acts according to the principle that the end justifies the means. A third maxim is, that there may be situations in which a man, and especially a Christian, cannot be unaware of the fact that he must sacrifice everything, even his life, in order to save his soul. Of this we are reminded by all the martyrs. . . . Did they, in the face of the "situation" in which they found themselves, use-lessly or even mistakenly incur a bloody death? No, certainly not, and in their blood they are the most explicit witnesses to the truth against the "new morality." [16]

The foregoing are the principal points to be noted about the address of April 18, 1952. It might be well to add, how-ever, that in this discourse the pope explicitly stated that the new morality stemmed from existentialism, "which either prescinds from God or simply denies Him, and, in any case, leaves man to himself." He conceded that the present-day (postwar) conditions had furnished fertile soil for the growth of this system and for its partial adoption by Catholics "in order to make the hardships of Christian life more bearable." Toward the end of his discourse he ad-mitted the difficulties frequently had in judging the

[16] *Ibid.*, pp. 417–18.

morality of some situations, but he insisted that the proper use of the virtue of prudence not only affords a sound means of solving these acute problems but also allows for the "creative activity" for which the situationists plead. (This last point will be discussed in the next chapter.) Furthermore—and this in answer to the claim that the new morality means real adulthood—he made it clear that the goal of true Christian education is also maturity, a maturity which implies "the perfect man, according to the measure of the fulness of the age of Christ." Finally, returning to the theme of the congress, he stated that the dangers to the faith of youth are very numerous, but certainly among the most dangerous is the new morality. Just as true morality is rooted in faith, so a false morality would destroy faith.

THE *Magnificate Dominum*

The addresses of 1952 are the most comprehensive and best known of the papal statements on the new morality. However, this chapter would be incomplete without a quotation from the allocution, *Magnificate Dominum*, in which the pope explicitly referred to the discourses of 1952. On this occasion he said:

. . . Not a few moderns, men and women, think that the leadership and vigilance of the Church is not to be suffered by one who is grown up; they not only say it, but they hold it as a firm conviction. They are unwilling to be, like children, "under guardians and stewards" (Gal. 4, 2). They wish to be treated as adults who are in full possession of their rights, and can decide for themselves what they must, or must not, do in any given situation.

Let the Church—they do not hesitate to say—propose her doctrine, pass her laws as norms of our actions. Still, when there is question of practical application to each individual's life, the Church must not interfere; she should let each one of the faithful follow his own conscience and judgment. They declare this is all the more necessary because the Church and her ministers are unaware of certain sets of circumstances either personal or extrinsic to individuals; in them each person has been placed, and must take his own counsel and decide what he must do. Such people, moreover, are unwilling in their final personal decisions to have any intermediary or intercessor placed between themselves and God, no matter what his rank or title.

Two years ago, in Our allocutions of March 23 and April 18, 1952, We spoke about these reprehensible theories and We examined their arguments (*Discorsi e Radio-messagi*, vol. 14 [1952] pp. 19 sq., pp. 69 sq.). Concerning the importance given to the attainment of a person's majority, this assertion is correct: it is just and right that adults should not be ruled as children. The Apostle speaking of himself says: "When I was a child, I spoke as a child, I felt as a child, I thought as a child. Now that I have become a man, I have put away the things of a child" (I Cor. 13, 11). That is not a true art of education which follows any other principle or procedure, nor is he a true shepherd of souls who pursues any other purpose than to elevate the faithful entrusted to his care "to perfect manhood, to the mature measure of the fulness of Christ" (Eph. 4, 13). But to be an adult and to have put off the things of childhood is one thing, and quite another to be an adult and not to be subject to the guidance and government of legitimate authority. For government is not a kind of nursery for children, but the effective direction of adults toward the end proposed to the state.

Since We are speaking to you, venerable brothers, and not to the faithful; when these ideas begin to appear and to take root in your flocks, remind the faithful: 1) that God placed shepherds of souls in the Church not to put a burden on the flock, but to help and protect it; 2) that the true liberty of the faithful is safeguarded by the guidance and vigilance of pastors; that they are protected from the slavery of vice and error, they are strengthened against the temptations which come from bad example and from the customs of evil men among whom they must live; 3) that therefore they act contrary to the prudence and charity which they owe themselves if they spurn this protection of God and His most certain help.[17]

INSTRUCTION OF THE HOLY OFFICE

The foregoing papal statements are essential to a proper understanding of the instruction of the Holy Office on situation ethics. Some of the points discussed by the pope, as well as some expressions in the instruction, will need further elucidation. It seems better to reserve such comments for the next chapter and to conclude the present chapter simply by giving a literal English version of the Instruction:

Contrary to the moral doctrine and its application which is traditional in the Catholic Church, there has begun to be spread abroad in many regions even among Catholics an ethical system which generally goes by the name of a certain "Situation Ethics." This ethics, they say, does not depend on the principles of objective ethics (which is ultimately based on "essence"); rather it is not merely put on the same plane with objective ethics, but is ranked above it.

The authors who follow this system hold that the decisive and ultimate norm of conduct is not objective right order, determined by the law of nature, and known with certainty from that law, but a certain intimate judgment and light of the mind of each individual, by means of which, in the concrete situation in which he is placed, he learns what he ought to do. And so, according to them, this ultimate decision a man makes is not,

[17] *AAS*, 46 (1954), 673–74; *The Catholic Mind*, 53 (1955), 317–18.

as the objective ethics handed down by authors of great weight teaches, the application of the objective law to a particular case, taking into account at the same time and weighing according to the rules of prudence the particular circumstances of the "situation," but that immediate, internal light and judgment. This judgment, at least in many matters, is not measured ultimately, is not to be measured, and is not measurable with regard to its objective correctness and truth, by any objective norm situated outside man, and independent of his subjective persuasion, but is entirely sufficient unto itself.

According to these authors, the traditional concept of "human nature" does not suffice; but recourse must be had to the concept of "existent" human nature which in many respects does not have absolute objective value, but only a relative and therefore changeable value, except, perhaps, for those few factors and principles which pertain to metaphysical (absolute and unchangeable) human nature. Of the same merely relative value is the traditional concept of the "law of nature." Furthermore a great many things which are spread about today as absolute postulates of the natural law, according to their opinion and doctrine rest upon the aforesaid concept of existent nature, and are therefore but relative and changeable, and can always be adapted to every situation.

Having accepted these principles and applied them to the present matter, they assert and teach that men are preserved or easily liberated from many otherwise insoluble ethical conflicts when each one judges in his own conscience, not primarily according to objective laws but by means of that internal, individual light based on personal intuition, what he must do in the situation at hand.

Many of the things set forth in this system of "Situation Ethics" contradict the truth of the matter, and the dictates of sound reason, betray traces of relativism and modernism, and wander far from the Catholic doctrine handed down through the centuries. In not a few assertions they are akin to various systems of non-Catholic ethics.

Having considered all this, in order to avert the danger of the "New Morality" of which the Supreme Pontiff Pope Pius XII spoke in the Allocutions delivered on March 23 and April 18, 1952, and in order to safeguard the purity and security of Catholic doctrine, this Supreme Sacred Congregation of the Holy Office forbids and prohibits this doctrine of "Situation Ethics," by whatever name it is designated, to be taught or approved in Universities, Academies, Seminaries and Houses of Formation of Religious, or to be propagated and defended in books, dissertations, assemblies, or, as they are called, conferences, or in any other manner whatsoever.

Given at Rome, from the offices of the Supreme Sacred Congregation of the Holy Office, February 2, 1956.

J. CARDINAL PIZZARDO
Bishop of Albano
Secretary [18]

---

[18] *AAS*, 48 (1956), 144–45.

8

Situation Ethics: Some Further Observations

T HE HOLY SEE's analysis of situation ethics, especially as given by the pope himself, is so complete that further comments might seem superfluous. But the topic is so important and the literature on it has been so abundant that our treatment might reasonably be considered deficient if we gave only a report of the Holy See's statements. Some further remarks are undoubtedly in order. The observations to be made here are not intended as a synthesis. Our purpose is rather to present a further development of a few of the main points and to include some especially illuminating comments of theologians who have written about situation ethics.

GENERAL OBSERVATIONS

It is clear enough both from the official documents and from other sources that situation ethics is a product of external conditions and of a philosophy which readily flourished in those conditions. As Karl Rahner, S.J.,[1] pointed out in 1950, World War II and the turbulence that followed in its wake made acute moral problems that had previously been of rare occurrence a matter of everyday experience. The problems of cooperating with the invading conquerors, of joining resistance movements, of the black market, of retaliation, of avoiding torture, of professing the faith in the face of diabolical persecution, of observing rigid laws of conjugal morality in the midst of the most dire poverty, of having children who would be just so much "gun fodder," of preserving premarital chastity when almost every form of innocent entertainment seemed beyond the reach of youth—these and countless other difficult problems became a part of the very atmosphere created by the War and its aftermath. And more than this, there was the preconditioning of men's minds by the dominance of the Nazi and Communist rejection of moral standards. With this dark picture in mind, it will be easy to see how the various tendencies that came to be known as "situation ethics," and that stem from existentialism, could be fostered. This will

[1] Cf. "Situationsethik und Sündenmystik," *Stimmen der Zeit*, 145 (1949–50), 330–42. With reference to this article, Dietrich von Hildebrand and Alice Jourdain (*True Morality and Its Counterfeits* [New York: David McKay Inc., 1955], p. 5) have written: "It is the merit of the great German theologian, Karl Rahner, S.J., to have been the first to lay his finger on this new ethics, which plays a great role in contemporary youth movements and literature. He distinguished two different trends, 'circumstance ethics' and 'sin mysticism.' He mentions no names and quotes no authors. He simply characterizes the two tendencies. They manifest themselves in various forms today, especially among Catholics. They are not philosophical theories, but rather lived, existential approaches to moral problems." Frequent references to Father Rahner's article are also found in P. De Letter, S.J., "In Defence of Christian Conscience," *The Clergy Monthly*, 17 (1953), 81–88. Father De Letter's article is a very clear summary of and commentary on the papal discourses of 1952.

be clear, we think, as some of these tendencies are more fully discussed.

We have suggested that situation ethics is a "series of tendencies." By this we mean that it is not a formally organized system of morality. Such is the way the pope chose to describe it and condemn it—i.e., by referring to various tendencies or tenets. And the existentialists themselves, who fathered this new morality, seem to protest consistently that they have no system of philosophy. Nevertheless, the Holy Office has called the new morality a "system." If "system" is taken in a somewhat wide sense, the word is certainly accurate, because the tendencies that constitute situation ethics are not completely disparate things. Rather, they are so closely connected that one cannot understand any of them without considering the others. Thus, the study of the situationists' proposed "autonomy" from the ecclesiastical magisterium leads one to consider their attitude toward moral laws; and this leads to their theory of the primacy of individual judgment; and this, finally, can be rightly understood only in the light of their exaltation of such things as personal responsibility, personal freedom, individual activity and creativeness—in a word, of their demand for what might be called "self-assertion." Because of this interweaving of the various tendencies, the new morality may be rightly designated as a system, even though its advocates do not propose it as such.

Another important general point to be kept in mind is that practically every tendency of the situationists has various degrees. This may be briefly illustrated by reference to the papal discourses of 1952. In one place the pope said the proponents of the new morality "do not deny outright general moral concepts and principles"; yet in different parts of the addresses he seemed to visualize degrees varying from crass existentialists who admit no general principles to Catholics who would soften the rigor of the law by minimizing its prohibitions, or who would remove its complexity and "casuistry" by returning to a primitive simplicity, or who would escape its sanctions by rationalizing that their own situations are "different" and that God, a loving Father, understands them even though the Church does not. These gradations are sometimes subtle. Because of them it is difficult to appraise many writings which seem to have the "flavor" of the new morality but which may have an acceptable orthodox explanation or which, though not acceptable, are not at all in the same category as situation ethics. For instance, as we shall explain later, some Catholic authors have gone entirely too far in their theories of diminished subjective responsibility, but this is not the same as the situationist tendency to change or abolish objective moral standards. Yet the language of the former is sometimes unfortunately somewhat similar to that of the latter.

Perhaps this last-mentioned difficulty is the reason why the critics of situation ethics seldom name names. They are content to speak in general and, with but few exceptions, they do not specify the writers who defend the new morality. No doubt this safeguards the law of fraternal charity. But it does not help to a clear understanding of situation ethics; and it may even defeat the purpose of protecting charity by leading the unwary reader to suspect orthodox writers. There is, however, a partial compensation in the fact that many critics do cite concrete examples of solutions and expressions that are typical of situationism. It may help to an understanding of this difficult matter if we give some of these examples before discussing the various tendencies of situation ethics.

The pope himself cited abandoning the faith, premarital unchastity, and frustration of the marriage act as things that might be sometimes justifiable by the new morality. He also made it clear that the tendency to restrict the authority of the Church to purely religious matters is a mark of the new ethics. Francis Hürth, S.J., suggested that the Moral Rearmament movement is an example of situation ethics because MRA is a system of morality without faith or dogma, is based on the notion of immediate contact of the soul with God, without external norms of guidance, without the magisterium, and so forth.[2] Later, Father Hürth gave examples of theologians who taught that contraception, therapeutic abortion, direct masturbation, and direct suicide are sometimes permissible.[3] Father Hürth was speaking of (unnamed) Catholic theologians, sincere men, who held that all these actions are generally wrong but who were tainted with situationism in the sense that they thought such actions could be justified by reason of special circumstances. Joseph Fuchs, S.J., writing some time before Father

[2] This analysis of MRA is taken from a *monitum* written by the Cardinal Archbishop of Milan and quoted by Father Hürth in *Periodica*, 41 (1952), 237. This number of *Periodica* contains the original texts of the papal addresses of 1952, with a Latin translation and a commentary by Father Hürth. For more complete discussions of the history and nature of MRA, see John McCarthy, *Irish Ecclesiastical Record*, 81 (1954), 32–36; also Ralph J. Bastian, S.J., and John A. Hardon, S.J., *American Ecclesiastical Review*, 135 (1956), 217–26.

[3] Cf. *Periodica*, 45 (1956), 185–87. These examples are given in a 65-page commentary on the instruction of the Holy Office on situation ethics. For a briefer, and much clearer, commentary, see J. Fuchs, S.J., "Éthique objective et éthique de situation. A propos de l'Instruction du Saint-Office du 2 février 1956," *Nouvelle revue théologique*, 78 (1956), 798–819. References to writings by Father Fuchs that antedated the instruction will be given in footnotes 4 and 9.

Hürth, mentioned the same examples, as well as refusal of military service; but Father Fuchs apparently had Protestant theologians chiefly in mind.[4]

Two other examples that may help toward an understanding of some of the individual tendencies to be discussed can be culled from existentialist literature. The first concerns the very different conduct of two girls, one of whom courageously gives up a love affair with a man whom she decides she has no right to marry, the other of whom continues a love affair with a married man because, according to her, the one thing that counts is the *grand amour*. The existentialist solution is that, though the conduct of these two girls is diametrically opposed according to traditional moral standards, yet each is in reality right because she is sincere with herself.[5] The other example is Kierkegaard's celebrated analysis of the scriptural account of Abraham's willingness to sacrifice his son Isaac. Abraham manifested his willingness to act against the universal moral law because through faith he recognized a higher relationship— the direct relationship of the individual to God. In Kierkegaard's analysis, the moral law itself was really a temptation to Abraham; and he rose above the temptation by conforming to the will of God which he perceived through faith.[6] Both these existentialist examples must be kept in

[4] Cf. "Situationsethik in theologischer Sicht," *Scholastik*, 27 (1952), 161–82. A condensed English version of this article is in *Theology Digest*, 2 (1954), 25–30. The same number of *Theology Digest* includes other helpful references concerning the new morality: cf. pp. 24, 30–32.

[5] Cf. the analysis of Sartre's ethics given by Jeremiah Newman in "The Ethics of Existentialism," *Irish Ecclesiastical Record*, 77 (1952), 321–32; 421–32. For the example in our text, see p. 331. There is an abstract of Father Newman's article in *Theology Digest*, 2 (1954), 30–31.

[6] Cf. Frederick Copleston, S.J., *Contemporary Philosophy* (Westminster, Md.: The Newman Press, 1956), pp. 151–52. See also *Encyclopedia of Morals* (New York: Philosophical Library Inc., 1956), p. 285. The

mind as the tendencies and tenets of the situationists are unfolded.

ATTITUDE ON THE MAGISTERIUM

It is clear enough that existentialism, whether atheistic or Protestant, can find no place for the living magisterium, as Catholics understand it. But the official documents cited in our last chapter have undoubtedly been concerned with a reprehensible and at least dangerous, if not positively wrong, attitude of Catholics regarding the function of the Church. One such attitude consists, as Pius XII has clearly described it, in relegating the authority of the Church to matters that are purely and exclusively religious. It seems that in our preceding chapters enough has been said to show both the un-Catholicity and the absurdity of this manner of thinking.

Another attack on the function of the teaching Church has been phrased in a superficially appealing form. Why, it is asked, cannot one be a Catholic and adopt a freer and easier way of life based on prudence and charity and independent of all the norms dictated by ecclesiastical authority and specialists in moral theology? The gospel, according to these objectors, contains only general principles of charity, conjugal fidelity, respect for authority, for life, and for property. How, then, can the Church impose in the name of Christ all the accretions and refinements of moral doctrine that have occurred since His time? If the early Christians could serve Christ without all the rules laid down later, why cannot we do the same?

The general answer to this difficulty was aptly given by

encyclopedia is edited by Vergilius Ferm; the article on Kierkegaard is by Ria Stavrides.

Albert Stevaux when he pointed out that the objection is rooted in a misunderstanding of the role Christ Himself planned for His Church.[7] It was only natural that the moral precepts (and counsels, too) of the gospels, like the doctrines of faith, would need interpretation and development, and it was the role of the Church to give this interpretation and foster this development. Thus, some interpretation and some elaboration were essential to the growth of the Church and to its influence on the consciences of the faithful.

This is not to say that the moral theology treatises have no noisome accretions or no odious casuistry. No honest scholar would say, for example, that everything contained in the treatises on sacrilege or the Sixth Commandment is part of the necessary development of the precepts of the gospel, as explained by Father Stevaux; nor would the honest scholar deny that there is odious casuistry in some of the opinions which contradict common sense, but from which it is difficult to erase the label "probable"—for example, the case of burning the wrong house,[8] the case of mixing recent sins in the confession of past sins, and so forth. But the situationists' criticisms are not limited to such accretions and casuistry; they would do away with the whole development of moral theology and go back to the few laws of the gospel. And even these relatively few laws are stripped of their universal binding force, as will be seen later.

[7] Cf. "L'Église et la morale," *Revue diocésaine de Tournai*, 8 (1953), 305-19.

[8] A long-needed survey of theological opinion on this celebrated case has been made by Edouard Hamel, S.J., "L'erreur sur la personne dans la damnification. étude de théologie positive," *Sciences ecclésiastiques*, 8 (1956), 335-84. Father Hamel's conclusion is that there is no solid probability, either intrinsic or extrinsic, for exempting from restitution merely because of a mistake about the ownership of voluntarily damaged property.

ATTITUDE ON THE MORAL LAW

The atheistic existentialist can obviously admit no genuine moral principles or laws. In fact, it was this atheistic existentialism that prompted some modern Protestant theologians to work out a theory of ethics which they thought would preserve a Christian view of the moral law and at the same time allow for the higher law of love and the individual's direct relationship to God. Situationism, as it has affected Catholics, apparently stems from this Protestant version of existentialism, which was analyzed by Joseph Fuchs, S.J., in his article published in early 1952.[9]

According to Father Fuchs, these Protestant theologians wished to uphold some validity for the moral laws; yet they could not on principle admit an absolute binding force that would cover every concrete case. To them, this seemed to conflict with the liberty of God. They could not see how it would be impossible for God to give a permission or even a command that would be contrary to any so-called "natural law"; to hold otherwise would be to tie the hands of the Creator and Master of the universe. To solve this dilemma —of denying all objective moral law on the one hand, and on the other of admitting an absolute binding power that would conflict with divine liberty—these Protestants turned to the law of love in the New Testament. This law of love is superior to all other laws and may contradict them. More-

[9] See the reference to his article in *Scholastik* in footnote 4, *supra*. In June, 1954, Father Fuchs read a paper on situation ethics at a convention of moralists in Luxembourg. This paper was revised into an article entitled "Morale théologique et morale de situation," and published in *Nouvelle revue théologique*, 76 (1954), 1073–85. Father Fuchs has also written what he calls a "petit livre" entitled *Situation und Entscheidung, Grundfragen christlicher Situationsethik* (Frankfort on the Main, 1952). His latest contribution (at the time we now write) is the commentary on the instruction by the Holy Office mentioned above, footnote 4.

over, the individual knows this law as it applies to him in the concrete situations of everyday life, not through any verbal formula, but rather through a sort of divine inspiration received within his own soul. In a word, in the depths of the soul there is an immediate contact with the will of God. This is the meeting of "the 'I' of man and the 'I' of the personal God, not the God of the law, but of God the Father, with whom man must unite in filial love," which was described by Pius XII in his allocution on the new morality. The will of God is thus manifested directly to the individual and is received by him through an "intuition of love."

The foregoing analysis of Protestant situation ethics is illustrated graphically by a wagon wheel:

. . . The spokes of the wheel are moral norms which all tend to one point, the will of God. However, the moral norms, like the spokes of a wheel, never meet, because at the center is a hole, a vacuum, in which God makes known to me here and now His inscrutable will. Consequently, these moral norms are a general indication of God's will, but in the concrete situation, God indicates to me—as it were independently of these norms— His present will in my regard. Since at times He may even indicate to me a course of action contrary to that prescribed in a general norm, I must look to the actual situation to discover His will.[10]

In these Protestant theories it is easy to see a reflection of Kierkegaard's deductions from the scriptural account of Abraham and Isaac. And it is also easy to note a complete misunderstanding of the traditional Catholic teaching about the universality and absoluteness of the precepts of the

[10] Cf. *Theology Digest*, 2 (1954), 25. (This quotation is from the condensed version of Father Fuchs' article in *Scholastik*.)

natural law. Some laws (e.g., the prohibition of blasphemy) are so universal and absolute that they admit of no possibility of change or exemption. The precept, "Thou shalt not kill," does not have this same *de jure* absoluteness. Since God is the master of human life, He could authorize its destruction, even in the case of innocent persons; and if He gave such authorization, the destruction of life would be justified. Kierkegaard missed this point in judging that God commanded Abraham to act against the natural law; and so have the disciples of Kierkegaard. Their error, however, goes deeper than this and becomes more pernicious when they translate the Abraham-Isaac example into a matter of everyday life by allowing individuals to decide for themselves that the "voice of God" is exempting them from precepts of the natural law.

It is perhaps well to note here that the theory of moral laws, as just described, is by no means a "common opinion" of Protestant theologians. There is another view which is certainly similar to, if not identical with, the traditional Catholic explanation of natural law. The contrasting Protestant views are labeled by Edward Duff, S.J., following Dr. Joseph H. Oldham, as the "ethic of inspiration" and the "ethic of ends." Father Duff writes:

As described by Dr. Oldham, 'the ethic of inspiration' insists that the fundamental and characteristic Christian moral attitude is not obedience to fixed norms or to a moral code but a living response to a living person, a fellowship with God who is sovereignly free and whose Will is sought for a present personal decision. Archbishop Temple once evidenced this outlook in declaring that revelation is not truth about God but the living God Himself. An 'ethic of ends', on the other hand is based on an idea of the proper ordering of society and its parts whose overall purposes and particular functions are discoverable by a rational examination of their nature and operations.[11]

THE PERSONAL DECISION

All the situationists make much of the "personal decision" that must be made in an individual's ethical problems. And, as they differ in their attitudes toward the moral law—from absolute denial of the law to mere denial of the law's absoluteness—so they differ in their explanation of this personal decision. And, whatever be their explanation, it is necessarily somewhat baffling to one who is accustomed to thinking of judgments of conscience in terms of the application of general moral principles to concrete situations.

In the extreme existentialist position, God and moral principles are completely out of the picture. The sole ruling norm of "ethical" action is personal sincerity, acting according to one's convictions. One Catholic explanation of the personal decision consisted in postulating a moral sense—an intuitive power for recognizing moral good, a power that operates independently of reason.[12] The decision of conscience, according to this explanation, would be rather a feeling than a judgment. Its concrete expression would be: "This act is good because I *feel* it is good." In this explana-

[11] Edward Duff, S.J., *The Social Thought of the World Council of Churches* (New York: Association Press, 1956), p. 94. This book is an objective analysis of the history, nature, authority, social philosophy, and social policy of the World Council of Churches from the Amsterdam through the Evanston assemblies. Dr. Oldham, whom Father Duff cites, edited the report of the Oxford Conference of 1937, which was the predecessor of the World Council.

[12] For an analysis of this theory, see G. Bortolaso, S.J., "Etica dell' amore ed etica dell' obbligazione," *La Civiltà Cattolica* (May 17, 1952), pp. 368–79. *Theology Digest*, 2 (1954), 31–32, contains an abstract of Father Bortolaso's article.

tion—if we understand it correctly—there is an immediate and intuitive perception, not precisely of God, but of moral good (and also of moral evil). It differs, therefore, from the Protestant version which has been described by Father Fuchs and others. In the Protestant explanation, there is an immediate contact with God so that a person knows by a kind of divine inspiration what he is to do and not to do. This inspiration may, at times, contradict the moral precepts (as God commanded Abraham to sacrifice Isaac), but even if it does, it may and should be followed.

It seems to be the Protestant version, or some variations of it, that the Holy Office had in mind when it said that according to situation ethics, "the decisive and ultimate norm of conduct is . . . a certain intimate judgment and light of the mind of each individual, by means of which, in the concrete situation in which he is placed, he learns what he ought to do." Nothing would be gained by our trying to make a further analysis of this judgment; but it does seem worthwhile to point out that, according to situationist thought, actions performed in conformity with this internal light are not merely subjectively, but also objectively, well ordered. Situationists would not, therefore, accept the traditional explanation that an action contrary to the moral law, but performed in good faith—e.g., contraception—would be subjectively good but objectively immoral. In their view, the moral precepts known through reason and revelation (if they exist at all) are subordinate to this higher law, the will of God as known by this "*intimum lumen.*"

SELF-ASSERTION

One attitude common to the various degrees of situationists and which is shared by many of the orthodox critics of moral theology,[13] is a certain contempt for the mediocre man, for the man who is content with the minimum, who, as it were, simply swims with the stream of orthodoxy, who shows no personal initiative in his moral problems—if he has such problems—and no desire to rise above the commonplace. This man, say the situationists, is merely passive in his moral life. By this they seem to mean that he simply accepts what the Church, or his pastor, or perhaps his confessor says he must or may not do. He is, as a consequence, not "creative": that is, he assumes no personal responsibility for his moral decisions; he does not make himself what he is, but he is molded by others. Moreover, his goodness is largely negative; it consists in abstention from doing wrong. In fact, the situationists (and some others [14]) would question whether this kind of life is really good, whether the virtue practiced by this mediocre man is really virtue or merely "pseudo-virtue."

The situationists do not stop here. One of their captivating slogans is "liberty"; and the theists among them translate this into the "liberty of the children of God." Here, as in other matters, there are degrees and variations. According to one explanation, liberty means acting with joy and spontaneity; there is no real liberty, therefore no real virtue, in "acting against the grain." Hence, even the saints, and especially the martyrs, as well as many military heroes, would fall under the strictures of the situationists; for certainly many of those who practiced heroic virtue constantly in ordinary life have had to do much that was against the grain; and some of the martyrs have faced the prospect of

[13] Cf. *supra*, chapters 4 and 6.
[14] E.g., Gerald Vann, O.P., "Unconscious Motivation and Pseudo-Virtue," *Homiletic and Pastoral Review*, 57 (1956), 115–23.

torture and death with a sense of dread and were impelled to be heroes through a sense of duty and not through any feeling of elation.

Such ideals as freedom and personal initiative or creativeness can certainly have soundly orthodox meanings and can even express what is best in traditional Christian morality. But not as the situationists propose them. The liberty they want is freedom from the established plan of God: from the teaching authority constituted by Christ and from the imperatives of the moral law. Thus, the freedom they sponsor makes the individual himself his sole norm of action when the chips are down. As Pius XII has pointed out, this would defeat its own purpose. There is no real sense of interior freedom without a concomitant sense of security; and it is hardly psychologically possible for a person to have this sense of security in his moral judgments unless he makes them in accordance with norms that he knows to be correct. This is the reason, no doubt, why the pope specified the removal of all objective norms of morality as the central weakness of the new morality. Freedom, as the Church has always explained it, is a regulated freedom; the power of thinking and acting within a divinely-outlined pattern. This is true both of theological speculation and of moral action.

The situationists say that the liberty they propose would free men from many frustrations, would solve many otherwise insoluble moral conflicts. In this they show a woeful lack of knowledge of human nature. Man left to himself, without clear norms for his actions, is much more apt to experience frustration and much less likely to solve difficult problems with a sense of security than if he had such norms, even though the norms might at times require great sacrifices.

A similar lack of insight into human nature is found in the criticism of the mediocre man. Any priest who has dealt intimately with consciences over a number of years comes to realize that there are many people who are capable of leading the negatively good lives criticized by the situationists, but who simply do not respond to exhortations to do more. Moreover, it is to be noted that it is not only mediocrity in the spiritual sense that the situationists (and some others) criticize. Equally subject to their censures are those large numbers of Catholics who lead good, simple lives, who do their duty as the Church through their pastors or their confessors has explained it to them. These devout persons, who will one day take their places in the ranks of the uncanonized saints honored on November 1, are criticized because of their "passivity," their lack of spiritual initiative, their lack of "creativeness."

A final word about self-assertion, initiative, or creativeness. Within the scope of traditional morality and asceticism there is ample room for personal responsibility for decisions of conscience. The key to this is found in the correct notion of Christian prudence, which supposes the knowledge of general norms and applies them to concrete situations. Thus in the sphere of obligation, there is much room for, and need of, individual mental activity in deciding how the principles concerning occasions of sin, cooperation, scandal, epikeia, and so forth apply to the individual situation; and the answers may differ from person to person, as well as for the same person in different situations. It was very likely to cases such as these that Pius XII referred when he distinguished between absolutely binding precepts and cases in which there are no absolutely binding standards. Concerning these latter cases, he said:

[139]

Where there are no absolutely binding standards, independent of all circumstances or eventualities, the situation which "happens only once" demands, it is true, in its unicity, an attentive examination, in order to decide which rules are to be applied, and how. Catholic morality has always, and extensively, treated this problem of forming one's own conscience by first examining the circumstances of the case to be decided. The whole of its teaching offers a precious aid to the definite guidance of conscience, whether theoretical or practical. Let it suffice to mention the explanations of St. Thomas, still of value, on the cardinal virtue of prudence and the virtues connected with it. His treatise shows his understanding of a sense of personal activity and of actuality which contains whatever true and positive elements there may be in "ethics according to the situation," while avoiding its confusion and wanderings from the truth. Hence, it will be enough for the modern moralist to follow the same line if he wishes to make a thorough study of the new problem.[15]

The pope's words apply primarily, as we have suggested, to cases in which an individual must decide what is his duty; but they apply also to that almost infinite field of personal decisions that are concerned, not with obligations, but with counsels, with actions "beyond the call of duty." Particularly in this sphere of supererogation is there room for personal initiative and for responsiveness to the voice of God (through the inspirations of grace) in the soul; yet even here the principles of true Christian prudence must be followed to avoid self-deception and great spiritual harm.

[15] *AAS*, 44 (1952), 418; *Catholic Documents*, 8 (July, 1952), 19. The reference to St. Thomas is to 2ª, 2ªᵉ, qq. 47–57. For a clear, brief exposition of St. Thomas' teaching on prudence, see John R. Connery, S.J., "Prudence and Morality," *Theological Studies*, 13 (1952), 564–82.

9

Occasions of Sin

MORALISTS NOT UNCOMMONLY discuss occasions of sin in the treatise on the sacrament of penance. The reason for this is practical: they wish to give pastoral rules for the confessor when he deals with a penitent who is or may be in the proximate occasion of serious sin. Logically, however, this topic belongs more properly in general moral, either in the treatise on sin or, even better, in the treatise on law. It is a commonly accepted principle that every law implicitly includes the obligation of taking the ordinary means of fulfilling the law; and one such means is the avoidance of things that create an unjustifiable danger of violating the law.

The foregoing is one reason why we include a discussion of occasions of sin in the present volume. Another reason is that the topic has a special pertinence to a number of the questions already covered in our earlier chapters. For instance, the critics (both orthodox and unorthodox) of moral theology show a pronounced dislike for casuistry. Yet, as we have already pointed out, casuistry has a place in moral theology—so much so that there can be no really practical moral theology without good casuistry. And there is perhaps no better example of the need of casuistry, as well as of its difficulties, than the attempts of eminent theologians to formulate principles and practical rules concerning occasions of sin.

Moreover, the problem of occasions of sin is an excellent illustration of the Holy Father's statement that there can be situations to which no absolutely binding precepts are immediately applicable, and in which, therefore, there is special need of the virtue of prudence. This does not mean, of course, that there is any moral problem that is solved independently of a general principle. It simply means that for the application of some principles there is need of an unusually careful examination of all the concrete circumstances. Prudence makes this examination and draws the conclusion, not by means of the mysterious *"lumen internum"* of the situationists, but by applying a sound principle to the situation.

Thirdly, as we mentioned more than once in our early chapters, there are among Catholic theologians many legitimate controversies—controversies which the Holy See allows and which only the Holy See can authoritatively solve. The dispute among moral theologians concerning the nature of a proximate occasion of mortal sin is such a controversy, and a very important one.

Finally—to point out one more link between the present chapter and the preceding material—we should like to recall what we said in chapter 6 about the rash publicizing of opinions of individual moralists as if these opinions were the authoritative teaching of the Church. Unfortunately, this has happened all too frequently in our country during the last decade or so, with the result that the faithful have become profoundly confused about certain important moral problems of everyday life. Some of these practical problems are concerned with duties relative to occasions of sin.

The foregoing remarks not only show the pertinence of our present topic but also suggest the logical manner of developing it. We shall first outline the main points concerning occasions of sin, with special reference to the controversy over the meaning of a proximate occasion; then we shall discuss the two practical problems of company-keeping and dancing.[1]

THE GENERAL CONTROVERSY

Points of Agreement

Before we attempt to delineate the general controversy concerning the proximate occasion of mortal sin, we should like to touch briefly on the points that are matters of common agreement among moralists. First, according to all authors, an occasion of sin is an external circumstance which implies an impulse or allurement to sin with a consequent likelihood or danger of sinning, and this likelihood or danger would not be present, or would be notably diminished,

---

[1] Company-keeping, dancing, and attendance at theatrical and screen productions are the problems most commonly discussed by moralists in their treatises on occasions of sin. We discussed the third problem in "The Legion of Decency," *Theological Studies*, 18 (Sept., 1957), 387–433. We intended to include this article as a chapter in the present volume; but shortly after the article appeared, the National Office of the Legion of Decency announced a new classification of movies. Our moral appraisals and opinions remain unchanged but it would require a certain amount of rewriting to put them in terms of the new classifications. We think this can best be done after a year or so of experience during which the meaning of the new classification will become clearer. It seems advisable, therefore, to reserve our discussion of the National Legion of Decency for a later volume in this series on contemporary moral theology.

if the external circumstance were avoided. The purpose of this definition is to distinguish between a danger of sin which results primarily from the external circumstance and a danger which exists primarily because of a personal weakness. Thus, if a boy indulges in impure thoughts only when he reads a certain type of magazine, there is a presumption that for him the reading constitutes an occasion of sin. On the other hand, if he entertains impure thoughts at almost any time and under almost any conditions, the reasonable conclusion is that the source of the trouble is *within* him; he is not an *occasionarius* in the technical sense. Furthermore, a circumstance which is deliberately chosen as a means of committing sin should not be confused with an occasion strictly so called. Such a choice is a direct choice of sin, not the choice of an occasion of sin. An occasion is not chosen for the purpose of committing sin. By supposition it is chosen for some other reason and thereupon becomes an inducement to sin. Thus if a man, after making up his mind to sin, seeks out the person or place which will enable him to do so, this person or place is not the "occasion" of his sin. A confessor who would demand that such a penitent "promise to avoid the occasion of sin" would be giving harmless but inapplicable advice. He would be failing to recognize the penitent's real problem and failing to come to grips with it.

Also, though they disagree in explaining the distinction, all authors speak of *remote* and *proximate* occasions. Moreover, in speaking of the proximate occasion of mortal sin, they generally distinguish between the common, or absolute, and the personal, or relative, occasion. The latter refers to an occasion which is known to be proximate for this individual, for instance, through his personal experience; the former refers to an occasion which is presumably proximate for men in general, or for all the normal members of a certain group, e.g., adolescents. There is no disagreement on these notions (except the controversial question of the meaning of proximate occasion); but it is well to observe that there may be and there are differences of opinion regarding the appraisal of certain situations—that is, whether these situations as a matter of fact do or do not constitute a common, or absolute, occasion of serious sin.

One defect in the present treatises is the fact that authors seem too ready to call an occasion a common or absolute one, and that they do not make sufficient allowance for relativity as to time, locality, or differences between groups. What was true of St. Alphonsus' time, or of the people with whom he personally dealt, may not be true of our day or of our people. Pius XI, in *Vigilanti cura*, excluded the idea of a world-wide office for classification of films because the considerable differences in national habits and attitudes make such universal classifications impractical.[2] Theologians who make estimates that a given proximate occasion is such for the generality of men do not usually base their estimates on statistical samples scientifically controlled and calculated. They are based rather on common opinion (and too often perhaps on the opinion of other moralists in other lands), or on personal experience with penitents (which is necessarily limited), and probably to some extent on the optimistic or pessimistic views they entertain as to human nature and human frailty. At any rate, it seems to us that an estimate of common proximate danger is more likely to

[2] *AAS*, 28 (1936), 261.

be accurate when it is predicated of a certain class or group, rather than of the generality of men, for example, the educated or the uneducated, male or female, married or unmarried, fully mature, immature, and so forth.

Differences of opinion concerning absolute occasions in the two practical examples to be discussed later would often have to do only with the factual appraisal of the situations; but sometimes these differences can be traced to the more fundamental question concerning the meaning of proximate occasion.

Another point on which there would be no theoretical dispute (even though practical cases might present difficult problems and admit of differences of opinion) is the distinction between *voluntary* and *necessary* occasions of sin. An occasion is termed *voluntary* when it can be avoided with ease or at least with relatively little difficulty; whereas it is *necessary* when its avoidance is either physically or morally impossible. Also, insofar as theory is concerned, there is agreement that a person can be justified in remaining in or not avoiding a necessary occasion, even of mortal sin. This latter point is true even of necessary occasions which are, according to the varying terminologies, *proximate* occasions of mortal sin. The usual condition, of course, is that proper means be taken to render the proximate danger of sin remote.

Finally, there is no disagreement among theologians that given an occasion of serious sin which is voluntary and truly proximate, there is a grave obligation to remove it or to avoid it. This is the doctrine implied in the condemnation of the following proposition: "Potest aliquando absolvi, qui in proxima occasione peccandi versatur, quam potest et non vult omittere, quin immo directe et ex proposito quærit, aut ei se ingerit." [3]

Even the strictest authors are generally willing to waive the question of occasions of venial sin—and this for two reasons: first, a penitent's dispositions concerning such occasions would seldom, if ever, have any bearing on the validity of absolution; [4] and secondly, occasions of venial sin are so numerous that it would be impossible to avoid them all, and in many specific cases it would be impossible to determine whether the occasion was necessary or voluntary. For similar reasons, some authors lay little stress on the duty of avoiding truly remote occasions of mortal sin; and many explicitly deny that there is any obligation to avoid such occasions. [5]

The Controversy

There might be some controversy over one or another of the foregoing points, but it would be so slight as to amount to a mere *lis de verbis*. But, despite the fact that the question is sometimes complicated by differing terminologies, there is clearly more than a *lis de verbis* in the controversy over the definition (and therefore the real meaning) of a proximate occasion of mortal sin in contradistinction to a

[3] DB, 1211; proposition 61 of a number of errors condemned on March 4, 1679 (under Pope Innocent XI).

[4] It seems theoretically possible that an unwillingness to give up the proximate occasion of a venial sin would affect the validity of absolution, e.g., if this venial sin constituted the *sole* matter for confession, so that nothing else would be included even generically.

[5] Among those who explicitly deny the obligation are: Genicot-Salsmans-Gortebecke, II (17th ed., 1952), n. 356; Piscetta-Gennaro, V (6th ed., 1938), n. 763; Prümmer, III (8th ed., 1936), n. 449; Varceno-Loiano-Grizzana, IV (1940), n. 335; Tanquerey-Cimetier, I (12th ed., 1936), n. 531; Vermeersch, III (4th ed., 1948—edited by Creusen), n. 535. The references are all to the manuals of moral theology prepared by these authors.

remote occasion.[6] This controversy is neatly pinpointed by
the following examples of A. Regan, C.SS.R.:

. . . A man goes into an hotel and drinks in circumstances
which make it impossible for him to assert definitely that he will
not get seriously drunk. Perhaps in these same circumstances he
has frequently been drunk in the past, or perhaps the hold drink
has upon him is rapidly becoming such that serious abuse is
definitely likely. Yet no one can definitely say that on this or
that occasion he will get drunk, for we can suppose that the
chances in both directions are roughly equal. According to St.
Alphonsus such a man is guilty of mortal sin—at least objectively—each time he goes deliberately into these dangerous
circumstances. Company keepers see each other at places or
times or in other circumstances which are likely to lead them
into mortal sin: they know this because perhaps they have fallen
in the past, or perhaps because they must honestly acknowledge
that their sense of modesty is so breaking down that to court
temptation *even once more* is seriously to risk a fall. To take
such a risk even once is in the eyes of the Holy Doctor a mortal
sin, even though it may also be probable they will not fall, for
the vital point is that as long as a fall remains probable there is
no room for a prudent judgment that sin will actually be
avoided.[7]

[6] The varying definitions are briefly summed up by Genicot-Salsmans-
Gortebecke, II, n. 356 (n. 371 in the last edition by Salsmans) as follows:
"Alii, ut S. Alphonsus (n. 452), *proximam* dicunt occasionem in qua
homines communiter *ut plurimum* peccant, vel etiam in qua homo expertus
est se *frequenter* cecidisse.—Unde, etiam in posterum, peccatum est saltem
probabile.
"Alii, ad mentem Lugonis et aliorum, proximam dicunt occasionem in
qua homo *semper* aut saltem *frequentius* peccat.—Unde, etiam in posterum,
peccatum *est moraliter* certum aut saltem *probabilius.*"
A very complete historical exposition and analysis of the definitions has
been given by P. Napholc, S.J., "De vera proximæ occasionis peccati
notione," *Periodica,* 21 (1932), 1*–34*; and 129*–57*.
[7] Cf. "The Proximate Occasion of Sin according to St. Alphonsus,"
Australasian Catholic Record, 26 (1949), 97–109; our citation from pp.
101–02.

Regarding the examples chosen by Father Regan, it should be noted that these are often presented to the confessor as habits of entering occasions in which one often sins mortally. This is not the point of controversy. Almost all authors, it seems, would agree that one has a serious duty to give up the *habit* of frequenting a voluntary occasion in which one *often* sins mortally, because the habitual frequenting of the occasion includes a practical certainty that sin will take place.[8] Obviously, this is not the point that Father Regan is stressing. His thesis concerns the duty of avoiding a single act. Moreover, it is not limited to the examples in the text. It is a general thesis that refers to every mortal sin, whether internal or external, whether committed alone or with others. The thesis is that, as regards any of these sins, an occasion is proximate when the danger of sinning is truly probable, even though it is equally probable that, in spite of the occasion, the sin will be avoided. And, since this degree of danger constitutes a proximate occasion, a mortal sin is committed (objectively) *each time* one exposes oneself to the danger without a proportionate reason.

Father Regan's text also contains the principal argument

[8] Thus, even Genicot, one of the strongest defenders of the lenient opinion (an opinion later abandoned by Salsmans), wrote:

"Fatemur tamen, propter imprudentiam in salute exponenda, leviter peccare eum qui se, absque justa causa, probabili seu serio gravis peccati periculo obiciat: immo sæpe veram occasionem proximam reperiri in consuetudine, quamvis in singulis actibus quibus frequentatur non habeatur nisi probabile periculum. Sic ponamus juvenem, qui crebro peccavit cum amasia, sæpe etiam eam adire quin graviter contra castitatem delinquat: hunc censemus sub gravi teneri ad abrumpendam hanc consuetudinem, in qua pergere nequit sine morali certitudine novorum lapsuum, quamvis in tali casu forte singulæ visitationes grave peccatum non constituant, nisi quatenus renovetur pravum propositum in his relationibus periculosis perstandi." Quoted from his *Institutiones theologiæ moralis*, II (5th ed., 1905), n. 372. This is the last edition of the work prepared by Genicot alone.

used in defense of this thesis: namely, that a man who, without sufficient reason, exposes himself to this probable danger of mortal sin is guilty of a serious violation of prudence. The reasoning behind this statement is that actual grace is required for successfully resisting a serious temptation and that one who is not doing what he can to obtain the grace will not get it. Subsidiary arguments that have been advanced are the following: such a man acts in the state of practical doubt; he is tempting God; he is violating the precept of charity toward himself in the same way (in fact, a *fortiori*) as the man who, without good reason, exposes himself or others to the probable danger of serious bodily injury.

Father Regan's thesis, of course, is not new; nor are the arguments that are advanced to support it.[9] Over the course of many years, numerous theologians have carefully considered these arguments. A great many have been sufficiently impressed to sponsor the thesis; many others have remained unconvinced.[10] For one reason or another these latter theologians do not believe that the stricter opinion can be proved; or at least they do not believe it can be proved universally, so that a confessor would be justified in refusing absolution as soon as he has established that any penitent is voluntarily (that is, without proportionate rea-

[9] St. Alphonsus is usually considered the father of the opinion. Its principal modern exponent is Francis Ter Haar, C.SS.R., *De occasionariis et recidivis* (Turin: Marietti, 1927), and *Casus conscientiæ de praecipuis hujus ætatis peccandi occasionibus* (2nd. ed.; Turin: Marietti, 1939).

[10] A scholarly presentation of opinions expressed up to 1932 is given by P. Napholc, S.J., in the article cited *supra*, footnote 6. Father Napholc's own conclusion favors the stricter opinion; but he cautiously leaves it to others to judge whether his conclusion is morally certain and whether his reasoning is sufficiently cogent to warrant setting aside the views of many great authors who believe that a less severe opinion must be followed in practice.

son) entering any occasion which includes the probable danger of any mortal sin.

The position of those who hold a milder opinion will be better understood in the light of the following considerations.

In the first place, we are not dealing here with the question whether it is a sin to enter a probable danger of mortal sin without proportionate reason. All are agreed that this is sinful. The question is: How sinful? Is it necessarily gravely sinful?

A duty under pain of mortal sin must be proved, and the burden of proof is on those who assert the obligation. According to those who hold the more lenient opinion, all the arguments advanced by Father Regan and others merely prove that there is *some* obligation to avoid in every case the probable danger of mortal sin; they do not prove that that obligation is always a serious one.[11]

If we were to arrange a scale of danger of mortal sin as contained in various occasions, the dangers would range all the way down from certain, to morally certain, to highly probable, to more probable, to equiprobable, to probable, to less probable, to slightly probable, to hardly probable, to possible, to hardly possible, to impossible. In other words the degrees of danger are indefinitely numerous. With the gradually diminishing probability of sin there is a gradually diminishing malice until finally a point is reached where all would agree that there is no longer mortal malice at all, but only venial malice.

Now since the strongest and most telling argument for

[11] This is the position taken, e.g., by M. Fabregas, S.J., "De obligatione vitandi probabile periculum peccandi," *Periodica*, 30 (1941), 20–45; and by M. Zalba, S.J., in Regatillo-Zalba, *Theologiæ moralis summa*, I (2nd ed.; Madrid: Biblioteca de Autores Cristianos, 1957), n. 1155.

asserting mortal sin at any given point is an appeal to the virtue of prudence, how can it be shown that Ter Haar and others have the right understanding of what prudence demands *sub gravi* when they draw the line at "less probable" or "equiprobable," and who can say that Vermeersch is wrong when he puts it at "more probable," or that Genicot is wrong when he puts it, as De Lugo and other great theologians have done, at "highly probable" or "morally certain"? The virtue of prudence, which looks to the infinite complexities of future human conduct and future contingencies, refuses to be constrained by such narrow formulas.

Essentially, therefore, some theologians merely take this negative position: grave guilt is not proved to be universally present whenever probable danger is voluntarily entered. A formula based merely on the notion of probable danger is too rigid.

In the second place, one must consider the degrees of gravity in mortal sins. It will obviously be more imprudent to expose oneself to the probable danger of committing a very great mortal sin than a lesser mortal sin. Mortal sins admit of indefinite degrees of gravity, too, from a solitary internal sin of thought, to an external sin, to a sin that affects one or several other persons, to sins that damage the goods or bodies or souls of others, to sins that damage the public good of the community or the nation or the Church of Christ itself. Since prudence is the criterion, it will take a much greater necessity to justify entering an occasion of one of these greater sins. And a lesser degree of danger will be seriously rash when the sin is one of greater gravity. Accordingly, some theologians who would not admit that voluntarily entering probable danger is always mortally sinful, would agree that it is so in the case of particularly scandalous sins.[12]

In the third place, the following reason may be put forward for doubting the universality of the stricter view. In a case where the penitent has no proportionate cause (i.e., no truly adequate justifying reason) for entering the occasion, the occasion is called a free or voluntary one. And yet he might have *some* reason for entering it. He would be entering a free occasion and a probable danger of mortal sin without proportionate cause, but not without any cause. In such a case, though acting sinfully and imprudently, his imprudence might fall short of grave guilt. There are good theologians who, speaking of indirectly voluntary venereal excitement, say that it is mortally sinful to expose oneself to the danger of orgasm without *any* justifying reason, but only venially sinful to do so for a reason which is real but inadequate.[13] Analogically, it would not be unreasonable to maintain that grave guilt is not proved at least in those cases where the penitent has *some* justification for entering the "free" occasion.

The distinction between free and necessary occasions is terminologically clear and complete. But when the notion of necessity is examined we find that this, too, like probability, admits of indefinite degrees, ranging from mere preference (which cannot be called necessity at all) to slight moral necessity, to real moral necessity, to grave moral necessity, to very grave moral necessity, to practical physical necessity, to absolute physical necessity. Since it is not

[12] Thus, e.g., G. Kelly, S.J., in *Theological Studies*, 11 (1950), 64–65, and *The Good Confessor* (New York: The Sentinel Press, 1951), p. 86.

[13] Cf. Genicot-Salsmans-Gortebecke, *Institutiones theologiæ moralis* I (Brussels: Editio Universalis, 1951), n. 401; Noldin-Schmitt-Heinzel, *De castitate* (Westminster, Md.: The Newman Press, 1952), n. 37.

entirely clear at what point along this line an occasion ceases to be free and can be considered in some sense necessary, reasonable doubts can be raised as to the grave guilt of a person who enters an occasion of sin in these borderline cases. If one were to go further and hold that there is excuse from grave sin *only* when such a quasi-excusing cause is present, then this position would be stricter than that of De Lugo and Genicot, who do not, apparently, demand any such qualification. Theologians who take a middle position in the controversy seem to have in mind considerations of this kind. But at all events, the simple formula that "it is always mortally sinful to enter the probable danger of mortal sin without proportionate cause" is too absolute. It may admit of exceptions.

In the fourth place, there are practical considerations which make some theologians hesitate to accept the stricter view. This view easily leads to an unpredictable multiplication of proximate occasions of mortal sin in everyday life, and sometimes ends by defeating itself. "Men are in nowise withdrawn from the mire of sin, but are plunged into it all the more deeply because all the more despairingly." [14] Michael Fabregas, S.J., says that the argument that man must do what he can to avoid sin can easily be pressed so far that it would include even a slight or less probable danger.[15] He shows furthermore, from the writings of Father Ter Haar himself, that the logical consequence of the stricter opinion is the almost indefinite multiplication of proximate occasions of mortal sin, not only for the laity but also for religious and clergy. Thus Father Ter Haar writes:

[14] Gerson, as cited by St. Alphonsus; cf. *infra*, p. 156.
[15] See pp. 42–43 of the article cited *supra*, footnote 11. Father Fabregas also candidly expresses the opinion that the stricter view is but a practical application of equiprobabilism.

"Probable dangers, i.e., dangers of probably sinning gravely against some precept of God or of the Church, are innumerable and of quasi-everyday occurrence especially in our society." [16]

The foregoing considerations help us to understand that there really is a controversy about the meaning of proximate occasions of sin and to understand the speculative and practical reasons underlying it. They help us to appreciate the position of those theologians who refuse to admit the universal validity of a rigid formula expressed in terms of "equiprobable" or of "less probable" danger of sin.

Obligations Must Be Certain

It has been charged more than once that the milder view in this controversy can readily lead to abuses in directing penitents and in the public statements of preachers—e.g., by saying: "It is only a venial sin to expose oneself to the probable danger of mortal sin." We agree with this. But we think it is equally an abuse to insist that a penitent must follow the stricter view or to make an unqualified public statement to the effect that it is a mortal sin to expose oneself to the probable danger of mortal sin. And in this connection we should like to recall some of the remarks that St. Alphonsus himself makes at the beginning of his treatise on restitution.[17]

First, he states it as a recognized principle that obligations are not to be imposed under pain of mortal sin unless the gravity is evident. Next he cites St. Antoninus to the effect that no one is to be accused of mortal sin unless this is

[16] *De occasionariis et recidivis*, n. 30. Father Ter Haar applies the same idea to priests and religious in *Casus conscientiæ*, n. 7.
[17] *Theologia moralis* (Gaudé ed.), 1. 3, n. 547.

backed by the express authority of Holy Scripture, or of the Church, or by a convincing reason. And he concludes this little section with the following reference to Gerson:

Hence Gerson, taking note of the evil consequences of excessively rigid opinions, comments as follows: "The result of such public statements, which are too severe, too general, and too strict, especially in matters not completely certain, is that men are in nowise withdrawn from the mire of sin, but are plunged into it all the more deeply because all the more despairingly."

It should be noted that the principle here enunciated and explained by St. Alphonsus—that obligations are not to be imposed under pain of mortal sin unless the gravity is certain—is a universal principle and that it is proposed as such by the saint himself, even though he adds that it has special application in matters of restitution. It applies therefore to all truly controversial questions, including those concerning occasions of sin. According to the principle, it is not right to impose on a penitent the stricter view concerning the duty of avoiding occasions of sin, and (in keeping with the quoted words of Gerson) it is still less justifiable to make public statements about mortal sin when the reason for asserting mortal sin is not truly certain.

It seems to us that the theoretical dispute we have been considering, and the enunciation of simple formulas, whether in terms of probable danger, or of highly probable danger, or of morally certain danger of sin, may easily distract our attention from the real, practical problem which confronts the confessor. It is true that theologians dispute about the definition of proximate occasion. But they are all agreed that those occasions are to be called proximate which one must avoid under pain of mortal sin. Even when they permit one to enter a necessary proximate occasion it is only on condition that it can first be made remote. Therefore the real problem about proximate occasions is to decide when this penitent has a grave obligation not to expose himself to this danger. The complete prudential judgment on this question in any given case will have to take into account, in our opinion, not only proximity in terms of degrees of probability of sin, but also the degrees of gravity of the sins in question, and the degrees of utility or necessity which may exist for entering the occasion.

It would be presumption on our part to attempt to end the dispute over the nature of a proximate occasion of sin with a sweep of the pen. Our purpose has been not to end the controversy, but merely to show that there is a controversy—a controversy which affects the whole Church and which can be authoritatively settled only by the Holy See.[18] In the absence of such an authoritative solution, no prelate, preacher, spiritual adviser, or confessor is justified in imposing the stricter view on others.

COMPANY-KEEPING

The same St. Alphonsus, who so eloquently defended the principle that obligations under pain of mortal sin must not be imposed unless they are certain, held an almost unbelievably stern doctrine about courtship. After mentioning that Roncaglia would allow a young man to visit the girl he intended to marry, on the score that one should not be obliged to marry an unknown person, St. Alphonsus added:

Speculatively, this opinion seems reasonable. But, having learned through experience, I would not permit a young man to go to the home of his betrothed more than once or twice; nor would I permit the girl or her parents to receive him [more than

18 See our discussion of this point in chapter 3.

that]. For I have rarely found one who does not sin in such a visit, at least in word or thought; because all the looks and conversations between such betrothed are incentives to sin, and it is morally impossible for them to deal with each other and not experience impure urges to those things that will take place after they are married.[19]

After repeating this same teaching in his *Praxis confessarii,* he observed:

Generally speaking, as regards boys and girls who love each other, although they are not all to be charged indiscriminately with mortal sin, I believe they ordinarily find it difficult to be outside the proximate occasion of sinning mortally. This is abundantly clear from experience; because out of a hundred youths in this occasion, scarcely two or three will be found free from mortal sin.[20]

With reference to this opinion of St. Alphonsus, John R. Connery, S.J., has commented: "I think everyone would admit that this would be a very severe norm to set down in this day and country. It would be a mistake, though, to conclude that St. Alphonsus did not know what he was talking about. But what may have been true in his day is not necessarily true today." [21]

A similar appraisal of the Alphonsian teaching was given by a writer in *L'Ami du clergé* [22] at the conclusion of an excellent discussion of courtship. This writer insisted that the youth of today are as good as those of former generations. They live, it is true, in a different atmosphere, an atmosphere that requires an even more solid character train-

---

[19] *Theologia moralis* (Gaudé ed.), 1. 6, n. 452.
[20] *Praxis confessarii* (in the Gaudé ed. of *Theol. moral.*), n. 65.
[21] *Theological Studies,* 16 (1955), 584.
[22] Aug. 17, 1950, pp. 519–22.

ing. To give them this training, we must have their confidence; but we shall not gain or preserve this confidence by imposing on them regulations and a regime that have long since gone out of date.

Perhaps this is the most prudent way of dealing with the Alphonsian teaching on courtship: to explain it as pertaining to another time and another social milieu. Yet it seems advisable to add that his teaching is not easily harmonized with the following words of Pope Pius XI, in the encyclical *Casti connubii:*

To the proximate preparation for a good married life belongs very especially the care in choosing a partner; on that depends a great deal whether the forthcoming marriage will be happy or not, since one may be to the other either a great help in leading a Christian life or, on the other hand, a great danger or hindrance. And, so that they will not deplore for the rest of their lives the sorrows arising from an indiscreet marriage, those about to enter into wedlock should carefully deliberate in choosing the person with whom they must henceforward live continually. They should, in so deliberating, keep before their minds the thought, first of God and of the true religion of Christ, then of themselves, of their partner, of the children to come, as also of home and civil society, for which marriage is, as it were, a fountainhead. Let them diligently pray for divine help, so that they will make their choice in accordance with Christian prudence, not indeed led by the blind and unchecked impulse of lust, nor by any desire of riches or other base influence, but by a true and noble love and by a sincere affection toward the future partner; and then let them strive in their married life toward those ends for which this state was constituted by God. Lastly, let them not fail to ask the prudent advice of their parents regarding the partner and let them seriously consider this advice, so that through their [the parents'] more mature knowl-

[159]

edge and experience of human affairs they may guard against a baneful mistake, . . .[23]

Would anyone seriously claim that either youth or their parents could obey this admonition of the Holy Father if a boy were allowed to visit the girl's home only once or twice? Fortunately, even the most severe theologians would not recommend that norm in our country today. And from the discussion in *L'Ami du clergé* previously referred to, one may infer that this norm is not acceptable in France, either. Nevertheless, one would be blind to the facts if one did not recognize that the judgment of St. Alphonsus on the weakness of youth has had a profound influence on the theological treatises written since his time. Authors too often imply that courtship is *per se* a proximate, though necessary, occasion of serious sins against chastity. It would be more consonant with the tone of the encyclical on marriage and more in conformity with the genuine moral wholesomeness of our young people to say that courtship usually creates *some danger* to chastity, but that proximate danger of serious sin arises, not from the nature of courtship, but rather from special circumstances: for example, the inferior moral caliber of one or both of the parties, the undue protracting of the engagement, the places in which the young people meet, and other like circumstances.

Teen-age Company-keeping

A problem that has been much to the fore in recent years is that of juvenile company-keeping when there is no prospect of an early marriage or, even more frequently, when there is no thought of marriage. In keeping with his custom

[23] *AAS*, 22 (1930), 585-86.

of frankly and courageously facing and solving current problems, Francis J. Connell, C.SS.R.,[24] published an article on this topic entitled "Juvenile Courtships." A most laudable aspect of this article is the extreme care with which Father Connell describes what he means by steady company-keeping. To be such, he says, an association between a boy and a girl must be (1) *frequent,* (2) *exclusive,* and (3) motivated by *some measure of affection.* Less laudable, we think, is the fact that Father Connell seems to overstress the aspect of danger to chastity, and especially the idea of proximate occasion of mortal sin. It is not our purpose to discuss his remarks in detail. It seems better simply to quote the following words of John R. Connery, S.J., who summarizes the main points of Father Connell's article and adds personal comments:

The ordinary prelude to modern marriage is company-keeping or so-called "going steady." When this practice is engaged in by those who have hopes of getting married within a reasonable period of time it is not only unobjectionable but highly desirable. It offers prospective partners the opportunity to foster mutual love and affection as well as the occasion to adjust to each other's personality. It thus gives them the necessary experience to make a prudential judgment regarding their ability to live together in harmony. But when "going steady" is engaged in by adolescents who because of their youth have no prospects of getting married, besides being premature and devoid of any intelligent purpose, it also constitutes a danger to chastity if continued over any period of time.

In an article on the subject which appeared in the *American Ecclesiastical Review,* Francis J. Connell, C.SS.R., asserts that the practice of "going steady" among youths with no prospects

[24] *American Ecclesiastical Review,* 132 (1955), 181–90.

of marriage is sinful. He agrees with Ærtnys-Damen that it is generally a proximate occasion of sin. He also maintains that even where there has been no sin in the past and no danger of sin in the future, it is still a remote occasion of sin and therefore venially sinful. Briefly, then, according to Father Connell, "going steady" is always sinful; generally a mortal sin; sometimes only venial.

In this opinion Fr. Connell is following the judgment of European moralists. These moralists are certainly respected in their field but on this particular subject I think it is somewhat risky to rely too much on the opinions of moralists living in a different social milieu. Occasions of sin will often vary according to time and place. . . .

I would hesitate to label the practice itself as sinful. I think that it can be dangerous and should be discouraged but I would prefer to settle the question of sin on an individual basis. To my mind there are several good reasons for this position. First of all, the term "going steady" is often used in a broad sense, as Fr. Connell admits, and not in the restricted sense which he condemns. For youngsters who ordinarily do not make distinctions, labeling "going steady" as sinful could easily result in false consciences. Secondly, to be a proximate occasion of sin, the practice would have to result in frequent sin for those who engage in it. I am not prepared to say that this is generally the case for the Catholic boy or girl of ordinary virtue. As for the rest, I am not sure that the virtue of purity comes off any worse in steady company-keeping than in individual dating. Also, as for those cases where it must be considered only a remote occasion of sin, there are enough moralists who say that one can ignore a remote occasion of sin to make it risky to call the practice venially sinful. Finally, I think that we moralists at times think that we have solved a problem whenever we can label something sinful. This somewhat false security tends to make us neglect motivation which might be much more effective.

There are many reasons against going steady which might be very effective with youth but which we tend to overlook or ignore just as soon as the practice can be labeled sinful. Even if one agrees with Fr. Connell's thesis, I think it would be wise to put the stress elsewhere.[25]

Father Connery's concluding remarks remind us of a statement which, we believe, will be more impressive with a brief historical introduction. In the summer of 1940, a group of approximately fifty priests assembled for an institute on religious education. In the course of that convention, the members of the institute (mostly student counselors and professors of religion) thoroughly discussed the need of a text on chastity adapted to the intellectual and practical requirements of young men and women just entering college. To be more specific, they wanted a text that would not only state clearly the moral principles relative to extra-marital chastity but would give the Christian ideals as well. Moreover, they considered it imperative that the text should include something on the proper preparation for Christian marriage.

A committee of three was appointed to write the text. This committee was composed of a moral theologian, a psychologist, and a professor of religion. All had had considerable experience in youth counseling. At the end of a year the text was ready and it was unanimously approved for experimentation by the members of the institute. After a year of experimentation in the classroom, the text received another unanimous approval—this time for publication.[26]

[25] *Theological Studies*, 16 (1955), 583–84. The section omitted from this quotation contains Father Connery's remarks about St. Alphonsus, which we have already cited.

[26] The published work is *Modern Youth and Chastity* (St. Louis: The Queen's Work, 1943), by Gerald Kelly, S.J., in collaboration with B. R. Fulkerson, S.J., and C. F. Whitford, S.J.

We would not wish to imply that the unanimous approval of fifty priests constitutes an argument for infallibility. But we can say, *teste experientia*, that it is an unusual phenomenon! Moreover, the history of the text since its publication has been a confirmation of the original approval. A half-million copies of the English edition have been used, mostly in the early years of college and in the later years of high school, as well as in the armed forces. The booklet has been translated into French, Spanish, Italian, Portuguese, German, Dutch, and Japanese. Reviewers and other critics have all spoken favorably of it.

The purpose of this historical prelude is to suggest that the booklet has offered a presentation of youth problems that has been and still is satisfying to earnest youth and their educators and counselors. One of its special features is an analysis of sex attraction in its relation to the social activities of youth, to the goals of Christian marriage, and, of course, to the proper preparation for marriage. Under the heading of "Personal Sex Attraction," it describes an exclusive companionship of a boy and a girl that is based on emotional fascination. It shows how this kind of companionship, when animated by a truly spiritual love, can be an ideal basis for a wholesome preparation for marriage and a God-given aid to a happy and holy marriage. It also shows the limitations and dangers of personal sex attraction itself. Then, under the caption, "Not for Everybody," it has the following statement:

Evidently persons who are ineligible for marriage should not foster an affection of this kind. Nor should those for whom marriage must necessarily be a thing of the rather distant future. We are referring here particularly to young men and women in the early years of college and, of course, to all others who are in somewhat similar circumstances: for instance, those who will be separated by war conditions or other exigencies. We base this judgment on the following solid reasons:

1. The affection may rush you ahead faster than you thought of going, and you will contract a hasty and regrettable marriage. This has happened often.

2. You will be tied down to one person, and you will thus lose the general social advantages and contacts that should mean a great enriching of your life in the future.

3. By cultivating this affection, you expose yourself in a special way to the dangers to chastity already mentioned, because this love affair may be a very prolonged one, and the danger of violating chastity increases as the affection is prolonged without its logical culmination in marriage.

4. For a college student in particular: you will find it almost impossible to do full justice to your studies, and you may lose or seriously damage the very thing that you came to college to get—an education, a profession.

There may be exceptions to these rules, but one cannot count on exceptions.[27]

Every word of the foregoing statement was carefully chosen by the writers and carefully examined by the members of the institute. All agreed that there should be no undue stress on the danger of unchastity; attention should also, and even especially, be called to other evils of these too-early courtships. Association of groups of boys and girls in such things as parties, dances, study clubs, and apostolic activities can be very beneficial, a basis for mutual understanding and respect and an excellent preparation for their adult business, social, and religious life; but many of these benefits are lost when there is an exclusive concentration of one boy on one girl.

[27] *Ibid.,* p. 25.

At the time we write this, a widespread movement against juvenile courtships has already begun in Catholic schools. Although some of the publicized statements we have seen have overstressed and even exaggerated the danger to chastity, most of them have put the emphasis on the social and educational disadvantages of such courtships. This seems to us to be the soundest policy, both morally and psychologically. And certainly the movement against too-early company-keeping cannot be too strongly endorsed.

DANCING

It will be of interest and profit, before we consider the morality of dancing, to survey the canonical legislation pertinent to our country. The Second Plenary Council of Baltimore,[28] without mentioning dances in particular, insisted that there could be no good reason for raising money for the Church by anything that is an occasion of sin, a source of scandal, and a basis for holding the Catholic name up to ridicule. In this category it listed picnics, excursions, and the like, that were held near large cities. These things should either be absolutely forbidden or so regulated as not to become seed-beds of sin.

The Third Plenary Council of Baltimore,[29] in the chapter "De modis prohibitis pecunias ad pias causas colligendi," repeated the warning of its predecessor; laid down certain rules to correct abuses connected with picnics, excursions,

[28] *Acta et decreta,* n. 396. Although dancing is not mentioned in this decree, the attitude of the bishops is clearly manifested in the Pastoral Letter, where they warn the people "against those amusements which may easily become to them an occasion of sin, and especially against those fashionable dances, which, as at present carried on, are revolting to every feeling of delicacy and propriety, and are fraught with the greatest danger to morals" (p. cxxi).

[29] *Acta et decreta,* n. 290.

and fairs conducted to raise money; and then briefly absolved the matter of dancing with this strong precept: "Mandamus quoque ut sacerdotes illum abusum, quo convivia parantur cum choreis [Balls] ad opera pia promovenda, omnino tollendum curent."

A decree of the Sacred Consistorial Congregation, March 31, 1916,[30] told how dances "for pious purposes" began in the United States, how it gradually came about that pastors themselves organized them, how the Council of Baltimore, noting the abuses likely to be connected with dances that go far into the night, had forbidden such dances to be given for Church purposes. The congregation observed that the abuses condemned by Baltimore had again crept into the United States and had even spread to Canada; it was therefore the purpose of the new decree to insist that the prohibition of the Council of Baltimore be upheld. For this reason, with the approval of Benedict XV, all priests, whether secular or regular, and other clerics were absolutely forbidden to promote and favor the above-mentioned dances, even though they were held to aid pious works or for some other holy purpose. Moreover, all clerics were forbidden to attend such dances, should they be given by lay people.

To clear up a doubt created by this decree, the congregation was asked: "Are dances given in the daytime, or at night but not protracted to a late hour, or not accompanied by a dinner, but conducted in the manner commonly called

---

[30] *AAS*, 8 (1916), 147–48. The text of the mandatory section is as follows: ". . . sacerdotes quoslibet sive sæculares sive regulares aliosque cleros prorsus prohiberi, quominus memoratas choreas promoveant et foveant, etiamsi in piorum operum levamen et subsidium, vel ad alium quemlibet pium finem; et insuper clericos omnes vetari, quominus hisce choreis intersint, si forte a laicis viris promoveantur."

a picnic, included in the condemnation of March 31, 1916?"
The reply, dated December 10, 1917,[31] and again approved
by the pope, stated that such dances were included in the
condemnation. Clerics, therefore, were forbidden to promote or sponsor them, even in the circumstances mentioned, and they were forbidden to attend the dances if
they were promoted by others.

In a scholarly discussion, John Rogg Schmidt reviewed
the foregoing documents, as well as various comments and
interpretations, and reached the following conclusions: (1)
the prohibitions refer only to dances given for some pious
cause; (2) they forbid both priests and laity to promote
dances for the purpose of raising money for the Church;
(3) they do not forbid the holding or promoting of dances
for recreational and social purposes; (4) they do not forbid
priests to be present at dances held for recreational and
social purposes; (5) the reasons for the prohibition of
dances in the interest of pious causes were the morally questionable features which were formerly considered as generally associated with dancing; and (6) in a properly
supervised parish dance these features are now lacking;
hence it seems that the legislation has now ceased as law
"because its subject matter has changed, . . . and because,
as consequent to such change, its purpose, namely, to
obviate at least a probable suspicion of moral danger common to the participants and the obloquy of prudent and
upright men, has likewise ceased." [32]

It seems to us that Father Schmidt's analysis and argu-
mentation are reasonable; and we leave it to the canonists

---

[31] *AAS,* 10 (1918), 17; cf. *Canon Law Digest,* I, 137–38.

[32] "Attendance of Priests at Dances," *The Jurist,* 11 (1951), 77–99, and
251–85; quoted words are on p. 284.

themselves to offer expert objections, if there are any, on the juridical side. Up to the time we write, we have seen no such objections printed.

Prominent in Father Schmidt's discussion, however, is a matter of distinct concern to moralists. We mean the question of the moral dangers of dancing, and especially the question of occasion of sin. Father Schmidt's article contains an account of one of the private sessions of the Third Council of Baltimore, in which the bishops frankly discussed the feasibility and advisability of absolutely forbidding dancing, especially the so-called "round dances." Their judgment seems to have been less severe than that of their predecessors, and they were clearly not unanimous in thinking that dancing, even the round dances, was always an occasion of sin. Nevertheless, it does seem that their final pronouncement against using dances to promote a pious cause was based on the supposition of what Father Schmidt calls the "morally questionable features often associated with dancing."

Whatever be the judgment concerning the attitude on dancing and its dangers that prevailed in the nineteenth century, and that may exist even now in other countries, we would certainly agree with Father Schmidt that in our country today dancing as such is not an occasion of sin. Nor is it looked upon as a questionable pastime by good and prudent men. Any occasion of sin connected with dancing will usually be traced to some entirely extrinsic circumstance such as drinking, the place where the dance is held, and so forth. This seems to argue, not for a prohibition of dancing, but for providing youth with the opportunity of dancing in surroundings conducive to good morals.

Without wishing to be unduly critical, we confess that

moral manuals often impress us as being entirely unrealistic on the question of dancing, particularly with reference to the "round" dances.[33] The authors apparently think that any dancing involving physical contact is bound to cause grave temptation in a majority of cases. Some years ago a moral professor in Rome made the statement in class that the modern dances are *per se* proximate occasions of grave sin. His North American students immediately objected to this assertion; they told him plainly that, before entering the seminary, they had danced these modern dances and had not found them occasions of sin. We think that these seminarians expressed the typical attitude of what we might call the flower of our Catholic manhood and womanhood. Good Catholics can dance without qualms of conscience on the day they receive Holy Communion; and with an equally good conscience they can receive Holy Communion, without the need of confession, on the day after they dance. They certainly would not do this if they found dancing to be a proximate occasion of mortal sin; and we doubt that they would do it if they found *any real* occasion of sin in dancing.

Father John McCarthy, of the *Irish Ecclesiastical Record*, makes a strong defense of the position we are taking here. Speaking of Ireland he has this to say:

It seems to me that it is a completely unwarrantable generalization to describe the vast majority of the dances which are performed in our halls today as being in themselves dangerous

[33] An American theologian can hardly refrain from smiling as he reads the catalogues of dances that moralists have considered to be gravely dangerous to morals (cf., e.g., Arregui, n. 170). But our devout fathers and mothers would probably not share our amusement. They would be astounded at the strong indictment of many dances which they always regarded as an innocent pastime.

occasions of sin. The fact is that many good and conscientious Catholics . . . can and do take part in modern dances without scruple or fear of sin. When they attend these dances, they do not feel that they are going into an occasion of sin. Indeed, they would be greatly shocked at the suggestion that they are.[34]

The present writers happened to be in Rome when the late Daniel A. Lord, S.J., talked to a large group of seminarians on the activities of the Sodalists in the United States. At one point in his talk, Father Lord told how the Sodalists had prepared for a dance by decorating the hall in such a way that everything centered round a beautiful statue of the Blessed Mother. The seminarians listened to this with unconcealed amazement. Here was a man describing how our youth used what the moral books called an occasion of sin as a sign of their devotion to Mary—how not only their devotions but also their recreations were under her patronage! But this was not the only reason for the seminarians' wonder. Another thing that visibly impressed them was Father Lord's unbounded confidence in the goodness and wholesomeness of our youth.

We share this confidence in the moral wholesomeness of our youth; and we agree with the writer in *L'Ami du clergé* that the youth themselves will not have confidence in us if we impose on them the external customs of former generations. The things they enjoy often differ from the things we enjoyed; but their enjoyment is not less innocent for that reason. The music that thrills the adolescent of today might be obnoxious to his parents and his advisers; and his dances might appear to be occasions of sin. But it is the judgment of experienced youth counselors with whom we have dis-

---

[34] *Irish Ecclesiastical Record*, 78 (1952), 293–94.

cussed this matter that today's dances are no more occasions of sin than were the dances of former times. The occasions of sin still arise mainly from external circumstances associated with the dances and not with the dancing itself. These circumstances are drinking; the time and place of the dance; the lack of prudent supervision; the abuse of automobiles; the time when adolescents are expected to be home; and so forth. There is, no doubt, much negligence on the part of parents regarding these various points; and this negligence should be corrected. But, granted the proper precautions against extrinsic dangers, there seems to be no solid reason for considering modern dances as such to be proximate occasions of serious sin.

CONCLUSION

In this chapter we have treated not only the theoretical dispute about proximate occasions, but the practical problems of company-keeping and dancing. The position one takes on the theoretical dispute will have its influence on one's solutions of cases in pastoral practice. It may even appear to some that the theologians who take the more lenient view in that dispute are bent on excusing people and are setting themselves up as advocates for the accused. Actually, however, these theologians are just as much concerned about getting at the truth of the matter and just as eager to save souls as their confreres of a stricter persuasion. They, too, urge and exhort their penitents to avoid the unjustifiable probable danger of mortal sin; they tell them they are obliged (but *sub levi*) to avoid such danger; and they try to lead them to a better way of life. But they insist that the penitent's conduct must be clearly shown to be mortally sinful before any confessor is justified in refusing him absolution. They do not allow the confessor to set himself up as a lawmaker or to impose his own system of morality on a penitent. On the Day of Judgment we shall know where the speculative truth lies and which method in practice saves more souls. Until then: *in necessariis unitas; in dubiis libertas; in omnibus caritas.*

10

Imputability and Unconscious Motivation

T HE THEOLOGIAN, AS well as the layman, has always been
interested in the question of human responsibility;
and this interest is perhaps especially keen concerning a
negative aspect of the question, the problem of grave responsibility for serious sin. Human sympathy instinctively
leads us to hope that men are not guilty of the apparently
vast number of serious sins they commit; for mortal sin
deprives a man of eternal life, and delivers him, if unrepent-
ant, to eternal death. Situationists would reduce the number
of mortal sins in the world by diminishing the objective
binding force of the moral law; even by completely abolish-
ing it in certain peculiarly difficult situations. Orthodox
theologians know that the problem cannot be solved in this
way. They are more likely to seek a solution on the subjective side, by appealing to factors which prevent man from
being fully responsible for the deeds he actually commits.
Unfortunately, however, one can go too far in this direction
also. A recent, and prominent, example of this kind of

thinking was manifested by Abbé Marc Oraison in his book
Vie chrétienne et problèmes de la sexualité.[1]

ORAISON'S BOOK

This book was a doctoral dissertation. The author is a
gifted and zealous priest, who is also a physician and a
psychiatrist. He did not deny traditional standards of the
objective order of sexual morality. Rather, he insistently
defended these standards and claimed that modern scientific sexology confirms them. In this he differed from the
situationists and from many Freudians, although his work
was inspired by Freudian psychoanalysis and Freudian
sexological theory. Nevertheless, the practical consequences
of his theory, as far as sexual sins are concerned, would be
scarcely distinguishable from the consequences of applied
situation ethics. In his book, he finds a solution for the
sexual crises of Christian conscience by urging to the limit—
and considerably beyond—the distinction between material
and formal sin, that is, between objective malice and subjective responsibility.

Almost all mankind, in this theory, is so sexually immature, and so much dominated consciously or unconsciously by passion, that in practice and as a general rule
we must presume that sexual sins are only materially grave,
that is, the person who commits them is not subjectively
guilty of mortal sin. Man's unconscious profoundly influences his "voluntary of execution," depriving him, practically, of the power of inhibiting his sinful sexual acts. But
he still has his "voluntary of choice" by which he approves
or disapproves these acts and actions. It is only in the rare

[1] Marc Oraison, *Vie chrétienne et problèmes de la sexualité*, Paris:
Lethielleux, 1952.

case in which he deliberately approves of them that he will be guilty of formal mortal sin. The sin consists, formally, not in being sick, or in exhibiting the symptoms of the sickness, but in not wanting to get well. This doctrine is applied not only to people who suffer from obvious mental, emotional, or sexual pathology, but also to all those persons whom most of us would describe as normal.

The inevitable inference from this is that sins of masturbation (p. 98), homosexuality (p. 117, pp. 250–51), fornication and adultery (pp. 195–97), and conjugal onanism (pp. 223–27) must be presumed in the vast majority of cases to be only material mortal sins. Those who confess them should be properly instructed as to their grave malice, and gradually educated to that (rare) stage of sexual maturity where they will no longer occur. But while they continue to occur, the sacraments are not to be refused, and the victims of this pathology should be instructed that it is permissible to receive Holy Communion after these things happen without first confessing them (e.g., pp. 223, 251). The reason is clear: They have not been guilty of formal mortal sin.

This brief summary picks out only the objectionable points and in doing so doubtless oversimplifies, omitting a great deal that is instructive and worthwhile. These good points, as well as the author's courage in confronting an acute moral problem, probably account for the fact that some of the reviews, while definitely critical, had been surprisingly temperate and sympathetic.

Underlying these practical conclusions of Abbé Oraison there seems to be a fundamental misconception, the idea that normality is illusory, that everyone is a victim of sexual pathology. And this in turn is based not only on Freudian theory but on a misconception as to what original sin did to human nature.

Of course there is a certain improper sense in which it can be said that we are all emotionally sick, or sexually sick, as a result of original sin. Concupiscence itself can be broadly described as a sort of sickness of human nature in its fallen state. But it is only in some topsy-turvy world that everyone is a pathological problem in the real sense of the word—certainly not in the world of common sense, nor in the world of Christian tradition and Catholic practice.

At about the same time as Abbé Oraison's book was published, Pius XII delivered his address on the education of the Christian conscience, in which he solemnly and authoritatively rejected the thesis that sexual passion as a general rule destroys the freedom necessary for the commission of a grave fault.[2] A year later, in his celebrated address to the psychotherapists, the pope emphatically reaffirmed the principle of the responsibility of the normal man, with special reference to modern psychoanalytical theories. In this address the Holy Father insisted that the soul with its free will, not the instinctive drives of the unconscious, is the fundamental governing force in man: "That these energies may exercise pressure on an activity does not necessarily signify that they compel it." Even in cases of psychological sickness, the misdirected instincts should not be prematurely considered "as a sort of fatality, as a tyranny of the affective impulse streaming forth from the subconscious and escaping completely from the control of the conscious and the soul."

Pius XII was most emphatic of all in repudiating the idea

[2] *AAS*, 44 (1952), 270–78; translated in *Catholic Documents*, 8 (July, 1952), 1–7.

that in the reality of everyday life and as a general rule passion excludes subjective guilt and subjective responsibility. He said:

It is not possible therefore, when studying the relationships of the ego to the dynamisms that compose it, to concede unreservedly in theory the autonomy of man—that is, of his soul —but to go on immediately to state that in the reality of life this theoretical principle appears to be very frequently set aside or minimized in the extreme. In the reality of life, it is argued, man always retains his freedom to give his internal consent to what he does, but in no way the freedom to do it. The autonomy of free will is replaced by the heteronomy of instinctive dynamism. That is not the way in which God fashioned man. Original sin did not take away from man the possibility or the obligation of directing his own actions himself through his soul. *It cannot be alleged that the psychic troubles and disorders which disturb the normal functioning of the psychic being represent what usually happens.* [Italics ours.] The moral struggle to remain on the right path does not prove that it is impossible to follow that path, nor does it authorize any drawing back.[3]

Abbé Oraison's book appeared in 1952. The papal statement just quoted (which did not name Oraison) appeared on April 13, 1953. The book was put on the Index early in 1953, but this fact was not made known until January, 1955. Soon after the announcement was made Abbé Oraison submitted to the decree of the Holy Office, and has since publicly signified in the press his acceptance of the decision.[4]

[3] *AAS*, 45 (1953), 278–86 at 279.
[4] The decree of the Holy Office condemning the book is dated March 18, 1953, but the condemnation was not publicly announced until Jan. 3, 1955. See *AAS*, 47 (1955), 46. The following issue of *AAS*, 47 (1955),

Imputability and Unconscious Motivation

It is to be deeply regretted that at a moment when the baffling problems of subjective morality and formal guilt are in need of careful scrutiny and development, and when the moralist needs to reappraise his norms for estimating subjective guilt, especially where the mentally or emotionally sick are concerned, a serious work of this kind should appear, which clearly passed the limits set by traditional Catholic doctrine and practice. An official condemnation was the inevitable result. But we may express the hope that this condemnation will not discourage other serious, but more conservative, efforts to solve what Vermeersch referred to, almost thirty years ago, as one of the great challenges to the modern moralist, the "grave and thorny problem . . . of subjective imputability." [5]

Vermeersch was undoubtedly thinking of the problems that are distinctive of our own age—problems that have been brought to the fore by the theories and discoveries of modern medicine, and especially by modern psychology and psychiatry. Oraison's views of subjective responsibility, and the application he makes of them to problems of sex, are based in large measure on psychoanalytical psychology. The investigations of this school of psychology pose a general problem of moral imputability. It is the problem of the relation between unconscious psychic life and the free human acts of men. For the remainder of this chapter we shall consider this problem: *Does unconscious motivation pervade human conduct to such an extent that it destroys or*

89, gave formal notification of Abbé Oraison's submission. A letter of his to a French newspaper (*Le Monde*, Feb. 9, 1955), in which he acknowledges the authority and judgment of the Holy Office is reprinted in *La documentation catholique*, 52, n. 1194 (Mar. 6, 1955), col. 288.

[5] Arthur Vermeersch, S.J., "Soixante ans de théologie morale," *Nouvelle revue théologique*, 56 (1929), 880.

[179]

seriously impairs human responsibility even in normal individuals?

THE PROBLEM OUTLINED

An example or two of the dynamic unconscious at work will clarify what we mean by this problem. A famous case in Freud's early experience was that of a young woman patient referred to as Anna O. She suffered from a serious mental illness and exhibited symptoms of a hysterical kind. Among these symptoms was the inability to take a drink of water from a glass. Under hypnosis she revealed the fact that as a very young child she had beheld, with great disgust, a governess giving a pet dog a drink of water from a glass. It was Freud's explanation that this early emotional experience, buried deep beyond the recall of ordinary efforts of memory, was exerting its influence on Anna, all unknown to her, so many years afterwards. It was her unconscious that prevented her from raising the glass of water to her lips.

This conception of the unconscious as a dynamic factor, influencing, or controlling, or possibly determining conscious psychic life, is one of the most fundamental and characteristic tenets of psychoanalytical psychology. It has been found very useful not only by psychiatrists of the psychoanalytical school but by others, in the diagnosis and treatment of mental ailments.

But the theory of unconscious motivation is applied not only to explain morbid symptoms but to explain the moods, attitudes, feelings, and prejudices of those who would ordinarily be regarded as mentally healthy, normal people. "It is quite possible that Paul is always so self-conscious when he meets people in authority because, as a child, he had a strained relation to his stern, authoritarian father and because he unconsciously relives that relationship when he meets men in authority; or that Mary dislikes her new teacher at first sight because, unknown to her, that teacher reminds her of a woman whom she hated when she was a child." [6]

Furthermore, many psychoanalysts would invoke the dynamic unconscious to explain not only moods and feelings, but the decisions we think of as free, for instance, the decision to choose a state of life, or a marriage partner, or a confidential consultant. A good example of unconscious motivation affecting conscious decisions is offered by the psychoanalyst Frink from his own experience. Dalbiez relates the story:

Frink tells us that he was one day in some perplexity about his private affairs. He soon realized that he would not be able to surmount his difficulty without having recourse to a friend. The choice lay between three men. He was very intimate with all three, and knew beforehand that each of them would do all he could to help him settle the matter. Instead of choosing one of the three, he made up his mind to approach a fourth individual, with whom he was but slightly acquainted, and whom he could scarcely call a friend. He had no logical reason for supposing that this man, whom we shall call X, was really in a position to give him suitable help. When Frink made his overtures, he was quite unaware that he was doing something very illogical and perhaps very dangerous. In seeking for the causes of so strange a decision, it came to his mind that the night before his visit to X, he had had a dream in which he experienced certain difficulties, representing his present fix, for the solution of which he invoked the aid of a certain T, who had been a member of the household when Frink was a boy. He at once understood

[6] Joseph Donceel, S.J., "Second Thoughts on Freud," *Thought,* 24 (1949), 470.

why he had had recourse to X in the actual situation. He now noticed for the first time that there was a great physical resemblance between X and T, although they were of very different ages. This had led Frink unconsciously to identify X and T, and to feel toward the former the confidence which his childhood experience had legitimately caused him to feel toward the latter. . . . Frink's whole behavior, involving his rejection of his three friends and his choice of X, was merely a repetition of a fixed reaction of childhood.[7]

This example is particularly apropos because it deals with the conscious decision of a presumably normal individual. Moralists lend a ready ear to the thesis of diminished or even nonexistent responsibility of the mentally ill. It offers, it is true, many practical problems, but not the semblance of a denial of the doctrine of free will. But psychoanalytical psychiatry as the above example shows, generates a difficulty even about the responsibility of the normal individual. The genesis of the difficulty seems to run somewhat like this: In his clinical practice, the psychiatrist becomes so deeply impressed by the influence of unconscious motivation that he suspects the existence of such influence in every apparently human act, even to the extent of taking the act out of the realm of "full responsibility" as described by moralists. In other words even the Catholic psychiatrist, who holds fast to the theoretical doctrine of free will, is apt to find himself inclined towards this pernicious conclusion: "We do have the power of free will, but in any concrete case we cannot be sure of the measure of our responsibility."

If this conclusion merely meant that in no concrete case could we be sure that our responsibility is perfect (i.e.,

[7] Roland Dalbiez, *Psychoanalytical Method and the Doctrine of Freud*, 2 volumes, translated by T. F. Lindsay. London and New York: Longmans Green, 1941 and 1948. See Vol. II, 296–297.

100%) one would not label it pernicious. It might even be true. But it seems that in many cases it does not have this limited meaning; it means that the normal man in his ordinary apparently free acts is probably so much influenced by unconscious motivation that his freedom to act and his corresponding responsibility for his actions are substantially impaired or vitiated.

It is not enough to tackle the problem of freedom in general, or the problem of unconscious motivation and its effect on freedom, with a mere speculative conviction of man's power to act freely; the Catholic must also be convinced that in many of his acts the normal man does have sufficient freedom to merit great praise or blame before God, and also that in many of his acts the man is certain of this responsibility. This must be true; otherwise such doctrines as the necessity of confession, the canonization of saints, and many others, are bereft of all practical meaning. Our religion, taken as a whole, is a religion to be lived, and it presupposes not only the remote power of responsibility, but also actual, serious responsibility, recognizable as such, in a large number of our acts. This applies to good and meritorious acts as well as to blameworthy ones.

In considering this problem the first task would be to decide whether psychoanalysis has proved its point, namely, that unconscious motivation does influence, or pervade, or even dominate the conscious psychic activities both of the mentally sick and the mentally well. Unfortunately the theologian and moralist are not competent to decide this point. It is in the field of scientific psychology.

No one doubts that some of our psychic life is below the level of actual awareness, and that some of it is easily accessible to attention or recollection while some is more

[183]

difficult of access. There is abundant evidence of the unconscious in this sense. Dom Moore appealed to memory,
reasoning processes, sensory judgments determined by unconscious elements, universal ideas, etc., as proofs that there
is unconscious psychic activity within us. The phenomena
of hypnotism and dreams and all the examples furnished by
psychoanalytical techniques provide evidence of some unconscious psychic material and activity.[8]

But when the question is about the dynamic unconscious,
as psychoanalysts understand the term, there is a great deal
of disagreement among the scientific psychologists and psychiatrists themselves as to the existence of such an unconscious, or at least as to its nature and the extent of its
influence on conscious life, especially among normal people.
An impressive amount of scientific opinion unfavorable to
psychoanalytical fundamentals could be quoted.[9] One of
the difficulties is that some of the psychoanalytical claims
cannot, apparently, be demonstrated by the methods of
positive science, although they are put forward as scientific
discoveries. It would be premature, therefore, to conclude
that the treatise *De actibus humanis* is now obsolete and
that we have all along been basing our morality on something illusory—a man or a conscience which does not exist.

On the other hand, there is an immense body of psychoanalytical literature, and a growing accumulation of
clinical data, which go to support the psychoanalytical position. Making use of dynamic concepts, psychiatrists and

[8] Thomas Verner Moore, O.S.B., *The Driving Forces of Human Nature
and Their Adjustment* (New York: Grune and Stratton, 1950), pp. 68–80,
explains how all these psychic activities presuppose an unconscious in the
general sense of the word.

[9] John C. Ford, S.J., *Depth Psychology, Morality and Alcoholism*
(Weston, Mass.: Weston College Press, 1951), pp. 20–34.

psychologists (of different schools) have had fruitful results, especially in the treatment of the mentally ill. The evidence for the existence of a dynamic unconscious has convinced so many serious thinkers that it would be arbitrary merely to brush it all aside as if it did not exist and could create no problems. The doctrines of Freud have revolutionized psychological thinking and have left a deep impress on the thought of mankind. The moralist, who by profession must be concerned with human conduct and misconduct, cannot shut his eyes to any source of information which can shed light on human motives and human responsibility.

This leaves moralists in something of a quandary. All we can do is to leave it to the scientists to determine the scientific facts. Meanwhile, we can profit by accepting, for the purposes of our discussion, the supposition that the dynamic unconscious does exist and that unconscious motivation does play a significant role in the conscious life of normal people.

In that hypothesis, is there created for the moralist a new and critical problem as to free will and human responsibility? Before replying to that question, there are several considerations which will put the question in clearer relief, and mitigate, perhaps, the seriousness of our hypothetical problem.

SOME CLARIFYING CONSIDERATIONS

The first consideration is that much of our everyday psychic activity is not free anyway. In fact none of it is free, here and now, except the deliberate acts of the will. We are responsible *in causa* for many acts that are not themselves deliberate; but not even all the acts of the will are free: only the deliberate ones. Unconscious motivation of all these indeliberate psychic activities presents no problem for the doctrine of free will. Pertinently, Dalbiez observes:

Psychoanalysis can claim very real successes. But wherein do these successes lead us to modify the philosophical position of the problem of free-will? What psychoanalysis has contrived to explain is such phenomena as failed acts, dreams, neurotic symptoms. But what sensible person ever dreamt of denying that the facts in question are determined, and of dragging in free-will in this connection? . . . It is astonishing that Freud imagines that his opponents could regard the lapsus as a free act. Let us repeat that the problem of free-will needs no discussion in a field in which it does not arise.[10]

Dalbiez would undoubtedly agree, however, that some psychoanalysts also explain our free, deliberate choices by means of unconscious motivation and rely on such motivation so exclusively that they end by giving a deterministic explanation.

In this connection a comment on the term "psychic determinism" is in order. Sometimes it means psychological determinism, that is, a philosophical doctrine that denies freedom of the will and explains the choices we call free as the necessary product of prevailing psychological pressures and motives. But more often the term "psychic determinism" is used in a context which does not involve free will at all. When psychic events, or symptoms, or attitudes and moods, are explained in terms of psychic causality, as opposed to organic or physiological causality, this is called psychic determinism. Psychic causation would be a clearer term. Disputes among psychologists as to whether certain phenomena are to be explained as having a physiological or

10 Dalbiez, *op. cit.*, II, 296.

psychological origin need not involve the doctrine of free will at all. They can and usually do prescind from it. It is only when psychic determinism is used to explain the deliberate choices of the will, and explains them in terms which exclude the self-determination of the will, that we have a direct conflict with the doctrine of free will. Of course there are psychologists and psychiatrists who hold this position, in common with other men of science and other philosophers. Freud was one of them.[11] But this position is not essential to a theory of the dynamic unconscious.

The second consideration which diminishes the problem somewhat is this: Many of the motives which are loosely referred to as unconscious are not really unconscious at all. Even psychoanalysts themselves do not always distinguish well between truly unconscious motivation and other similar phenomena. One author, for example, gives an illustration of a "dynamic concept in the unconscious."[12] It is the case of a psychotic individual who murdered his two children to keep them from growing up to lives of immorality like their mother's. But the man in the case acted from motives of which he was aware. He described them in detail. They were not only conscious motives but compulsive ones. The psychoanalyst suspected, but did not uncover, deeper motives based on the unconscious desire to murder the mother. We must be careful, therefore, not to refer to unconscious motivation except in cases where psychoanalytical psychology itself uncovers such motivation. Psychoanalysts do not agree among themselves as to the amount and extent of unconscious motivation in everyday life.

[11] Dalbiez, *op. cit.*, II, 298, quotes passages from Freud at random to show that "Freud categorically denies the existence of liberty."

[12] Moore, *op. cit.*, p. 74 sq.

Then there are the motives which we do not like to admit to ourselves. We dismiss them more or less deliberately and more or less successfully from consciousness; but it does not require psychoanalytical techniques to bring them to light. Ordinary reflection often suffices. Donceel throws light on this point:

The motives we allege for a given decision may not always be the real or the only motives for that decision. A student of literature who reads a well-written, pornographic novel, overtly for its style, covertly for its salacious contents, is not unconscious of the motives which prompt his decision; he knows them but he does not want to admit them to himself. He is "rationalizing" according to the terminology of the psychoanalysts; in plainer terms he is deceiving himself. The extensive ascetical literature devoted to the problem of purity of intention contains many pages which foreshadow some of the deepest probings of modern psychoanalysis.[13]

One should distinguish carefully, therefore, between the unconscious motives known to psychoanalysis and these rationalizations, disguised motives, self-deceptions, and insincerities of which spiritual writers speak so frequently. The unconscous motivation of psychoanalysis results from automatic psychic mechanisms operating deep within the personality. The motivation is completely unknown to the person who is affected by it, and the sicker and more abnormal he is the greater is the domination it exercises over him and the more difficult it is to uncover the motivation. Sometimes, the analysts tell us, it takes years on the office couch.

It is an error to speak indiscriminately of such motivation and of those rationalizations which can be uncovered by a

[13] Donceel, *art. cit.*, pp. 476–77.

sincere examination of conscience or perhaps with the help of the spiritual director. These insincerities may range all the way from almost explicit hypocrisy through the various degrees of self-deception, down to the hazy borderland where the conscious merges with the unconscious and is submerged in it. Some of them, therefore, are hard to classify. But in general they must be considered conscious activities (certainly not unconscious in the strictly psychoanalytical sense), though the consciousness may be more or less attenuated and the activities accordingly more or less imputable. We are constantly amazed at the ability of human beings (other human beings of course) to deceive themselves. The matter is complicated further by the fact that men act from "mixed motives." For instance, a deliberately chosen, rational, and morally good motive for a certain activity may not be without an admixture of attraction, perhaps instinctual, for what is morally evil in the same activity—or may not even be free from an admixture of a subsidiary less-worthy motive which is deliberately chosen.

As a result of such half-conscious acts we are confronted, it is true, with a tantalizing problem of subjective imputability. But it is not the problem of unconscious motivation and its effect on freedom. It is the problem of diminished imputability of partly conscious motives. If a man really succeeds in deceiving himself he may end by having a *conscientia erronea*. If he does not quite succeed he is to some extent lying to himself, and ends with a *conscientia mendax*. But in both cases we are dealing with *conscientia* not with *inconscientia*. Which is which in practice? What is the criterion of a completely pure intention? Is there any such thing? And what connection has all this with the rather hazy psychology of the virtual intention? These are all old problems, not new ones.[14]

There is a third consideration which will help us to clarify our problem. It is the equivocal use of the word *motivation*. The unconscious activities of psychoanalysis, even though they are shown to be the wellsprings of human activity, are not *motivations* in the theological sense of that term. The word "motive" to the theologian (who conceives man as a rational being whose will makes decisions on the basis of rational deliberation) means a good which is consciously apprehended by reason; a good for the sake of which the agent acts. It operates in the order of final causality. It is a *finis operantis rationabiliter*. For such a motive to be unconscious is a contradiction in terms. Since it is consciously apprehended and accepted as a motive for action it is imputable to the agent in various degrees, for praise or for blame, for better or for worse.

But the unconscious motives of psychoanalysis belong to an altogether different level of human nature. They are instinctual urges or attractions; they are emotional impulses or repulsions. They are beyond intellectual apprehension as long as they remain in the unconscious. They are almost always nonimputable because the agent is hardly ever responsible for their existence within him. They may stem from a traumatic experience which occurred long before he had the use of reason, or may result from an emotional experience over which he never had any control. They are not known to reason, are not deliberately accepted by the person as goals of his human activity, and never have been.

[14] See Gerald Vann, O.P., "Unconscious Motivation and Pseudo-Virtue," *Homiletic and Pastoral Review*, 57 (Nov., 1956), 115–23; and *ibid.*, 124–27, "Reply to Father Vann," by John C. Ford, S.J.

They may be called motives in the sense that they provide motive power and emotional energy, thereby influencing his human acts; but they are not the motives of scholastic philosophy and theology. They belong to the order of efficient, not final, causality.

Our problem is not clarified when these two essentially different conceptions are described by the same word. And yet it is impossible to avoid using the equivocal terms "motivation" and "motive," because they have acquired established, but different, technical meanings in theology and psychology. The existence of possible unconscious *sources* of our moral activity is one thing. And to call them *motives* may be legitimate in psychology. But the use of that term is bound to confuse the issue before us, which is that of the effect or influence which these sources may have on the freedom and imputability of our conscious activities.

It will help to clear the ground then, if we keep constantly in mind that many of the so-called "unconscious motives" are not really *unconscious* in the psychoanalytical sense, and that a great many more of them are not really *motives* in the theological sense.

PSEUDO-VIRTUES OF THE UNCONSCIOUS

A fourth consideration concerns the so-called "pseudo-virtues" of the unconscious. Usually it is responsibility for evil actions and the attenuation of such responsibility that occupies the mind of the moralist. But as mentioned earlier, responsibility for virtuous conduct may also be affected by unconscious factors in our psychic life. The "pseudo-virtues of the unconscious" are frequently referred to by religious-minded psychoanalytical writers. Conscious conduct which is objectively in accordance with the moral law and ostensibly virtuous is discovered to be based on unconscious motives of a far from virtuous kind. There is question here not of half-conscious rationalizations and insincerities, but of strictly automatic processes buried deep in the unconscious. A man may think that he is practicing the virtue of penance when actually he is a masochist in disguise. His continence may result not from virtue but from inhibition, frigidity, obsessive disgust. The idealist may be unconsciously homosexual. Love of God may be a false transference of the father-feeling. The *voie d'enfance* may reflect an infantile attitude toward the father. All these false, neurotic qualities that look like virtues may be pathological symptoms. They may be the symptoms of retarded affectivity, infantile fixations, or unconscious instinctual drives.

The idea of the pseudo-virtues has been elaborated in a book of Dr. Charles Odier: *Les deux sources, consciente et inconsciente de la vie morale.*[15] Dr. Odier shows great respect for religious and moral values, and his work is an attempt to separate the true religious and moral values from pseudo-religious and pseudo-moral values deriving from the unconscious. He gives many examples of what he considers to be pseudo-virtue and pseudo-morality; and he includes a long, comparative table of the essential elements of the two moral systems: the unconscious morality of the Super-Ego and the conscious morality of the moral conscience. He believes that psychoanalysis has contributed enormously to

[15] Cf. Charles Odier, *Les deux sources, consciente et inconsciente de la vie morale,* Neuchâtel, Switz.: Éditions de la Bacconière, 1943–1947 (Cahiers de Philosophie: Étre et Penser"); also Father Tesson, S.J., "Moral Conscience and Psychiatry," *New Problems in Medical Ethics,* edited by Peter Flood, O.S.B., vol. III (Westminster, Md.: The Newman Press, 1956), 85–102; C. H. Nodet, "Psychoanalysis and Morality," *ibid.,* pp. 103–17; F. Pasche, "Psychoanalysis and Moral Conscience," *ibid.,* 118–21.

the solution of the fundamental problems of the human spirit precisely because it has thrown relentless light on the pseudo-moral values of the unconscious.

We leave it to professional psychologists to evaluate these theories. Anyone who recognizes the existence of the dynamic unconscious should find no difficulty in admitting that there are cases, especially among neurotic individuals, where, underlying their conscious conduct and its conscious motivations, there are forces of this kind; and that the more seriously ill a person is, the more likely it is that these unconscious forces hold sway over him. But possibly a word of warning is in order lest one appeal prematurely to the theory of pseudo-virtue, and deny without sufficient reason the reality of the virtue that appears at the conscious level.

Let us imagine this example: Titius, an unmarried man, shuns all occasions of unchastity and lives a life of complete purity in thought, word and deed. In fact he has few if any temptations of a sexually attractive kind and for the most part feels repugnance, rather than attraction for sexual stimuli. Whether or not unconscious elements far removed from virtue underlie this attitude of Titius may be difficult to discover. His conduct being considered "abnormal" or at least unusual, a person of a psychoanalytical turn of mind might be tempted to look immediately for such explanations as pathological frigidity or obsessive disgust stemming from unconscious mechanisms. Getting at the root of such elements, if they do exist, might be of great ascetical value, and might lead to a deepening and strengthening of his spiritual life. But granted all this, it is a mistake to characterize his conscious conduct as only pseudo-virtuous.

Let us look first at the objective morality of his acts. The law of chastity requires of the unmarried man continence.

Titius observes this law and is continent. Objectively that is real virtue, not pseudo-virtue. The conduct of Titius in its immediate object, its circumstances and its end is good conduct. Those are the three objective determinants of good conduct. Titius' actions are objectively pleasing to God.

Then let us look at his conduct subjectively, that is, as it appears to him in the light of his own conscience. Titius knows what is right and wrong. He knows it is wrong to indulge himself sexually. He believes and knows that his continence is in accord with the law of God. After deliberation he chooses to be continent. He finds it easy so to choose, but he is convinced that he could have chosen otherwise. Have we any reason for saying that he is deceived? Is not the testimony of his own conscience before, during, and after his acts the best criterion we have of his freedom? In the absence of positive evidence of serious illness we ought not to conclude that he is so abnormal that he cannot choose freely to do what is right. Common sense would agree with the teaching of the treatise *De actibus humanis.*

How will God judge him? Certainly not on the basis of the unconscious influences that may actually be at work within him. Nobody is responsible for these. God does not ask us to be psychoanalyzed in order to know how we stand with Him. Titius is no hero, but he must be judged to be practicing real, not pseudo, virtue.

TO INFLUENCE IS NOT TO COMPEL

With all these preliminary considerations disposed of, we can now approach the solution of our problem by making a familiar distinction between pressures which *influence* a man in making his choices and those which compel or determine those choices.

It is a commonplace of psychological experience that human beings, even when acting deliberately, are subject to all sorts of influences both conscious and unconscious, over which they have little or no control. We shall enumerate later the principal elements which moralists take into account as modifiers of human freedom—recognizing that some of them, at least in unusual circumstances, not only modify it but eliminate it. It is part of our very concept of free will that the will can be "motivated" in both directions, can be under stronger pressure in one direction than the other, and can even recognize the stronger pressure without being forced to succumb to it. In fact, an act of the will could hardly be called free in choosing one alternative if there were no motive at all for choosing the opposite.

Can we not, therefore, look upon unconscious motivation and the activity of the dynamic unconscious as merely one more of these influences? It exerts its pressure on human activity along with many other factors, without necessarily forcing it. It is a newly discovered factor, it is true. It may turn out to be of immensely greater significance for education, for morality and for human life generally, because so universal, or so pervasive—though so elusive. That remains to be seen. But it is not essentially different, or essentially more embarrassing for the doctrine of free will than other influences of which we are aware in daily life. This includes other unconscious influences (as we shall see) which exert their pressure on man without forcing his will.

Let us recall again the example of Frink and his choice of a consultant described above. And let us listen again to Dalbiez' reflections:

Let us grant without cavil that Frink has correctly interpreted the unconscious determinants of his attitude toward X. Do facts of this kind adduce anything at all *novel* against the belief in free will? We believe not. Ever since the world has contained philosophers, they have been well aware, and have often repeated, that our past, our stock of previous experience, has,— without any need to reappear in the field of consciousness,—a great influence on our resolutions. All are agreed hereon, and yet some accept and others reject free will. The novelty which psychoanalysis has to contribute is the possibility of ascertaining which elements of the past have been active in any given case. This is a splendid scientific result, but of no philosophical importance whatever.[16]

In other words the mere fact that the unconscious influences our conduct, or influences a great deal of it, or influences it to a great extent, is no direct proof that our freedom and responsibility are notably impaired, much less eliminated. We cannot immediately conclude that since there is a great deal of unconscious motivation in a given act, therefore the agent lacks that amount of freedom which is necessary to be guilty of mortal sin, or worthy of the highest merit before God.

A good deal of misunderstanding (and of possible harm to consciences) could be avoided, if when the unconscious sources of a person's conduct are revealed to him he were not left under the impression that these unconscious factors had *compelled* him to act as he did, whether sinfully or virtuously. This universal, and, as it were, automatic inference seems to be a common error among those who deal with psychoanalysts, or at least who dabble in depth psychology. The words of Pius XII, cited above, bear repetition:

[16] Dalbiez, *loc. cit.*, p. 298; and compare Donceel, *art. cit.*, p. 476.

"That these energies may exercise pressure on an activity does not necessarily signify that they compel it." [17] Even in cases of psychological sickness he suggests that the misdirected instincts should not be prematurely considered "as a sort of fatality, as a tyranny of the affective impulse streaming forth from the subconscious and escaping completely from the control of the conscious and the soul." [18]

One author compares the agent under the influence of unconscious motivation to an airplane pilot, who is not familiar with all the workings of the machinery which he nevertheless substantially controls. He may discover by analysis elements that contribute to the direction that the ship is taking—elements of which he was previously unaware—but though these elements were always there and always operative he was nevertheless master of the ship. It was the pilot not the mechanism that determined the course of the ship.[19]

A. Willwoll, S.J., a German psychologist, describes a kind of unconscious motivation (not Freudian), which nevertheless influences our free activity without determining it. Bihler summarizes the teaching as follows:

It would be hard to explain some of our conscious life and activity, without admitting what he terms the "psychological a priori" in that group of experiences. This would consist of certain factors, certainly not fully conscious,—some subconscious or even unconscious, yet affecting now more, now less, our conscious experience. Then, too, there are unconscious dispositions and tendencies. In a very illuminating article on this same topic, he has carefully examined the manifold character of

[17] *AAS,* 45 (1953), 278–86 at 279.
[18] *Ibid.,* p. 281.
[19] Joseph Géraud, "Procédés actuels d'investigation de la conscience," *L'Ami du clergé,* 58 (1948), 518.

these influences on our conscious life. In the pathological area you meet with these compulsive ideas and impulses, repressions, emotional blocks and prejudices. Not pathological, but none the less definitely influencing us at times, are the effects of our cultural and social milieu, which may influence our judgments and action. All these have their influence upon us and often without our awareness, or at least full awareness.[20]

If unconscious influence is obvious to the philosopher and psychologist it should be still more so to the Catholic theologian who knows something of the workings of grace in the human soul. It is the teaching of theology that even under efficacious grace, and even under a special abundance of God's grace, the soul is free to do good, and wins merit accordingly. And those good impulses of the will in which actual grace partially consists are not necessarily present in the consciousness of the recipient.[21] He cannot explain why it is that the good he chooses seems so attractive, why it is that his heart can relinquish the *amor terrenus* which hitherto bound it, and be drawn by the *amor cœlestis* which hitherto left it cold. He is aware, on reflection, of the attraction, but he was not conscious of the "motivation." We say it is God's grace. In the case of the saints we say it is the overwhelming grace of God. And yet we do not say that this overwhelming grace, this "unconscious motivation," destroys or notably impairs the freedom of the will.

We must confess to a mystery here. It has always been a mystery how God's grace and the freedom of the will can be

[20] Hugh Bihler, S.J., *Psychology of Instinct* (Manuscript, Woodstock College, Woodstock, Md., 1950) refers to A. Willwoll, S.J., "Vom psychologischen Apriori in unseren Urteilen," *Feldkircher Festschrift, 75 Jahre Stella Matutina*, pp. 417–41; "Vom Umbewussten in Aufbau des religiösen Erlebens," *Rätsel der Steele*, p. 50.

[21] Blasius Beraza, S.J., *Tractatus de gratia Christi* (Bilbao: Elexpuru Hermanos, 1916), nn. 44, 45, 55 sq., and n. 64.

reconciled. From the time of St. Augustine until the present day, theologians have struggled with the problem. But Catholics have never doubted the freedom of the will. The analogy is obvious in the problem of unconscious motivation, to whatever extent it exists in normal men and women. To influence is not to compel.

CONCLUSIONS

The questions we have been trying to answer are these: In the supposition that psychoanalysis has established its fundamental position as to unconscious motivation, does this create for the moralist a new and critical problem as to free will and human responsibility? Does unconscious motivation pervade human conduct to such an extent that it destroys or seriously impairs human responsibility even in normal individuals? The answer to both these questions must be in the negative.

This is not to belittle or to underestimate the important consequences that may eventuate from these discoveries, important for general education, important for ascetical direction, important for pastoral counselling and for the administration of the sacrament of penance. But it is to emphasize the fact that we have here not a really new problem, but an old one in a new form. It is the old and everbaffling problem of trying to measure the influence of "impediments" which detract from the freedom of human acts. It is new because the dynamic unconscious as conceived by psychoanalysis is a factor hitherto undreamed of in its far-reaching implications.

Yet the discoveries brought to light, up to the present, are far from demonstrating that this unconscious so pervades the everyday activities of normal men that it creates a critical general problem as regards their freedom. The thing that Catholic moralists must defend (because the faith itself forces them to the conclusion) is this: that normal men and women *per se* have sufficient freedom in the concrete circumstances of daily life to merit great praise or great blame before God. This conclusion does not seem to us to be endangered by the discovery of the dynamic unconscious.

Nor do we believe that the treatise *De actibus humanis* has been made obsolete and must be completely rewritten on the ground that it deals with a man and a conscience which no longer exist.[22] The discoveries are not that revolutionary. Besides, even if revolutionary, the revolution is still going on and we do not know what will come of it. Our task is rather to incorporate new findings into the treatise, and with the expert help of professionals, give our students the benefit of whatever new knowledge there is about human nature, human responsibility, and the wellsprings of human conduct. Meanwhile the enlightened testimony of a man's own conscience will continue to be the most valuable help we have in trying to estimate the state of his soul.

[22] This somewhat exaggerated position was taken by Jean Rimaud, S.J., "Les psychologues contre la morale," *Études*, 263 (1949), 3–22 at pp. 11–12.

Freedom and Imputability Under Stress

I N THE LAST chapter we saw an exaggerated and untenable
version of the doctrine that passion takes away subjective imputability; and since that opinion was based on psychoanalytical theory, we attempted to clarify some of the
general questions raised by the new psychology of the
dynamic unconscious.

It is possible to go too far in the opposite direction also,
and make little or no allowance for the modification of
human responsibility due to emotional disturbances. There
is little danger nowadays that anyone will return to the outmoded doctrine of interpretative advertence, according to
which a man was guilty of his objectively sinful conduct
even if he did not actually advert to the malice of that conduct at all, provided he *could have* and *should* have ad-
verted to it. Still less is there any danger that we would ever
go back to the crude estimates of earlier ages, in which the
mere external performance of an act was, in effect, almost
the only criterion of guilt.

But there is a danger that some may be too mechanical in applying inadequate rules of thumb. There are such things as compulsions and uncontrollable urges. There are such things as neurotic disturbances which may fall far short of any stereotyped picture of insanity and yet have very serious effects on human acts. Any priest who has spent long hours in the confessional knows of the difficulties and the weaknesses that often manifest greatly diminished culpability. We are learning more and more about the internal and emotional obstacles to the exercise of freedom. If we do not take them into account we run the risk of judging consciences too severely. The problem is how to take them into account justly, without endangering the principle of human responsibility.

When insisting on human responsibility the theologian and moralist should not be thought of as prosecuting attorneys, bent on finding men guilty of their misdeeds—while the psychiatrist is cast in the role of defense counsel. The thesis of diminished responsibility may not be as comforting as it appears on the surface. The shoe of nonresponsibility fits both feet. If it excuses from sin, it also eliminates merit; if it reduces blame, it also minimizes virtue. For good actions are not imputable to a man, either, unless he is free. They are not his in the moral sense. It is no compliment to human dignity to deprive man of the most human powers he possesses.

When this matter of responsibility is discussed with a materialistic psychologist, therefore, the point at issue is a basic one as to man's nature, and how he is to arrive at his destiny. Is he basically and essentially a self-governing being? Is it through reason and free choices for which he is responsible that he governs himself and reaches his last end?

Or is he a complicated automaton who is the creature of his unconscious, or of other forces, driven this way and that by hidden emotional and instinctual forces? The theologian answers that the essential governing force in man, the thing that differentiates him from other animals, is his reason and his free will.

But when the problem is discussed by psychologists and theologians who accept man's rational nature and free will (as we intend to discuss it here), it is a problem as to *degrees* of responsibility, and especially as to the degree of responsibility required in the concrete for the commission of mortal sin. For heaven and hell are at stake when a decision involving mortal sin is being made.

We shall try to explore the question with the help of established theological principles and whatever psychological information we have at our disposal. As will appear, it is a thorny problem indeed, and one we cannot hope to solve completely. Our purpose is rather to clarify it somewhat, by focusing attention on what we consider the nub of the problem, and by eliminating if possible some misunderstandings. We hope thus to encourage others to make more profound studies in the light of the philosophy of liberty, the psychology of will and emotion, and the theology of grace.

FREE WILL

Sometimes the psychiatrists and psychologists with whom we discuss these problems do not understand how absolutely basic free will is to all Catholic theology and scholastic philosophy. It is not merely a theological inference or a philosophical speculation. It is a fundamental article of faith. But more than that, it happens to be an article which is confirmed by the universal, spontaneous, and ineluctable conviction of mankind. In practical life all men are convinced that at times they act freely, that is, they could have chosen to do the opposite in the same circumstances. Even those who deny the freedom of the will when writing theoretically, cannot escape the compelling force of this inner conviction as regards their own freedom. They have to speak and act exactly as *if* they and others were free almost in the same breath with which they deny it.[1]

When we say the will is free we mean that the human being endowed with such a will has the power, given certain prerequisites of knowledge and motivation, of saying yes or no, freely, to a proposed action, or of choosing freely between two alternative courses of action. "Freely" does not mean easily or without reluctance, although sometimes free choices are easily made. "Freely" means that at the time the choice was made, the man could have made the opposite choice—even if with difficulty or repugnance. He was not compelled by external or internal pressures to choose as he did. He did it himself. He made the choice when he could have made the opposite one, and for that reason, *and only for that reason*, he is responsible for it. If he chooses what

[1] John R. Cavanagh, M.D., "Criminal Responsibility and Free Will," *Bulletin of the Guild of Catholic Psychiatrists*, 3, n. 2 (Dec., 1955), 24–33 at 27, gives the following considerations to show that human beings are responsible and therefore free: "This responsibility is easily recognized if one gives a moment of thought to these facts: 1) Everyone recognizes his own responsibility. 2) Everyone holds others responsible for various injuries or damage which one has suffered at their hands. 3) Everyone acts upon the belief in the power of his own initiative. *These three factors plus one's daily experience in the matter of free choice add up to free will.*" He cites Thomas Verner Moore, O.S.B., *The Driving Forces of Human Nature and Their Adjustment* (New York: Grune and Stratton, 1948), p. 329. For the scholastic exposition of the doctrine of free will, see St. Thomas, *De malo*, q. 8 art. *unicus.*

is morally good, he is worthy of praise as a man. If he chooses what is morally bad he is worthy of blame. But without freedom of choice the act is not his in the moral sense; he is not responsible for it; it cannot be imputed to him; he is worthy neither of praise nor of blame. No one is morally responsible for what he could not help doing. The words "moral responsibility" and "moral imputability," and the word "morality" itself, are all devoid of meaning, except in the hypothesis that man has the power of free choice, thus understood, in some of his acts.

Which ones? We say: the deliberate ones, that is, those done with knowledge and consent. We are interested most of all in those actions by which man chooses God or rejects God, chooses mortal sin or rejects mortal sin, administers a sacrament, makes a law, sentences a criminal, gives judgment in a lawsuit, binds himself by contract. And so of other important choices and decisions. Unless a man, acting with deliberation, is endowed *per se* with sufficient freedom to make such choices really his own and be fully responsible for them so that they must be imputed to him for reward or punishment, or as valid or invalid, then our religious beliefs and our social institutions do not make sense.

FULL DELIBERATION AND FULL CONSENT

Moralists have discussed the conditions for responsibility for mortal sin more thoroughly than the conditions for juridical and sacramental acts. In fact they sometimes refer to the discretion required for serious sin (presumably because better understood) as the measure of responsibility in other matters. For example we read that for valid matrimonial consent: "there is certainly required the discretion which is sufficient for sinning gravely, and in fact, greater discretion." [2]

As for mortal sin, moralists teach unanimously that to be guilty of it one must commit it with "full deliberation and full consent of the will." This phrase is even in the catechism. And since they use terms like "perfect advertence" and "perfect consent" one might easily get the impression that for mortal sin it is necessary to have the most clear-cut intellectual apprehension of the alternatives involved and an almost unmixed adherence of the will to the evil act which is chosen. Such an impression would be strengthened by reading a sentence like the following:

For as long as man is prevented by his subjective condition from evaluating his last end in accordance with its worth, and intending it with corresponding efficacy, he is unable to decide about that end by an act proportionate to it, with the result that his inordination is only venial. [3]

But it becomes quickly apparent, when the act of deliberation or advertence is described in greater detail, that moralists have in mind a degree of knowledge and consent which is far from being one hundred per cent perfect. For instance the author just quoted says of the advertence necessary for mortal sin:

It is not required, however, that the advertence last as long as the sinful action lasts, but it is enough that it was present at the beginning of the action, or even before the beginning if the sinner willed to begin the act and carry it out. . . . Nor is distinct advertence to a certain definite malice demanded;

---

[2] Genicot-Salsmans, *Institutiones theologiæ moralis* (17th ed.), II, n. 610, citing St. Thomas, *In IV Sent.*, d. 27, q. 2, a. 2, ad 2.
[3] Arthur Vermeersch, S.J., *Theologiæ moralis principia, responsa, consilia* (Rome: Gregorian University, 1947), I, n. 49.

rather, a consciousness *in confuso* of something gravely evil suffices. Nor must there be explicit attention to the *offense* against God, since philosophical sin does not exist. And *reflex* advertence is not required: the *direct* cognition which is drawn from habitual *knowledge* suffices. But perfect comprehension of the *substantial* malice is necessary; although with regard to some special circumstance known habitually it is said to be enough if it is present to the intellect in a subconscious or confused way.[4]

Such explanations (and they could be culled at random from the other authors) make it clear that the theologians who speak of full or complete or perfect deliberation and consent are really demanding only *sufficient* deliberation and consent.

DEGREES OF FREEDOM AND RESPONSIBILITY

"Sufficient" is a relative term. It implies degrees of freedom and degrees of imputability. This fundamental supposition underlies our entire discussion. But the concept of degrees of freedom is a confusing one, as we shall see. Nevertheless it is a commonplace among moralists and canonists. At the risk of laboring the obvious we would like to insist on this idea of degrees of freedom and imputability, because it is frequently not understood by psychologists and psychiatrists, who think the free will of the theologians is some sort of inexplicable omnipotence of choice; and is lost sight of at times, because of the equivocation in the use of the word "freedom," even by confessors and counselors.

The free will defended by theologians does not operate in an unreal vacuum. It is not a magic wand of the spiritual sphere which man can wave "at will" over his conduct and

4 Vermeersch, *op. cit.*, I, n. 383.

decisions. It is not independent of the hard facts of bodily existence and the baffling implications of human emotion. Every moral manual enumerates ignorance, passion (that is, emotion), fear and force as obstacles which diminish freedom and sometimes do away with it. Moralists also discuss temperament, organic disposition, endocrine glands,[5] drugs, acquired habits, education, environment, mental illness and unconscious motivation as modifiers of human acts. This modification implies that there are degrees of freedom and imputability.

Even in the criminal law of the Church, criminal imputability admits of an indefinite number of degrees. It is spoken of as being augmented (in a few cases) and diminished (in a great many cases) by such things as fear, passion, age, drunkenness, mental illness, and the rest. Since in modern canon law there can be no crime at all without grave subjective guilt to begin with, that is, without a subjectively imputable mortal sin, and since the degrees of criminal imputability attempt to follow as closely as possible the norms of moral imputability, it is evident that canon law takes it for granted that within the limits of mortal guilt there are many degrees of imputability. In other words, granted sufficient freedom for grave culpability, the criminal law raises the further question of degrees of this grave culpability.

In moral theology it is common teaching that given a sufficient diminution in the degree of freedom, the sub-

5 Cf. "Current Moral Theology and Canon Law," *Theological Studies*, 2 (1941), 527–77 at 532, discussing an article by H. S. Rubinstein, H. D. Shapiro, and Walter Freeman, "The Treatment of Morbid Sex-Craving with Testosterone Propionate," *American Journal of Psychiatry*, 97 (1940), 703. Other examples of physiological factors which affect conduct: the behavior of a diabetic deprived of insulin; effect of chlorpromazine on anxiety in psychotics; the new tranquillizers, etc.

jective guilt of what is objectively a grave sin can be essentially changed from grave culpability to venial culpability *propter imperfectionem actus*. We speak of semideliberate acts, and of imperfectly voluntary acts. These expressions mean that the acts referred to, though they are human acts, and *ex objecto* gravely sinful acts, are so lacking in deliberation or so imperfectly consented to that subjectively they cannot be more than venial sins.

Therefore the scale of imputability ranges all the way from the minimum that is compatible at all with the concept of a free, human act, up through all the degrees of venial culpability, across the dread threshold of mortal sin, through all the indefinite gradations of mortal guilt, to the highest point of the very limit of human malice. The two critical points on this scale are the point at the very bottom which distinguishes a free *actus humanus* from a nonfree *actus hominis*, and the point, surely very much higher on the scale, that distinguishes mortal guilt from venial guilt.

DEGREES OF FREEDOM FOR MORTAL SIN AND VALID ACTS

To put the matter fancifully, if one were given marks on malice and culpability where bad actions are concerned, or on virtue and merit where good actions are concerned, or on degrees of freedom where both are concerned, the marks might range all the way from one percent to ninety-nine percent. Zero percent would mean no human act at all; and we avoid one hundred percent because it seems more appropriate to angels or devils than to men. Still speaking fancifully, what is the passing mark for mortal sin? Certainly not ninety-nine percent freedom. The full deliberation and consent of the moralists does not demand that much. Is it ninety percent? Seventy-five percent? Sixty percent? Who can say? Some would put it higher, others lower. Only God knows the exact answer.

We might also ask whether the passing mark of freedom is higher for bad actions than for good ones. Should we require ninety percent freedom to be worthy of eternal punishment, but only sixty percent freedom to be worthy of eternal reward? [6] And how do sinful acts compare with juridical or sacramental acts? Do we need ninety percent freedom to be mortally guilty of a sacrilegious administration of a sacrament, but only sixty percent freedom to be able to administer it validly? And how do various juridical acts compare with one another? Does one contract require more freedom for validity than another? Does one need ninety percent freedom to be irrevocably bound by a contract of marriage, but only sixty percent freedom to be bound by a contract to buy an automobile? Should we demand only sixty percent freedom to benefit from a contract which is favorable but ninety percent to be bound by one which is onerous?

We make no attempt to answer these questions here.[7] There is nothing intrinsically repugnant, however, in the concept that a certain degree of freedom would be necessary in order that one's sins be gravely imputable, and a different

[6] Facility of operation is not by itself a criterion of imputability in general. A high degree of difficulty will exclude serious guilt and blame. But the converse is not true. Given a high degree of facility or complete absence of obstacles, it does not follow that there is no room left for high merit and praise. A man's good actions are imputable to him even if he loves what is commanded. Neither difficulty nor facility is the criterion of philosophical freedom, and the degree of psychological freedom is not the measure of imputability *ad meritum*. Virtue need not be odious to be meritorious.

[7] See G. M. Fazzari, S.J., *Valutazióne etica e consenso matrimoniale* (Naples: Editore M. D. D'Auria, 1951), pp. 45 sqq., for opinions of scholastics on the degree of discretion required for various important juridical acts, e.g., marriage, entering religion, etc.

degree in order to act validly in the juridical or sacramental order. The validity of some juridical and sacramental acts depends, besides, on standards and conditions freely determined by the legislator, human or divine.[8]

These questions are not altogether speculative. They have important practical bearings the moment one tries to estimate the moral or juridical responsibility of a mentally disturbed penitent, or of a person who has acted under great emotional stress. For instance, may the penitent go to communion without confession if this happens again? Must this penitent repeat previous acts (sacramental or juridical) because they were invalidly performed?

PHILOSOPHICAL FREEDOM AND PSYCHOLOGICAL FREEDOM

Our purpose in asking such questions, however, has been, at this point, merely to emphasize the important fundamental notion that there are indefinitely numerous degrees of freedom. We said above that to speak of degrees of freedom is confusing and that the word itself is equivocal. The reason is that moralists and theologians seem to use the word freedom (as we have in the preceding pages) in two very different meanings. We shall call these two meanings philosophical freedom and psychological freedom. The first does not admit of degrees, the second does.

By philosophical freedom we mean the *libertas indifferentiæ* which we attribute to the human will in scholastic philosophy. It is the kind of freedom which is required in order to have a human act. It presupposes advertence and

---

[8] For example, canon law requires a certain age for valid matrimonial consent. For centuries this was 12 for girls and 14 for boys; it is now 14 and 16 respectively. Special conditions are set down for the criminal imputability of minors. Marriage is invalid when contracted through *vis et metus;*—though some would deduce this latter effect from natural law.

rational deliberation, and has its metaphysical roots in the power of the intellect to make objectively indifferent judgments. There have been bitter theological controversies about its relation to grace and to God's concursus with human acts. Even in defining it, theologians have difficulty in prescinding from these disputes. But we believe the description we have given of free will in the philosophical sense would be admitted by theologians of all schools. It is "the power, given certain prerequisites of knowledge and motivation, of saying yes or no freely, to a proposed action, or of choosing freely between two alternative courses of action. 'Freely' does not mean easily, or without reluctance, although sometimes free choices are easily made. *'Freely' means that at the time the choice was made the man could have made the opposite choice—even if with difficulty or repugnance.*"

Is it not obvious that freedom thus understood does not admit of degrees? We can say of any action either "He was able not to have done it" or "He was not able not to have done it." It is either the one or the other. It cannot be a little of each. There is nothing in between. The absolute, physical power of choice, the freedom of the will from internal coaction, *stat in indivisibili.*

By psychological freedom we mean freedom from obstacles and pressures which make the exercise of philosophical freedom difficult. We call it psychological for want of a better word, and because it is the kind of freedom psychologists often speak about. Most if not all of the above-mentioned modifiers of human acts are obstacles to this freedom. Freedom in this sense, then, obviously does admit of degrees; it is by its very nature not absolute but relative. The fewer or weaker the obstacles the greater the freedom and facility with which the will can choose, and direct the execution of bodily activities.

It is unfortunate that the one phrase "freedom of the will" should be used to describe these two widely different things. Philosophical freedom is something positive and active. It is the power or faculty by which the will determines itself to this or that. It is freedom TO determine its own choices. Psychological freedom is passive and negative. It is freedom FROM the obstacles, pressures and impediments which make choices difficult. Philosophical freedom is the ability to choose IN THE FACE OF obstacles and pressures. Psychological freedom is the facility of a choice which results from THE ABSENCE OF obstacles and pressures.

Although these are such different things we frequently use the one word "freedom" to describe them both. When we say that passion interferes with freedom, sometimes we mean the kind of passion which prevents all deliberation and makes philosophical freedom impossible; sometimes we mean the degree of passion which leaves the fundamental human act essentially intact but creates greater or lesser obstacles to the exercise of freedom, thus diminishing the voluntary. We speak of diminished liberty, diminished sin, diminished voluntary, diminished responsibility and diminished imputability, in the same sentence in which we speak of the complete exclusion of the human act. Even careful writers will speak of diminished liberty when they mean diminished voluntary or diminished sin; or will speak of a diminished human act, when they mean diminished imputability of a human act. If we were more exact in our terminology and used the words *libertas, voluntarium, actus humanus, peccatum* and *imputabilitas* in their exact meanings we would probably avoid much of this confusion.

[213]

We have spent so much time on this question of degrees of freedom and the distinction between philosophical and psychological freedom because we believe it will throw light on our problem. To us it seems clear that for mortal sin both kinds of freedom are essential, the absolute, physical freedom which is the philosophical "liberty of indifference," and the relative psychological freedom from obstacles and difficulties, a sufficient degree of which is required before a human act can be gravely imputable.

We have now established with considerable accuracy what our problem is. Supposing that the prerequisites of philosophical freedom are present, and that a person is acting freely in the philosophical sense, how can we discover what is meant by sufficient psychological freedom for mortal guilt? We are especially interested in cases of severe emotional stress, of so-called "irresistible impulses," of obsessions and compulsive urges. On the scale of psychological freedom what is the passing mark for grave imputability? What follows will not solve completely this problem but will supply, it is hoped, some theological guideposts which will keep us from putting the mark too high or too low.

THEOLOGICAL GUIDEPOSTS

The first theological guidepost is this: We must start with the presumption that the normal individual is ordinarily capable of that degree of psychological freedom which is necessary to incur grave culpability. If this is not true, certain age-old practices of the Church are unintelligible. For instance, the way in which the Church has administered the sacrament of penance to the faithful, the way in which under her guidance confessors are prepared for their task, would not make sense except on the basis of this presumption. Furthermore the Church presumes that ordinary people have sufficient freedom to contract marriage validly, and we have seen that it is very likely that at least as much discretion is required for valid matrimonial consent as is required for subjective grave culpability.

Likewise in the administration of the criminal law of the Church it is presumed that the average individual is capable of a delict, and this presupposes a capacity for grave moral imputability. This presumption holds true in the criminal law even when a crime is committed through passion. The law considers the imputability diminished, it is true, but very often presumes that in spite of the impulses of passion there was still a crime. This could not be true according to canonical principles unless there was sufficient responsibility for mortal guilt, which is an essential element in every crime.

That the presumption remains true even when a man is put under considerable pressure from emotion, passion, or concupiscence has been recently reaffirmed on at least two occasions with great emphasis by Pius XII. One of these occasions was his address to the psychotherapists, when he said:

Original sin did not take away from man the possibility or the obligation of directing his own actions himself through his soul. It cannot be alleged that the psychic troubles and disorders which disturb the normal functioning of the psychic being represent what usually happens. The moral struggle to remain on the right path does not prove that it is impossible to follow that path, nor does it authorize any drawing back.[9]

There can be no doubt that the Holy Father spoke here of

[9] *AAS*, 45 (1953), 278–86 at 280.

a degree of autonomy which was compatible with grave guilt. But if it were not clear from this passage, it is explicit in his discourse on the Christian conscience as the object of education. There he taught in specially solemn terms that

the divine commandment of purity of soul and body still holds without any lesser obligation for the youth of today. They also are morally bound and, with the help of grace, are able to keep themselves pure. We reject, therefore, as erroneous the assertion of those who regard lapses as inevitable in adolescence, and therefore as not worthy of serious notice, as though they were not grave faults, because, they add, as a general rule passion destroys the freedom needed for an act to be morally imputable.[10]

On the other hand one should keep in mind that these passages refer to normal situations. One of them leaves room for a different presumption in the case of the mentally sick. In denying that "the psychic troubles and disorders that disturb the normal functioning of the psychic being represent what usually happens" the pope seems to imply that a different norm of imputability would apply to such troubles and disorders. Today the concept of mental illness has been broadened to include emotional illness of various degrees of severity. It is safe to say that in cases of real illness there is very frequently lacking that degree of psychological freedom requisite for mortal sin.

The second guidepost is the truth that there are a great many mortal sins in the world. Sometimes one hears exaggerated statements to the effect that a formal mortal sin is almost impossible to commit, or that a formal mortal sin hardly ever actually takes place. To hold such propositions

[10] *AAS*, 44 (1952), 270–78 at 275.

would be to contradict experience and the ordinary teaching and practice of the Church. Much of the Catholic teaching and practice in moral matters clearly supposes not only that formal mortal sin exists but that it is by no means a rarity. It may well be that the number of merely material mortal sins is very large, but this does not reduce the number of formal sins to a negligible number.[11]

Again let us appeal to the authority of Pius XII. In a sermon given in March of 1950 he called on the faithful to consider with courageous sincerity "the number, the gravity and the frequency of sins in the world." He continued:

Sin, the peculiar handiwork of man, defiles the face of the earth and disfigures the work of God. Consider the numberless sins, private and public, occult and manifest, sins against God and the Church, sins of men against their fellowman in soul and body, sins against the neighbor . . . against the family and society . . . And some of these sins are so cruel and unheard of that they need new names to be described.[12]

The third guidepost is the doctrine of grace. If it seems harsh to hold that there are so many sins, yet we must remember that they really are avoidable with the help of God's grace, and that God never refuses this grace. Perhaps if one were to consider merely the natural psychology of man, one would have to take a pessimistic view of his interior powers of self-control and self-determination. But we have the assurance from revelation that God's grace is sufficient for us and that He will not allow us to be tempted

---

[11] *L'Ami du clergé*, Jan. 17, 1952, p. 46; and Feb. 28, 1952, p. 140.

[12] Sermon of Pope Pius XII ("*La predica penitenziale*"), March 26, 1950, *Atti e Discorsi di Pio XII*, 12 (1950), 54–61 at 57; Rome: Editioni Paolini, 1954.

beyond our strength. That is why we can speak of Christian heroism and why we can demand at times fidelity to the teaching of Christ at the price of heroic sacrifices, and this under pain of serious sin. Such demands would be hard to understand unless we could count on God's special help for special difficulties.

However, we should not interpret the phrase "My grace is sufficient for thee" to mean that God promises to preserve everyone even from material mortal sin. Suppose a case of a madman who goes berserk and murders his custodian. He commits a material mortal sin. Did this happen because he failed to cooperate with the grace of God? Was God's grace sufficient to keep him from being tempted above his strength if only he had accepted it, then or earlier? No one believes any such thing, because such a person is simply incapable of any cooperation. Something similar could be true of one who is not so sick that he is incapable of a human act altogether, but is sick enough so that he is pathologically impelled to the commission of a sinful act. And so once more we see how important it is to distinguish between those who are sick and those who are well. This makes all the more damaging the error of those who would have us believe that as a result of original sin (or as a consequence of unconscious domination) everyone is mentally or emotionally ill.

At all events the promise "My grace is sufficient for thee" means sufficient grace to preserve from formal sin. It does not tell us that, no matter what the interior pressure, God's help is always so abundant that there will be no material sin by one who cooperates with it. We are in a mysterious realm here in which often enough we simply do not know when human helps are in vain and only the divine help of

[218]

grace can avail. But in doing battle against the *mysterium iniquitatis*, the tragedy that afflicts mankind, medicinal grace and mental hygiene do not exclude one another. The man of faith relies on all the help there is, both natural and supernatural. Even St. Paul could have invoked all his own natural powers of self-control, and in addition whatever assistance he could find from the philosophers and sages of his time, and still cry out with a whole heart: "Unhappy man that I am! Who will deliver me from the body of this death? The grace of God through Jesus Christ our Lord."[13]

Having seen some of the guideposts which keep us from being too lenient in setting the standards of grave culpability, we shall turn now to some considerations which will keep us from being too severe in our judgments of consciences.

Let us center our discussion around two questions which are sometimes put to penitents (and very usefully) in order to elicit from them information about their subjective dispositions at the time an objectively mortal sin was committed. The first question is: *"Did you realize fully that it was a grave sin?"* The second: *"Could you have resisted?"*

"DID YOU REALIZE FULLY?"

It will be seen that we have in mind here the type of case which involves, for instance, a deeply ingrained sexual habit, or an "irresistible" impulse, or an addictive urge, or an obsessive attraction, with its mono-ideistic narrowing of consciousness to a single object of sense desire. We are supposing, too, a case in which the penitent understands the import of these questions and is capable of giving an ac-

13 Romans 7:24.

curate account of his own inner experience at the time of the event.

Unless we are mistaken, it would be improper to conclude universally from an affirmative answer to either one of these questions, or to both of them, that there must have been a mortal sin.

The first question: *"Did you realize fully that it was a grave sin?"* has to do with sufficient advertence and deliberation. It is like the "right and wrong" test of criminal law.[14] Is it universally true that in the presence of sufficient advertence, there always follows automatically sufficient consent of the will? Moralists, canonists and scholastic philosophers have hesitated to admit that with the use of reason unimpaired, with intellectual perception intact, the will can be anything but sufficiently free.[15] They appeal to St.

[14] The so-called "right and wrong test" is taken from the Rules in M'Naghten's Case. See *infra*, chapter 12, note 5. English law, unlike Scots law, did not admit the doctrine of diminished imputability. A man was either guilty of a crime or not. One reason why the right and wrong test has been under severe attack by psychiatrists is that it does not take an adequate view of the psychological facts. It relies exclusively on an appeal to the intellectual perception of right and wrong, giving scant consideration to the disordered emotional factors that so frequently affect criminal conduct. The criticisms which are made of this test of criminal imputability, therefore, may well raise doubts as to the validity of a similar test (the sufficient advertence test) of moral imputability;—especially since the right and wrong test was undoubtedly based on the traditional moral philosophy of Christendom.

[15] Hence they repudiated the notion of "moral insanity" as it was first proposed (in England) because they considered it clearly incompatible with free will. In psychiatric terminology the person who was formerly called "morally insane" or "constitutionally immoral" now seems to have become the "constitutional psychopath." On moral insanity see: Franciscus Roberti, *De delictis et pœnis* (Rome: Catholic Book Agency, Piazza Ponte S. Angelo, 28, n.d.), vol. I, pars 1, n. 120 sq.; J. S. Cammack, S.J., *Moral Problems of Mental Defect* (New York: Benziger, 1939), p. 89 sq.; Coronata, *Institutiones iuris canonici* (Turin: Marietti, 1935), vol. IV, n. 1657; Vermeersch, *Theologia moralis*, etc., vol. I, n. 83; Benedict Merkelbach, O.P., *Summa theologiæ moralis* (3rd ed.; Paris: Desclée, de Brouwer, 1938), vol. I, n. 99, note.

Thomas: "To whatever extent reason remains free and not subjected to passion, to that extent the movement of the will which remains does not tend with necessity toward the object to which passion inclines." [16] Since the will is blind,

16 "In quantum ergo ratio manet libera, et passioni non subjecta, in-tantum voluntatis motus, qui manet, non ex necessitate tendit ad hoc ad quod passio inclinat."–1ª 2ᵃᵉ, q. 10, a. 1. Joseph S. Duhamel, S.J. comments on this passage: "To state that man is always free in his actions unless passion or other impediments interfere with the cognitive element of the human act is not what St. Thomas says here; nor is it a justified conclusion from the words of St. Thomas, as we shall see later. It is also contrary to fact. Apart from the testimony of psychiatry on the existence of compulsive acts and irresistible impulses, I am sure that every priest has met with this experience: a penitent has admitted clear knowledge of and actual advert-ence to the sinful and gravely sinful nature of a proposed action, yet has also protested sincerely but stubbornly that he had little or no power to resist and is convinced that he is not guilty of sin or, at least, of mortal sin." In a later part of the article Father Duhamel continues: "Man is an *unum per se*. All his appetitive faculties are radicated in his own soul. For this reason a spontaneous impulse of his sensitive appetite can trigger a spontaneous impulse of his rational appetite toward the same sensitive good even when it is known to be morally evil. But his executive powers are also radicated in his one soul. For this reason it is also possible that the im-pulse in his sensitive appetite is so strong that, despite evaluative cognition of the sinful nature of the act to which there is the impulse, the executive powers carry out the act completely or partially on the level of an *actus hominis*. In this case no will act is posited to command the external action. St. Thomas wrote that, to the extent that reason remains free and not sub-ject to passion, to that extent the *movement of the will, that remains*, does not tend with necessity to that to which passion inclines. In compulsive actions there is no movement of the will that remains; we are in the sphere of the *actus hominis*, not of the *actus humanus*. It is one thing to say that every act of the will that follows unimpeded deliberation is completely free; that is true, and St. Thomas said that. But it is a very different thing to say that every external action of man that takes place despite clear at-tention to the sinful nature of the action is a (denominately) free action and under the complete control of the will; St. Thomas did not say that, and it cannot be proved"–"Theological and Psychiatric Aspects of Habitual Sin. I. Theological Aspects" by Joseph S. Duhamel, S.J., "II. Psychiatric Aspects," by Jerome Hayden, O.S.B., *Proceedings of the Eleventh Annual Convention of the Catholic Theological Society of America* (1956), pp. 130–63 at p. 134 and at pp. 138, 139. In Thomistic psychology the final free choice of the will must always be in accordance with the *judicium ultimo-practicum*. But moralists should not forget that there are serious theoretical problems, disputed for many years among the scholastics, as to the nature of the mutual influence of intellect and will in the final produc-

they say, it must follow the act of the intellect and correspond with it.[17] Furthermore, since the will is a spiritual
faculty, passion and similar obstacles to human acts can
affect it only through the intellect, only inasmuch as they
can interfere with intellectual cognition.

But, apparently scholastic psychologists today would not
consider that given the mere cognition of the right and
wrong of an act the subsequent choice of the will is necessarily free.

For instance, J. S. Cammack, S.J., who demolishes philosophically and psychologically the theory of moral insanity,
is able nevertheless to say:

It is almost universally accepted now that real moral action is
not based on mere abstract knowledge, but on deeper "senti-
ments" which provide adequate motives for action by organizing
groups of emotions around, and in association with, certain
intellectual perceptions.[18]

Rudolf Allers describes the dissociation of emotional and
intellectual elements that is characteristic of schizophrenia.
It is not intended that what he says here of the incapacity
of the schizophrenic for human acts can be transferred to
the case of every emotionally disturbed or compulsive person, but it illustrates a scholastic philosopher's willingness
to admit that a person may be irresponsible while the operations of the intellect are still formally intact:

---

tion of the free act. No doubt the obscurities of our present discussion
originate in part from these disputes.

[17] See, for example, J. Noldin, S.J., *Summa theologiæ moralis*, vol. I, n.
61, ad fin.: "Quoniam voluntas in suis actibus *directe* solum a cognitione
dependet, ipsa, prælucente cognitione quae requiritur, semper expedita et
libera est. Hinc fieri nequit, ut morali libertate *omnino* careat, qui actionis
suæ moralem bonitatem et malitiam *sufficienter* apprehendit" (Italics ours).

[18] J. S. Cammack, S.J., *Moral Problems of Mental Defect* (New York:
Benziger, 1939), p. 95, note.

Though a normally functioning intellect is a *conditio sine qua non* of free consent, it is not the only factor influencing decision and volitional activity. Human acts are determined not only by reason but very much by emotional factors and by imagination (taking this term as used in Scholastic psychology). Schizophrenia is characterized especially by a dissociation of emotional and intellectual states; the normal emotional reaction to values or goods, by which the intensity of volition becomes reinforced, is destroyed. Influenced by abnormal emotional life and by a curious transformation of the general ideas on reality, though the operations of the intellect are still formally intact, the will can no longer be said to be free in a schizophrenic personality. The schizophrenic process is not one which would attack this or that faculty or operation, but is a definite and profound alteration of the whole personality. From the very moment this process has set in, normal personality ceases to exist. It is quite safe to advance as a general principle that whenever there is sufficient reason for supposing schizophrenic trouble to have existed at the time of contracting marriage, there was no possibility of free and rational consent.[19]

Dr. Allers speaks here of serious mental illness, and not of consent to sin but of consent to marriage, which may require a higher degree of discretion. We would like to see further studies by other students of scholastic philosophy and modern psychology which would explore the relationship between advertence and eventual consent in cases of less radical emotional disturbance. Meantime we offer some tentative considerations which incline us to believe that the advertence test, though it may be a criterion of philosophical freedom, is not apodictical as far as grave imputability is concerned.

[19] Rudolf Allers, "Annulment of Marriage by Lack of Consent because of Insanity," *American Ecclesiastical Review*, 101 (1939), 325-43 at 336.

The first of these considerations is the distinction between conceptual cognition and evaluative cognition, which has its principal application in practical judgments such as the judgments of conscience, and decisions in practical affairs. Conceptual cognition expresses, they tell us, what the object is; evaluative cognition appraises the value the object has. The normal adult, making everyday judgments in practical matters, perceives both in the same act of cognition. But there are cases, more or less pathological, in which, according to the psychologists, conceptual cognition is present without evaluative cognition. If this takes place, one could have full conceptual advertence but still might not have sufficient advertence for grave imputability. We will discuss this concept in more detail in a later chapter. Since the evaluation referred to may depend on emotional as well as on intellectual factors (see the passage just quoted from Father Cammack) this opinion leaves room for emotional interference with full consent even though the abstract or conceptual operation is intact. In the case of ingrained habits which affect the voluntary, this evaluative cognition of the grave sinfulness of an act may be habitually present in this individual; but under the influence of habit and passion (or the unconscious) the evaluative cognition recedes into the background of consciousness. The person knows that this is a gravely sinful act (conceptual cognition) and there is actual advertence to that conceptual cognition; however, the impediments to freedom rob that knowledge of its reality and implications (evaluative cognition). Hence despite sufficient conceptual knowledge that the act is a mortal sin, freedom and imputability should be measured not in proportion to that knowledge but rather in proportion to the evaluative knowledge which has been greatly disturbed or totally, though temporarily, suppressed.[20]

This distinction is further explained and exemplified in a very interesting comment by John J. Lynch, S.J.:

This notion of evaluative cognition is no novelty in moral theology. But it may be so taken for granted that some of its practical applications are overlooked. We would admit certainly that a child of four or five may have learned to distinguish between good and bad, and have come to predicate good or bad correctly of certain actions. But we would hesitate to say that the child appreciates the real significance of goodness or badness, that he has a full realization of their moral implications. The dawning of that evaluative concept is gradual in a child. It is impossible to say just when the realization comes, but until it does come it is impossible to conceive the child as guilty of real sin. That lack of appreciation, realization, evaluation of the meaning behind the concept of sin, while it need not in any way affect the freedom of the physical act, quite definitely affects its imputability as a morally culpable act. Knowledge requisite for subjective sin involves something substantially more than ability to identify an act as sinful.

Does not the same distinction explain what we mean when we speak of a person under the influence of liquor as losing his moral inhibitions? All moralists admit that responsibility for sinful acts committed in such circumstances may be diminished in varying degrees. And yet many a person under the influence is still able to recognize a contemplated act as sinful. The fact of its being sinful, however, no longer makes any impression on him, or makes far less impression than it ordinarily would. And can it also be said perhaps of the person of hardened conscience that he eventually becomes so familiar with sin as to be no longer swayed by the realization of sin? Has he lost—culpably,

[20] Duhamel, *art. cit.*, pp. 137–38.

of course, through his induced habit of deliberate sin—that evaluative concept of right and wrong necessary for unqualified guilt?

It is not destroying the notion of subjective sin to insist that this evaluative concept of evil is necessary for true guilt, or to admit the possibility of that concept's being temporarily or even permanently impaired, in people of otherwise normal intelligence, by some psychological abnormality. The difficulty in practice comes in the attempt to verify this exceptional phenomenon in individual cases. Usually it would be extremely hazardous to express the absolute conviction that an otherwise intelligent person lacks this moral perception. But there is reason to think that some do with respect to one or another or even all species of sin, and we should keep an open mind, . . . if legitimate psychological evidence to this effect can be presented.[21]

Pope Pius XII cannot be quoted, perhaps, in favor of the distinction between evaluative and conceptual cognition, but it is somewhat surprising to find him, in an address to representatives of the Italian film industry, speaking of the emotional or affective side of man as decisive in determining his judgment and action. He was speaking about the production of the ideal film in relation to the audience which will view it:

All you have to do in this matter is to let yourself be guided by good common sense. The normal man has what we might call an unlearned psychology, which comes from his very nature, and which enables him to make the proper decisions in the ordinary problems of daily life, provided that he follows his sound common sense, his knowledge of reality and the advice of his own experience. But, an even more important provision is

---

[21] John J. Lynch, S.J., "Notes on Moral Theology," *Theological Studies*, 17 (June, 1956), 167–96 at 169.

that the affective element in him be well-ordered and regulated, since in the last instance, the thing that determines a man's judgment and action is his affective disposition at the moment.[22]

The second consideration is an analogy between the dependence of the intellect on the phantasm and the dependence of the will on the emotions. In scholastic psychology continual stress is laid on the extrinsic dependence of the intellect on the phantasm, or imagination. It is emphasized that a disturbance of the phantasm can result in a disturbance of reason—even a complete disturbance. The authors are at great pains to account for and theorize about the mysterious process by which the phantasm exercises its causality on the intellect, bridging the gap between the material and the spiritual.

When the spiritual will, following upon the deliberation of the intellect, elicits an act which is philosophically free, may there not be an analogous dependence on the emotions as far as its psychological freedom is concerned? In other words may not the internal act of choice itself depend to some extent, that is for its psychological freedom, on healthy emotional functioning, just as the intellect depends on the healthy functioning of the phantasm? The result would be that passion, emotion, and concupiscence could have their effect on the will more directly, and not merely through the operations of the intellect. The mystery would not be greater in the case of emotion acting on will than in the case of phantasm acting on intellect. The emotions and

[22] "The Movies and the Nature of Man," address of Pius XII to Representatives of the Italian Film Industry, June 21, 1955, *AAS*, 47 (1955), 501–12 at 510. See *The Pope Speaks*, 2 (1955), 101–12. But see *Humani generis*, AAS, 42 (1950), 574, for a carefully-worded statement on the role of the will and emotions in knowing and embracing religious and moral truths.

[227]

the will are both rooted in the same fundamental principle of operation ("*radicantur in eadem anima*").[23] Perhaps this or some other philosophical principle could be used in an attempt to solve the mystery. But whatever the explanation, there seems to be no insuperable philosophical objection to making the attempt.

Furthermore, when the spiritual will, enlightened by the deliberations of the intellect, makes its choice and commands an external act of the body, is there not still an analogous dependence of the free will on the emotions, on the sense appetites and instincts? Is there not here, also, a bridge to be crossed?—from the spiritual act of the will to the material acts of bodily execution? Is there any philosophical objection to the assertion that emotional pathology can block that crossing, even though the intellectual operation of deliberation remains essentially unimpaired?

In this view, emotional disturbance could destroy freedom not only by blinding the intellect beforehand and preventing deliberation, but also during and after the act of the will, in the sense that it could diminish psychological freedom or even effectively block the execution of the free will's commands, thus depriving the individual of the power of disposing of his activities.

"COULD YOU HAVE RESISTED?"

The second question, "Could you have resisted?" has to do with the sufficient consent of the will, and is another way of asking whether the person acted from a so-called "irresistible impulse." We shall use the familiar case of a severe habit of masturbation to make more concrete the point we are discussing here. This will illustrate aspects

[23] Duhamel, *art. cit.*, pp. 138–39.

both of the first question, on sufficient advertence, and of the second one, on sufficient consent, as well as the distinction between philosophical freedom and psychological freedom. We are principally concerned here only with the question of subjective imputability under the severe stress of concupiscence and habit, but will make some incidental remarks as to the pastoral handling of these problems.

The phrase "irresistible impulse" is particularly unfortunate for the purposes of the moralist. Apart from the confusing connotations of criminal court usage, the word "impulse" means primarily an impulsive movement of passion such as occurs in a sudden eruption of intense anger, or a sexual outburst, also sudden and overpowering. In these impulses there is no question of deliberation, or at least no question of the kind of deliberation required for grave guilt; and so there is no great moral problem to be solved. The case we wish to explore is concerned rather with a continuing fascination, or attraction, or temptation, which may almost obsess the mind, but which does not usually exclude all advertence to the malice of the act. The word urge describes it more accurately than the word *impulse*. As for the word "irresistible," that is misleading, too, as regards our purpose. For an urge may be resistible as far as philosophical freedom is concerned, and yet be so inhibitory of psychological freedom that the person's acts are no longer gravely imputable to him.

The moralist's chief concern is not to find out whether a persistent urge was irresistible or not in the absolute sense, which precludes a human act entirely, but to find out whether it was so intense that even though philosophical liberty was not destroyed the possibility of mortal guilt was. Consequently the word "compulsive," though not entirely satisfactory is closer to our real meaning. It does not have an absolute connotation. Compulsions admit of degrees. They affect the mind with greater or lesser force and with greater or lesser frequency. We prefer, therefore the term *compulsive urge* to the term *irresistible impulse*. But in using it to describe the morbid attraction, or compelling fascination with which the mind of the habitual masturbator dwells on the thought of self-abuse for some time before the act takes place, we do not intend to prejudge the question of his moral responsibility. It merely describes an event in which his resistance *de facto* gives way to the compelling force of passion.

A compulsive urge in order to be compulsive need not be such in all circumstances. An urge which in some circumstances is very intense and dominating may be counteracted by other factors. It is no argument against the irresistibility of a kleptomaniac's impulse to steal that he would not have done it if there was a policeman at his elbow.[24] The fact that a compulsive drinker stops drinking after he joins A.A. is not a proof (as we have heard said) that he was not a compulsive drinker in the first place. The fact that a masturbator does not yield to his morbid urge in the presence of other people does not prove that the urge is not compulsive when he is alone. Consequently, it is impossible to say once and for all that a given urge is cumpulsive or not. In the same individual it may be compulsive one day and another day not compulsive. Even actions that require longer preparation or a series of preliminary steps may be compulsively performed. Dr. Rudolf Allers notes:

There are also within normality [i.e. apart from definite mental

[24] Rudolf Allers, "Irresistible Impulses: A Question of Moral Psychology," *American Ecclesiastical Review*, 100 (1939), 208–19 at 208–09.

disease] certain states of mono-ideistic narrowing of consciousness in which the subject may act quite reasonably in regard to his one dominant purpose, while no other thought can enter the mind and while, accordingly, no motives counteracting his idea ever become efficient.[25]

In order that the will can make a free choice with liberty of indifference, there must be an appearance of good in both alternatives. In this sense there must be present to the mind motives in each direction. On the other hand it is stated that the will is necessitated only when presented with infinite good. This would seem to mean that even with an enormous disparity of motives the will would remain philosophically free. Whether this is true or not, the same thing is not true of the degree of psychological freedom requisite for grave human imputability. Lindworsky remarks, much to the point: "We . . . call the will free if, at least within certain limits of value, it can consciously strive or not strive for a value, or if in view of two equal, or at least not too dissimilar values, it can deliberately choose the one or the other." [26] We believe that in order to have the degree of freedom necessary to commit mortal sin there must not be too great a disparity in the attraction of the values represented to the mind. In the case of mono-ideistic narrowing of consciousness and of pathological fascination with the object of desire such disparity often exists.

There is another reason, too, why compulsive urges become overpowering and are not *de facto* resisted: the conviction of the person that the urge is irresistible. This

[25] *Ibid.*, p. 210.
[26] Johann Lindworsky, S.J., *The Training of the Will*, (Milwaukee: Bruce, 1929), p. 70.

conviction may come from hopelessness induced by past experience of continual defeat, or it may be born of false teaching. For example, the person has been taught that any pathological impulse is *ipso facto* uncontrollable, or that once an unconscious factor is uncovered the act is caused with fatalistic necessity.[27] It makes little difference from the viewpoint of imputability whether the irresistibility comes from the impulse itself or only from the false but sincere interior conviction. But from the viewpoint of treatment the latter case will be much easier to deal with. A further distinction made by Professor Allers is useful to us:

Another necessary distinction is the one between irresistibility caused by the mere strength of the impulse and the one arising from the alleged intolerability of the situation which is going to be changed only by obeying the impulse. The first case is seen in certain actions caused by passion: in a fit of violent anger it is the strength of the aggressive impulse which overpowers all the other faculties. The second case is evident in many sexual acts: the impulse is not the important feature in the whole situation; it is the great tension, the craving for relief which is not to be resisted.[28]

In these latter cases the subject of the compulsive urge finally yields to it to avoid intolerable pain. He says afterwards: "I had to give in"; "I could resist no longer." Yielding involves an act of the will, and we agree with Professor Allers that there is "at least some little bit of freedom left

[27] Allers, *art. cit.*, p. 211. Dr. Allers discounts to a large extent the influence of the unconscious in these urges, *art. cit.*, p. 217. Those who are psychoanalytically inclined consider that pathological urges, e.g., to homosexuality, though they may not be less imputable by reason of their intensity, may be less so because they are more under the domination of the unconscious.

[28] Allers, *art. cit.*, pp. 214-15.

in these cases." A final remark of Dr. Allers is very searching and very illuminating:

There is one very curious and very important feature worthy of mention in those irresistible impulses. They become irresistible, so to say, before they have fully developed. People have a presentiment of the impulse arising; they know that within a short time they will become entangled in a situation from which there is no escape, much as they desire one. They know that they are still capable, this very moment, of turning away and that by doing so they will avoid the danger—but they do not. There is a peculiar fascination, a lurid attraction in this kind of danger, and there is evidently some anticipation of the satisfaction that the *partes inferiores animæ* will derive from indulging in the "irresistible" action. This action itself may, therefore, not carry any responsibility and nevertheless not be excusable, because in fact the person has assented to its development.[29]

The assent to the development of the impulse may also be only half deliberate, but it is often the disguised expression of a desire for sexual satisfaction. Hence it is important to point out to such persons the latent insincerity in their protestations that they "did not want it to happen."

RECENT VIEWS ON IMPUTABILITY OF HABITUAL SELF-ABUSE

Keeping these psychological points in mind, we can now go on to consider some recent views on the subjective imputability of habitual self-abuse. There is a strong tendency among modern Catholic writers to be lenient in the estimate of grave culpability where this kind of sexual difficulty is concerned. We already saw the opinion of Oraison, who for all practical purposes seemed to exclude mortal sin from these cases. Another author who exhibits a very similar

[29] Allers, *art. cit.*, pp. 216–17.

point of view is Baron Frederick Von Gagern, M.D. He writes:

It is not to be denied that self-abuse can be practised with conscious purpose and freedom of will; but I have never come across such a case. But is not every genuine onanist [masturbator] suffering from psycho-physical infantilism, a species of spiritual immaturity looked upon as diminishing the weight of guilt? In general terms, what is the position with regard to clear knowledge and freedom of the will? Medical science tells us that all states of sexual tension have a detrimental and inhibitive influence upon the cerebral centre of mental processes. The urge towards detumescence—expulsion of the semen—can be far stronger than the instinct of self-preservation. . . . A man given to self-abuse will go on doing it, even if he fully believes in the severe injury to health which he has been told will ensue. How much less will he be restrained by the much less tangible idea of spiritual injury. In truth he is quite unable to grasp the moral weight of what he does; he simply does not realize the mortal sin.

From my own observation I would say that the majority of those who practice self-abuse or extra-matrimonial intercourse would utterly repudiate the idea that they do anything contrary to the will of God or desire to separate themselves from Him. They are not able to think clearly in this field, so completely is it dominated by the sexual urge. The reality of God seems very dim and remote, even when He is thought about at all. . . .

In the field of mind, the processes are subject to domination by elements surging from the subconscious, forces of an instinctive nature bringing the personality more or less under compulsion. These subconscious motives give rise to an urge towards self-abuse, and the conscious will is not strong enough to check them; thus a position arises in which we can hardly speak of freedom of the will.[30]

[30] Baron Frederick Von Gagern, M.D., *The Problem of Onanism*, trans.

Dr. Von Gagern apparently believes that mortal sin is impossible as long as there is no clear and explicit repudiation of Almighty God. This is not the view theologians have taken. But one must remember that he does not profess to speak as a theologian and that his remarks are based on his own professional practice. Presumably the masturbators he encounters are persons who are sick enough to require medical or psychiatric treatment. Reduction of imputability beyond the point of mortal sin is very frequent in such patients.

There is an appendix to Dr. Von Gagern's work which includes "Moral and Theological Notes on the Problem of Self-Abuse." These notes were written by Rupert Angermair, a professor of moral theology at Freising. His comments on subjective imputability serve as a necessary corrective to the statements of the physician. He says, in part:

How far . . . we may regard each specific act as a sin, or a mortal sin, will depend upon the subjective conditions determining it: how far actual knowledge was present and how free was the will. In this connection it must be said that knowledge and will are more easily and more seriously diminished and weakened in the case of a sin of this sort—which is so bound up with the emotions and so immediately linked to the confused life of

from German by Meyrick Booth, Ph.D. (Westminster, Md.: The Newman Press, 1955), pp. 90–91. In *Clergy Review*, 41 (Nov., 1956), 678–82, a correspondent inquires whether Von Gagern's book should be included in the condemnation of Oraison's work, since the teaching seems to be so similar. Lawrence McReavy replies in the negative. The Holy Office did not publish the reasons why Oraison's book was put on the Index. Furthermore Von Gagern does not speak as a theologian, but provides an Appendix in which professional moralists of obvious competence treat the moral problem *ex professo*. Another difference may be that Von Gagern, a physician and psychiatrist, is speaking principally of pathological cases from his practice.

[235]

the senses—than with many other sins, such as the neglect of religious duties or of duty to love the neighbour. . . .

. . . If the set-backs become increasingly rare, that may be taken as a sign that the will to overcome can be lasting and effective. The physical act does not give rise to "sin," nor does the will that is innocent, but too weak; but only a *bad* will and the free personal decision to do wrong. One cannot climb out of a bog with a single stride. . . .

In specific cases, full consciousness and relatively free will is not readily to be assumed if the actual act occurs suddenly, following upon a lengthy period of indecision, when the subject is pulled this way and that by desire and resistance, and, looking back, cannot recollect a precise moment of consent. The penitent who acted with full consent will usually be aware of the fact. In other cases, it is perhaps more the *id*, the lower urges below the level of consciousness, which has swept the penitent away, than the real self, acting as a free agent of consent. If he has the impression that he did not "come to himself" until after the act, we can assume that beforehand he was not fully himself—at any rate not in the "existential depth" of his true ego. In the same fashion, we may doubt the presence of adequate consciousness and free will in cases of morbid depression of mind and spirit and of strong emotional excitement (not self-induced), or where we have a partially conscious state, as when half asleep. Similar reasoning may be applied to the penitent who normally regards a grave sin with horror and at once returns to his normal attitude in case of being overtaken by a sudden set-back, and is able to say that he would never have fallen had he been in full possession of himself; one who is sincerely struggling to find the right path may well argue thus. The sin of self-abuse, it must not be forgotten, invades the personality as a whole; and while bearing the foregoing in mind we must not forget that persons given to the practice are more inclined in many cases than are other sinners to bring forward somewhat weak excuses for their actions.

Above all the priest must not forget that, even if the subjective character of particular cases may be judged mildly, the attitude of the onanist [masturbator] in general must be looked upon as highly regrettable. For this reason the priest must never regard his task as finished when he has passed judgment upon the sins of the past; he is the shepherd of souls and his function as judge must be supplemented by giving responsible aid for the future.[31]

Also much more reserved in his judgment than Dr. Von Gagern, and likewise taking into account the data of modern psychology, is André Snoeck, S.J. He writes on masturbation and grave sin in a symposium which is principally concerned with masturbation among boys at about the age of puberty. He insists on the objective grave malice of even a single act of masturbation, and then adds that this objective judgment of Christian morality, though severe, "*is valid for an act posited voluntarily by a man who has reached his spiritual maturity and who acts with sufficient liberty.*" [32] (Father Snoeck's italics.) Later when speaking of subjective imputability he says:

[31] Rupert Angermair, "Moral and Theological Notes on the Problems of Self-Abuse," Appendix to Von Gagern, *op. cit.*, pp. 115–19 at 116–17. This article appeared originally in *Katechetische Blätter*, Munich and Kempton: Kösel Verlag, September, 1950. An excellent treatment of the moral side of this problem is found in another article from the same publication, also reprinted as an Appendix to Von Gagern's work, pp. 129–35, "The Moral and Religious Guilt of the Act of Self-Abuse," by Heinz Fleckenstein, Professor of Moral Theology, Würzburg. Like most modern Catholic authors of all schools he is ready to accept modern psychological findings and to judge subjective guilt leniently in the light of these findings. He is particularly clear in the points he offers confessors for judging subjective guilt.

[32] André Snoeck, S.J., "Masturbation et péché grave," *Cahiers Laënnec*, 10 (1950), 21–31 at 25. Translated in *New Problems in Medical Ethics*, edited by Peter Flood, O.S.B., I (Westminster, Md.: The Newman Press, 1953), 35–44 at 39.

The demands of the objective norm should be measured, *hic et nunc*, to the strength of each and adapted to the present structure of the personality. Whatever may be said of other cases which we cannot discuss here, the case of the child is clear to us. Indeed, to submit the child to demands which are imposed on the fully mature adult, would be not only to commit an injustice—because the child does not appreciate the data of the problem in the same manner as the adult—but also to occasion the risk of causing grave psychical damage by the fact that punishment, when not understood, always causes anguish. However, this is not meant as implying that the child is not capable of a free act; we merely consider that certain demands are in excess of what he is in a condition to understand and to give here and now. Law, both ecclesiastical and civil, has special dispositions for children, and accepts, as self-evident, attenuations of responsibility. Consequently, why should the same norm be applied to the child at the age of puberty and who does not know how to conquer his disequilibrium, as those applied to a person who has already attained his human maturity? [33]

Father Angermair, in examining the excuses from grave culpability, appeals principally to the struggle between desire and resistance in which resistance is finally overcome by the force of passion. This is the question of full consent and compulsive urges. Father Snoeck on the other hand relies principally on immaturity of appraisal in the adolescent. This may correspond to what we called above a lack of evaluative cognition. The two passages of Father Snoeck just quoted, when taken together, seem to imply that there is a general presumption against mortal guilt in masturbation that occurs about the age of puberty; but his thought is not quite clear on the point.

[33] Snoeck, *art. cit.*, p. 28; *New Problems in Medical Ethics, loc. cit.*, pp. 41–42.

Rather than admit any such general presumption we prefer to say that the cases in which grave subjective guilt is absent occur frequently but that each case has to be decided on its merits. We think this position is more in accord with the statements of Pius XII quoted on pp. 215–16. Just as it is improper to apply rigidly a mechanical rule based on mere intellectual advertence to the malice of the act, so also it is a mistake to rely on a mechanical rule based on a general presumption of irresponsibility. The only general rule which we would recommend at present is this: Subjective disabilities and impediments excuse the average man and woman from mortal guilt much more frequently than a reading of moral theology manuals might lead one to suppose.

PASTORAL PRACTICE

In making a judgment of grave guilt the confessor will have to rely first of all on the enlightened testimony of the penitent's own conscience. God judges men on the basis of their conscious motives and decisions. It may be that the unconscious is playing a significant role in this penitent's conduct, but the confessor is a poor judge of that. Even psychiatrists will disagree vigorously on the significance of unconscious factors in a given case. The authors quoted above attribute a great deal of influence to the dynamic unconscious, but others warn us not to conclude too hastily to psychoanalytical explanations, because hidden insincerities, habits, and other psychological factors may be to blame.[34] At any rate the confessor must rely principally on the conscious data supplied by the penitent himself. But we added "of an enlightened conscience" because so many

[34] Allers, art. cit., p. 211.

penitents are ignorant or confused and are poor witnesses to their own inner experience.

When exploring the conscience of the penitent, the two questions we have discussed at such length can be very useful: "Did you realize fully it was a grave sin?" and "Could you have resisted?" Our criticism of these questions was by no means meant to deny that they are frequently useful. We merely pointed out that affirmative answers to these questions do not indicate *conclusively* that mortal sin has taken place. Intelligent negative answers to them can indicate clearly that mortal sin has not taken place.

We mention here, without elaboration, some further criteria or considerations which when present should lead the confessor to judge leniently the question of mortal guilt in individual cases. When several of them are present together there is all the more reason for asserting that there is no grave culpability.

The first of these is a history of mental or emotional illness, nervous breakdowns, etc. With penitents who have been and still more who are presently under psychiatric or neurological care there is often a strong reason for doubting grave guilt.

Secondly, the fact that there is a severe habit, that is, one of long duration and inveterate frequency, but which the penitent is seriously trying to overcome, is itself an argument for lenient judgment. Some persons are much more prone to form enslaving habits, whether physiological or psychological, than others. They are spoken of as addictive personalities. Some quickly develop habituation or addiction to drugs or alcohol or almost anything of a sense-satisfying kind. Some seem to be peculiarly susceptible to the formation of compulsive, repetitious patterns of behavior. Such habits are more or less pathological; and it is the psychiatrist who is the judge of pathology. But when these habits do occur there is good reason for asserting that grave guilt is absent.[35]

Thirdly, the intensity of sexual passion when thoroughly aroused can be overpowering. It often precludes not merely grave guilt, but any human act at all during the moments when it is at its height. The scholastic theologians of the Middle Ages disputed as to the reasons which would justify or excuse the marriage act, because they took it for granted that a man was deprived temporarily of the use of reason during that act. "Ratio absorbetur in congressu sexuali," they said. Such a deliberate deprivation of the use of reason required a justifying cause. It is not to be thought that in every act of self-abuse passion is so intense; but if a person has resisted and refused consent up to the point where passion is very intense, or orgasm is almost at hand, he should be presumed not to be gravely responsible for what thereupon takes place.

Fourthly, the fascinated narrowing of consciousness to one all-absorbing object of desire can exclude any realistic appraisal of the alternatives to that desire, and thus reduce psychological liberty beyond the point where mortal guilt is possible.

[35] See Canon P. Tiberghien, "Vice et maladie," *Mélanges de science religieuse*, 5 (1948), 197–216. Father Duhamel, art. cit., p. 145, reaches a conclusion in agreement with our own: "If all the elements that diminish imputability are carefully assessed in each case, I suggest that, far more often than we have generally been willing to admit in the past, there will be serious doubt whether the subjective guilt of mortal sin was actually contracted, and, at times, there will be sufficient evidence to warrant the conclusion that there was no subjective mortal guilt." This is one of three general conclusions on the subjective guilt in the individual actions of the habitual sinner who is normal, and Father Duhamel states that although these conclusions have particular reference to the habit of masturbation, he considers them generally valid.

Fifthly, a sudden onslaught of passion that takes one unawares will hardly leave the opportunity for sufficient deliberation.

Sixthly, senseless, unsatisfying, frequent repetitions of the act of self-abuse within a short time are a sign of pathological impulse and an indication of greatly reduced responsibility.

Seventhly, the indulgence of fantastic ideas during the struggle with temptation, for example: "This is another person, not I, who is doing this," or "The natural law is different for me," or "I am dreaming that I am doing this," etc.,—all these and similar confabulations or irrational defenses show that a person is not himself and are arguments against grave culpability.

Finally, and perhaps most important of all in helping the confessor to make his judgment is a knowledge of the general state of the penitent's soul. If a penitent is making serious efforts to lead a life pleasing to God; if he is sincerely trying to overcome this habit and avoid the individual acts; if he avoids the occasions that are avoidable, frequents the sacraments and is constant in prayer; and especially if on the individual occasions when temptation comes he does not yield except after a long struggle or a hard one—the confessor should be lenient in judging the case.

A confessor or spiritual guide cannot form a prudent judgment about the state of the penitent's soul unless he takes the time and the trouble to do so. If penitents are rushed in and out of the confessional they may receive valid absolution, but the confessor will fail in his office not only as a teacher, father, and physician, but, in these difficult cases, in his essential role of judge. Many of these cases can be dealt with much more effectively by the spiritual counselor outside the confessional. When the confessor or spiritual father has taken the trouble to understand the penitent's case well enough to make a prudent judgment about it, he should then help him to know the true state of his soul, whatever it is.

He should tell him the truth as he sees it. His judgment is a human and imperfect one, but our Lord has instituted the sacrament of penance in such a way that He wants to make use of our human and fallible judgments in applying the grace of the sacrament to the soul of the sinner. Let the confessor tell the penitent the truth. Not the unexplained truth: "You committed mortal sin," or "You did not commit mortal sin"; but the truth with kindness and tact, the truth with appropriate advice and encouragement. For no matter what the truth is as to the mortal guilt of the penitent there is still work to be done: the eradication of the bad habit. Nothing will serve as a better foundation for helping the penitent to understand himself and accomplish this task than the truth about the state of his soul. Only on this basis can the confessor or spiritual father cooperate effectively in his restoration.

Consequently, if the priest is convinced that the penitent has sinned mortally he should tell him so, with kindness and with encouragement for the future; trying to bring him to a better disposition of sincerity and fervor in his Christian life, in accordance with the usual pastoral practice for dealing with sinners.

If he remains doubtful about grave subjective guilt but believes it is really probable that the penitent has not committed mortal sin, again he should tell him the truth as he sees it: that probably there was not grave sin and probably there was. Even this will be very encouraging to a penitent who has been sincerely trying. Furthermore it will keep him trying, when a lapse occurs in the future. Too often these penitents, after failing once, conclude that they have already sinned mortally when this point is actually doubtful. They then give up, say: "What's the use?," and make no effort to avoid further falls before the next confession. Telling them the truth as far as it can be discovered will be the best spur to continued resistance against temptation, besides being the best basis for collaboration in eradicating the habit.

Finally, if the confessor or spiritual father is convinced that the penitent has not been guilty of mortal sin he should tell him this also; again with kindness and encouragement, but being careful not to lull the penitent into a false sense of security. He should not allow the penitent to think that because the acts already performed were not gravely guilty this automatically absolves him from all responsibility for them. It would be worse to allow him to think he has no responsibility for the future. Besides being false—since in the great majority of the cases we are speaking about the acts seem to have been free human acts, and therefore venially guilty ones—this can be very demoralizing to the penitent. It may leave him with the impression that he is "not right" mentally, or that he is just an irresponsible person. Worst of all it might leave him under the impression that he is the helpless victim of his own passions, with neither the obligation nor the ability to do anything about his habit.

If a person is emotionally sick it is not bad tactics to tell him so, as long as you tell him at the same time that he can do something about his sickness and you will help him to do it. It is not bad tactics to tell this type of penitent, so many of whom are confused and overburdened with exaggerated, hopeless feelings of neurotic guilt, that he is not mortally guilty when this is the truth as you see it. It is not bad tactics to explain to him that he is suffering from a more or less pathological obstacle to liberty, if you tell him at the same time that he can get rid of the obstacle and that he should get rid of it and that you will help him to get rid of it.[36]

In other words with this type of penitent, who is sincerely trying to please God, it is often very helpful to treat his problem, for practical purposes, as a psychological one rather than a moral one. In this way one may discover the psychological source of the difficulty. At least one may correct the habit even though failing to find the source. By reducing the disproportionate feelings of guilt and tension, and by dealing with the difficulty in the calm, objective light of scientific discussion, it is often possible to bring the penitent to a clearer understanding of himself and of his problem.

Sometimes there comes to light a latent fear. The peni-

[36] The confessor or spiritual father must have the courage of his convictions, too, in accepting the logical consequences of the judgment "This penitent is not committing formal mortal sins." When he judges prudently that in the special circumstances of the given case future acts of self-abuse will not involve formal mortal guilt, he must not *forbid* the penitent to receive Holy Communion without confession after such materially sinful acts take place. Whether it would be *advisable* for the penitent to confess first would depend on the circumstances. In cases where the well-informed penitent's frame of mind after such an act is this: "I have probably not committed grave sin and am probably still in the state of grace," the penitent has the right, according to sound principles of probabilism, to receive Holy Communion after making an act of perfect contrition. However, depending on the disposition and intelligence of the penitent, the confessor may frequently think it more advisable that confession precede Holy Communion in such cases, especially if confession is easily available. Cf. Angermair, *loc. cit.*, p. 119.

tent is subconsciously fearful of sex and of this manifestation of sex. He is so afraid it will happen he becomes
convinced it will happen and it does.

At other times there is discovered a latent insincerity.
There are some personalities who get into the habit of
masturbation through a sort of interior compromise.[37] On
the one hand, they want to avoid mortal sin and the unpleasant consequences of having to admit that they committed a mortal sin. On the other hand they desire the
satisfaction that comes with sex acts, not with a really
deliberate desire of the will but at least with bodily desire.
In themselves these two things are incompatible, but they
are made compatible by a sort of subconscious compromise,
as a result of which the act is always committed with enough
mental confusion or hesitation to enable the person to say:
"I am not really acting with full freedom."

When such hidden insincerities are brought to light the
problem can be met head on and dealt with straight-
forwardly. It often yields to this approach. The same thing
is also true of other simple factors of psychological experience, which do not require the highly specialized knowledge
and technique of the psychiatrist or the deep probings of
the psychoanalyst. But there is needed the help of a spiritual
counselor who will take the time and the trouble to understand the individual case, who will have the courage to pass
judgment on it, and the patience to keep working with it.

CONCLUSION

In the present chapter we have tried to clarify rather than
to solve some of the formidable problems of subjective

[37] L. Hertling, S.J., *Theologia ascetica* (Rome: Gregorian University
Press, 1944), nn. 182–85.

moral imputability. These problems confront the moralist on every side. Self-abuse was merely a concrete case which we used as an illustration. We believe that all theologians are agreed that for formal grave culpability there is required not only liberty of indifference, which we have referred to as philosophical liberty, but also a certain degree of the liberty from obstacles and pressures which we have referred to as psychological liberty. This is implicit in the common teaching that objectively grave sins become only venially sinful *ob imperfectionem actus* in certain circumstances.

The problem is to determine what degree of psychological freedom is required and not to put the mark so high as to negate the fundamental moral responsibility of the average man and woman. We must confess that the problem is obscure and baffling. Frequently we can only admit our ignorance. We believe, however, that given the traditional conceptions of sufficient deliberation and sufficient consent, and given the psychological knowledge we now have as to emotional and instinctive obstacles to human acts, we are staying well within the bounds of the theological requirements in concluding that we should judge much more leniently than we have in the past a great many individual cases of human misconduct and frailty. "Though man may be more reasonable than the psychiatrists believe, he is less so than the philosophers think."

12

Juridical Aspects of Subjective Imputability

PROBLEMS OF IMPUTABILITY plague the jurist as well as the moralist. Questions arise as to criminal liability, as to the capacity for valid matrimonial consent, and as to contractual capacity in general. These problems are closely connected with the problem of moral imputability. We shall examine some of them here with the hope of throwing light if possible on the general question of human responsibility.

THE DURHAM CASE DECISION

When insanity or mental disturbance is alleged as a defense in criminal proceedings, questions of subjective criminal imputability immediately arise. Modern psychiatric science favors the view, of course, that there is a much wider area of irresponsibility than was hitherto suspected. Psychological impediments to human acts are multiplied. Crime itself is sometimes confused with mental pathology.[1]

[1] See, for example, Philip Q. Roche, M.D., "Criminality and Mental

Juridical Aspects of Subjective Imputability

But even for those who go all the way, and simply exclude human freedom—and who should logically on that account deny any such thing as subjective responsibility whether moral or criminal—the problem is inescapable.[2] We all have to deal with men as *if* they were normally responsible for their acts—no matter what our philosophy of human nature may be—and if we have a hand in criminal proceedings, we have to find some criterion, when mental abnormality is alleged, for separating the guilty from the not guilty, the responsible from the irresponsible. For very few would be hardy enough to take the position that no one should ever be treated as criminally responsible, on the ground that no one is ever really responsible at all.[3]

Illness—Two Faces of the Same Coin," *University of Chicago Law Review*, 22 (Winter, 1955), 320–24.

[2] See Alphonsus Bonnar, O.F.M., "Criminal Responsibility," *The Catholic Medical Quarterly*, 9, n. 4 (July, 1956) 67–73. Father Bonnar quotes an article by Eliot Slater, M.D., "The M'Naughton Rules and Modern Concepts of Responsibility," *British Medical Journal* (Sept. 25, 1954), pp. 713–18, in which Dr. Slater, despite later protestations, seems to do away with free will and responsibility. He had said: "Now if every act which a man performs is determined by his own nature on the one side and circumstances on the other, then no other way of acting was open to him. The application of such concepts as responsibility, innocence, and guilt becomes nonsensical."

[3] When moral responsibility for criminal acts is disregarded, the notion of punishment has to be repudiated also. But since society has to be protected against evil-doers, they have to be restrained and segregated by force. This force is then called treatment instead of punishment, even if it is administered in the State Prison. But if this use of force by the State is not ultimately based on guilt (which implies moral responsibility), then we can easily end up by punishing the innocent and calling the punishment treatment. See John F. Perkins, "Indeterminate Control of Offenders: Arbitrary and Discriminatory," *Law and Contemporary Problems*, Duke University Law School, Autumn, 1942; idem, "Defect of the Youth Correction Authority Act," *Journal of Criminal Law and Criminology*, 32 (1942), 111–18. And see "Notes on Moral Theology, 1943," *Theological Studies*, 4 (Dec., 1943), at p. 565, for comments on an article by Jess Spirer, "The Psychology of Irresistible Impulse," *Journal of Criminal Law and Criminology*, 33 (March-April, 1943), 457–62. Spirer favors "an established program of differential treatment. The criminal whose act grew out of

Questions in Fundamental Moral Theology

A recent decision, the much discussed Durham case in the District of Columbia Court of Appeals, has pointed up the impact of modern psychological thought on the established legal criteria for criminal responsibility. In this case the court held that the test of criminal responsibility established in the Rule of M'Naghten's Case, and widely used for over one hundred years, was inadequate.[4] According to the M'Naghten formula, the defendant, in order to escape responsibility, must show that "he was labouring under such a defect of reason from disease of the mind as not to know the nature and quality of the act; or, if he did know it, that

---

neurosis will be treated one way; the normal habitual offender will receive another form of treatment; the emotional criminal perhaps another. The point is that instead of permitting irresistible impulse as a defense, the law would hold that the stronger the impulse the greater the need for treatment."

[4] The doctrine of the Durham Case has been the subject of much discussion and criticism. See John R. Cavanagh, "A Psychiatrist Looks at the Durham Decision," *Catholic University of America Law Review*, 5 (Jan., 1955), 25–54; Natalie R. Yeager and Gennaro J. Consalvo, "A Proposal for a Fountainhead of Rationality in the Jurisprudence of Insanity," *Catholic University of America Law Review*, 5 (Jan., 1955) pp. 63–87; Paul Nolan, "Freedom of Will and Irresistible Impulse," *Catholic University of America Law Review*, 5 (Jan., 1955), pp. 55–62; a symposium on "Insanity and the Criminal Law: A Critique of Durham vs. United States," *University of Chicago Law Review*, 22 (Winter, 1955), pp. 317–404. This symposium contains the following articles: Harry Kalven, Jr., "Introduction," pp. 317–19; Philip Q. Roche, M.D., "Criminality and Mental Illness—Two Faces of the Same Coin," pp. 320–24; Manfred S. Guttmacher, M.D., "The Psychiatrist as an Expert Witness," pp. 325–30; Gregory Zilboorg, M.D., "A Step Toward Enlightened Justice," pp. 331–35; Frederic Wertham, M.D., "Psychoauthoritarianism and the Law," pp. 336–38; (the same author in the same issue of the *Chicago Law Review*, pp. 569–81, reviews Zilboorg's *The Psychology of the Criminal Act and Punishment*, New York: Harcourt Brace, 1954, and gives it a merciless lashing); Edward di Grazia, "The Distinction of Being Mad," pp. 339–55; Henry Weihofen, "The Flowering of New Hampshire," pp. 356–66; Henry Wechsler, "The Criteria of Criminal Responsibility," pp. 367–76; Warren P. Hill, "The Psychological Realism of Thurman Arnold," pp. 377–96; Wilbur G. Katz, "Law, Psychiatry and Free Will," pp. 397–404. See also, Gerard O'Brien, "Psychiatry and the Defense of Insanity," *Bulletin of the Guild of Catholic Psychiatrists*, 4 (April, 1956), pp. 3–20.

he did not know he was doing what was wrong." [5] This test is often referred to as the "right-wrong test." In the District of Columbia and a few of the states the "irresistible impulse test" was admitted in addition.

Following an old and little used New Hampshire rule,[6] the District of Columbia Court of Appeals stated:

We find that as an exclusive criterion the right-wrong test is inadequate in that (a) it does not take sufficient account of psychic realities and scientific knowledge, and (b) it is based upon one symptom and so cannot validly be applied to all circumstances. We find that the "irresistible impulse test" is also inadequate in that it gives no recognition to mental illness characterized by brooding and reflection and so relegates acts caused by such illness to the application of the inadequate right-wrong test. We conclude that a broader test should be applied.[7]

The broader test was stated thus by the court: "It is simply that an unlawful act was the product of mental disease or mental defect." But the court did not entirely reject a test based on right-wrong, on irresistible impulse, or on the will:

The jury's range of inquiry will not be limited to, but may include, for example, whether an accused, who suffered from mental disease or defect did not know the difference between right and wrong, acted under the compulsion of an irresistible impulse, or had "been deprived of or lost the power of his will. . . ."

The problem in our law is to find a criterion or test which can be given to a jury, so that after they have heard the evidence of the facts and the opinion of psychiatric experts,

[5] *Rex vs. M'Naghten,* 10 Clark and Finelly, House of Lords Cases, 200, (1843).
[6] *State vs. Jones,* 50 N.H. 369 (1871).
[7] *Durham vs. United States,* 214 F. 2nd 862 (D.C. Cir. 1954).

they will have a basis for judging the accused criminally responsible or not.[8] The problem is complex because it involves law, morals and psychiatric medicine, and because these disciplines are far from agreement with one another; even those who profess them, for example those who profess psychiatry, are far from agreement among themselves.

The report of the Royal Commission on Capital Punishment which studied this problem recently in Great Britain contained among its conclusions the following observations:

A just and adequate doctrine of criminal responsibility cannot be founded on legal principles alone. Responsibility is a moral question; and there is no issue on which it is more important that the criminal law should be in close accord with the moral standards of the community. There can be no pre-established harmony between the criteria of moral and of criminal responsibility, but they ought to be made to approximate as nearly as possible. The views of ordinary men and women about the moral accountability of the insane have been gradually modified by the development of medical science, and, if the law cannot be said to have always kept pace with them, it has followed them at a distance and has slowly adjusted itself to their changes. It is therefore proper and necessary to inquire from time to time whether the doctrine of criminal responsibility as laid down by the common law and applied by the courts, takes due account of contemporary moral standards and of modern advances in medical knowledge about the effects of mental abnormality on personality and behaviour. . . .

In our view the question of responsibility is not primarily a question of medicine, any more than it is a question of law. It is essentially a moral question with which the law is intimately concerned and to which solution [to the solution of which?]

[8] See Gerard O'Brien, "Psychiatry and the Defence of Insanity," *Bulletin of the Guild of Catholic Psychiatrists,* 4 (April, 1956).

medicine can bring valuable aid, and it is one which is most appropriately decided by a jury of ordinary men and women, not by medical or legal experts.[9]

The Durham Case decision has been criticized, not so much because it attempts to bring the law into line with psychological medicine, but because in doing so the formula adopted is so broad and so confusing that it is not a real improvement on the admittedly unsatisfactory right-wrong test.

CANONICAL NORMS OF CRIMINAL IMPUTABILITY

Canon law has its section on crimes and punishment and its own norms for determining criminal as distinct from mere moral imputability. The criteria that are set forth in the fifth book of the Code for measuring criminal responsibility in general, in mental illness, and when the offender has acted under emotional stress, etc., parallel very closely the teaching of Catholic theology on moral responsibility. In a sense this is a "pre-established harmony," because moral theology and canon law have grown up together under the unifying influence of one philosophical and theological system. It may throw some light on the questions raised by the Durham case to see how canon law approaches the same type of problem.[10] Let us first recall the difference between a sin and a crime and then look at a few of the pertinent canons, making some brief comments.

It is sometimes forgotten that the law of the Church, like the law of any sovereign society, must include penal sanc-

[9] Royal Commission on Capital Punishment 1949–1953 Report (Cmd. 8932) 79, 1953.

[10] See John C. Ford, S.J., "Criminal Responsibility in Canon Law and Catholic Thought," *Bulletin of the Guild of Catholic Psychiatrists*, 3 (Dec., 1955), 3–22.

tions. The fifth book of the Code of Canon Law is entitled "On Crimes and Penalties" not "On Sins and Penalties." Just as the codes of nations have a section on criminal law, setting forth definite crimes against the law of the land and definite penalties for such crimes, so also the Code of Canon Law has its criminal section which sets forth certain crimes against the laws of the Church and the penalties for them.

To understand this law it is necessary to distinguish between a sin and a crime. A sin is a violation of a law which obliges in conscience. It offends God. The violation may be of natural law, of divine positive law, or of human law, whether ecclesiastical or civil. It may be a violation in thought or in word or in deed. But not all sins are crimes. According to canon 2195, § 1, the first canon on crimes and penalties: "The word crime in ecclesiastical law means an external and morally imputable violation of a law to which has been added a canonical sanction, at least an indeterminate one." Every crime therefore, in ecclesiastical law, must be a sin to begin with, because it must be a "morally imputable violation of a law."

But not every sin is a crime. Some sins are merely internal, sins of thought. These are never ecclesiastical crimes, which always require "an external . . . violation of a law." Furthermore, not even external violations of Church law are crimes unless they are specifically treated as crimes in the fifth book of the Code, by having an ecclesiastical penalty attached to them. For instance one who without excuse fails to hear Mass on Sunday is guilty of a sin, and of an external violation of ecclesiastical law. But he commits no ecclesiastical crime, because canon law attaches no penalty to this violation. But to procure an abortion is a crime, the penalty for which is excommunication—if all the conditions for incurring such a penalty are fulfilled. Excommunication, suspension, interdict, removal from office, are examples of ecclesiastical penalties. Sometimes they are incurred automatically with the mere commission of the crime; at other times only after a trial and conviction in an ecclesiastical court.

The canons which follow lay down the fundamental norms for judging criminal imputability in canon law. The first of these canons, incidentally lays down the fundamental principle of *degrees of imputability*.

Canon 2199: The imputability of a crime depends on the criminal intent of the delinquent, or on his negligence in being ignorant of the violated law or in omitting proper diligence; accordingly, all the causes which increase, diminish, or do away with criminal intent or negligence, by that very fact increase, diminish, or do away with the imputability of a crime.

Canon 2200, § 1: Criminal intent here is the deliberate will to violate the law, and opposed to it on the part of the intellect is a defect of knowledge, and on the part of the will a defect of freedom.

§ 2: Once the external violation of the law has taken place, criminal intent is presumed in the external forum until the contrary is proved.

Canon 2201, § 1: Those who are actually without the use of reason are incapable of a crime.

§ 2: Those who are habitually insane, though they may have lucid intervals at times, or may seem sane in certain reasonings or in certain acts, are presumed nevertheless to be incapable of crime.

§ 3: A crime committed during deliberate drunkenness is not without some imputability, but it is less than when the same crime is committed by one who is fully in posses-

[255]

sion of himself, unless, however, the drunkenness was sought for on purpose to commit the crime or excuse it; but when the law is violated during indeliberate drunkenness imputability is banished entirely if the drunkenness destroys completely the use of reason; it is diminished if the use of reason is only partly destroyed. The same is to be said of other similar mental disturbances.

§ 4: Weakness of mind diminishes the imputability of a crime, but does not do away with it altogether.

Canon 2204: Nonage, unless the contrary is evident, diminishes the imputability of a crime, and that the more so the closer it comes to infancy.

Canon 2205, § 1: Physical force which destroys all power of action precludes crime entirely.

§ 2: Grave fear also, though only relatively grave, necessity, and even grave hardship generally do away with crime entirely if merely ecclesiastical laws are at stake.

§ 3: If, however, an act is intrinsically evil, or tends to the contempt of the faith or of ecclesiastical authority, or to the harm of souls, the causes mentioned in § 2 diminish indeed the imputability of the crime, but do not do away with it.

§ 4: The case of legitimate defense against an unjust aggressor, if due moderation is observed, does away with crime altogether; otherwise it merely diminishes the imputability, as does also the case of provocation.

Canon 2206: Passion which has been voluntarily and deliberately excited or fomented tends to increase imputability; otherwise it diminishes imputability more or less in proportion to the diverse heat of passion; and takes it away altogether if it precedes and impedes all deliberation of the mind and all consent of the will.

Under these rules it can be safely concluded that a great many psychotics would have to be classed as *definitely in-*

capable of committing an ecclesiastical crime, and the vast majority of psychotics, if not all of them, would probably be *presumed* to be incapable.[11] A large number of neurotics would be considered as having diminished responsibility; for canon law, like Scottish law, recognizes and incorporates the doctrine of diminished responsibility in criminal matters. Indeed it supposes that the degrees of responsibility are indefinitely numerous. It is noteworthy, too, as a corollary of the doctrine of diminished responsibility, that canon law supposes that the freedom and responsibility of the offender may be diminished to a significant degree but still be sufficient for the commission of a serious sin in the sight of God. For it is basic in the criminal law of the Church that without such serious guilt there can be no ecclesiastical crime at all.

To the lawyer of the common law, perhaps the most surprising thing about this jurisprudence is that it explicitly recognizes emotional factors as diminishng or eliminating criminal imputability even when the offender is not alleged to be insane or mentally ill at all. That is the plain meaning of canon 2206. Thus a man who was overtaken by a convulsion of rage and blindly attacked his bishop under the influence of such passion would not be guilty of crime, and would not incur the penalties attached to this act. The defense, if it were tried in court, would not have to allege mental illness or temporary insanity. It would allege passion, under this canon.

The lawyer will be surprised likewise, no doubt, by the rather lenient principle adopted for cases of drunkenness. And there is hardly any counterpart in our municipal law

[11] See Franciscus Roberti, *De delictis et pœnis*, (Rome: Catholic Book Agency, n.d.), vol. I, pars 1, n. 83 sq.

for the very wide provision whereby grave hardship excuses from criminal liability when merely ecclesiastical laws are at stake. This is based, of course, on the more general tenet that the laws themselves are not binding in the face of grave hardship.

This means that canon law is comparatively quite lenient in its treatment of criminal imputability in general and in cases of mental and emotional disturbance. At least, the canons as set forth are remarkably broad. It is hard to say, however, just how this works out in practice, because in modern times criminal trials are few and far between in the ecclesiastical courts, and when they do take place the proceedings are not made public.

The point that will strike the psychiatrist's eye, and which he will undoubtedly approve, is that instead of one test or criterion for criminal responsibility, there are many different ones for different classes of cases. Fundamental to all of them is the presumption of human freedom and responsibility. Fundamental also is a conception of man's spiritual nature, his spiritual intellect and will, which would not be accepted by many psychiatrists. But the individual criteria are stated in terms that are general enough to allow for an indefinite expansion of psychological knowledge about human motivation, and in terms that are elastic enough to allow the judges who apply them a very large measure of discretion in individual cases.

Such a multiplicity of criteria and such a measure of discretion might make for confusion in the hands of a jury. But in ecclesiastical trials there are no juries. The usual rule is that the majority vote of the three judges who hear a case decides the issue. The judges are the ones who would weigh the psychiatric evidence and apply the criteria to the individual case; consequently the law can demand of them a professional preparation and a maturity of judgment which could not be expected of a jury.

And since these canons are addressed not only to judges, but also to confessors, who must often act as judges in the internal forum of crimes to which *latæ sententiæ* penalties are attached, it is not out of place to emphasize that the law of the Church is exceedingly solicitous that penalties be not imposed unless both the internal and external components of the crime are realized.

PAPAL STATEMENTS ON CRIME AND PUNISHMENT

Recent papal statements have evinced an unusual interest in questions concerning the criminal process, the accountability, punishment and rehabilitation of the offender. In these statements, the pope is not talking about the restricted field of crime and punishment in Church law, but of the whole broad philosophy of crime and punishment in human affairs, both national and international. While recognizing pathological disturbances, and welcoming the aid of modern psychological science, his emphasis is on the fundamental principle of human responsibility. Speaking on October 15, 1954, to a group of delegates attending the Annual General Assembly of the International Criminal Police Commission, the pope took occasion to reiterate the most fundamental principle of all criminal jurisprudence. He said:

The entire development of the [criminal] process, from beginning to end, and the intervention of all the participants, accusers, witnesses, counsels, judges, experts, obey the same principle, tend toward the same goal: "pro rei veritate;" objective truth must shine forth. This objective truth involves certain

[259]

universal principles. First of all, there is the fact that the agent is a man endowed with liberty, not a thing, not an automaton whose functioning would depend on some inanimate mechanism; nor even a mere combination of feelings and impulses, which would pass over into act only under the effect of instinct and appetite. Objective truth means also that man, in virtue of his natural faculties, enjoys the capacity of self-determination and must consequently be considered responsible for his self-determined acts, at least until the contrary is proved or until there is a well-founded doubt.

We are not at all unaware that this implies a mass of questions and problems whose practical consequences are difficult to determine. We have treated of them at length in the allocution mentioned above, on International Penal Law, and We should like here merely to refer to that allocution; the pertinent passages will be recalled in a note. But We hasten to repeat: the judgment on the evildoer and his act must begin with the principle that every man is by nature possessed of a liberty which begets responsibility.[12]

The previous address to which he referred was an allocution delivered on October 3, 1953, to the Sixth International Convention on Penal Law. The pertinent passages follow:

There is an essential difference between the juridical and the physical order of things. In the physical order, nature works automatically; not so in the juridical order, where man's personal decision must intervene in conforming his conduct to the order established by law. "Man is the arbiter of each of his personal acts" is a phrase that expresses an ineradicable human conviction. Men will never admit that what is called the

[12] *AAS*, 46 (1954), 598–605 at 602–03.

autonomy of the will is only a tissue of internal and external forces.

There is much talk today of security measures destined to replace the punishment for the crime or to accompany it, of heredity, of natural dispositions, of education, of the extensive influence of the instincts at work in the depths of the unconscious or subconscious. Although such considerations may lead to useful conclusions, let us not gloss over the plain fact that man is a personal being, endowed with intelligence and free will, who decides finally himself what he will do or not do. This does not mean that he is free from every internal and external influence, from every inclination and attraction; nor does it mean that he must not struggle to keep on the right path, daily to fight a difficult battle against instinctive, and perhaps unhealthy, urges. But it does mean that despite all the obstacles, the normal man can and must assert his will; and it is the normal man who must serve as the rule for society and law.

Penal law would have no sense if it did not take into consideration this aspect of man, but penal law makes complete sense because this aspect is true. And since this aspect of man, personal and free, is a conviction of humanity, the effort to establish a universal penal code has a solid basis. . . .

At the moment of the crime, the delinquent has before his eyes the prohibition imposed by the juridical order. He is conscious of it and of the obligation it imposes. But, nevertheless, he decides against his conscience and, to carry out his decision, commits the external crime. This is the outline of a culpable violation of the law. By reason of this psychological process the action is attributed to its author as its cause. It is imputed to him as a fault because he has committed it as a result of a conscious decision; the order violated, and its guardian the state, demand an account of him; he falls under the penalties fixed by the law and imposed by the judge. The many influences exercised on the acts of intelligence and will, that is to say on the two factors which are the essential, constitutive elements of culpability, do not fundamentally alter this process, however great their importance in determining the gravity of the guilt.

The outline sketched above is always valid, because it is taken from the nature of man, and from the nature of a culpable decision.[13]

This last passage presumes, of course, the normal man referred to earlier. And although the word "normal" is unpopular in some schools of thought, it is impossible to avoid it or to ignore the thing it stands for in human relations, whether juridical or not. The description of the state of mind of the guilty delinquent who is really responsible for what he does, is reminiscent, in a way, of the Rules in M'Naghten's Case. And there is no doubt that those rules were formulated under the influence not only of the medicine of that time but of the philosophical and theological principles that were the common endowment of the Western world. The pope does not quite say, however, that whenever a person is conscious of the right and wrong of his action he is criminally responsible. He says rather that unless a person has this awareness of right and wrong and unless he *decides* to go against his conscience he should not be held criminally responsible.

This is undoubtedly meant to hold true of more serious crimes to which very serious penalties are attached, and most of all when capital punishment is involved. It does not seem likely that the pope would deny to the State the right to punish certain offenses even in the absence of moral fault and of criminal intent. There are many crimes and

[13] *AAS*, 45 (1953), 730–44 at 740–42. The translation, except for a few phrases, is taken from *The Pope Speaks*, 1 (Fourth Quarter, 1954), 365–66, note.

misdemeanors which are consummated legally by the mere performance of the forbidden act, for example, operating an automobile in excess of the speed limit. One may be justly punished for such offenses, even if there is no moral fault and no criminal intent, but only juridical fault.

In a later discourse the pope made more explicit reference to the effect of mental illness on criminal liability. On December 5, 1954, and on February 5, 1955, he delivered in two sections a lengthy and important statement on the Catholic philosophy of criminal guilt and punishment. This statement was addressed to the Sixth National Convention of the Association of Italian Catholic Jurists. Contrasting the infallible judgments of God with the imperfect judgments of human judges, the pope said:

The human judge, on the other hand, who lacks the omnipresence and omniscience of God, has the duty of obtaining moral certainty before pronouncing the judicial sentence, that is to say, a certainty which excludes all reasonable and serious doubt about the external act and the internal culpability. However, he has no immediate intuition of the interior state of the accused as it was at the moment of the action; furthermore, in most instances he is in no position to reconstruct it with full clarity from the evidence, and sometimes not even from the confession of the culprit. But this deficiency and impossibility ought not to be exaggerated, as if it were impossible, as a rule, for the human judge to obtain sufficient assurance and accordingly a solid basis for the sentence. According to the circumstances of the case, the judge will not fail to consult reputable specialists as to the capacity and responsibility of the accused, and will take into account the data of the modern sciences of psychology, psychiatry, and characterology. If, not withstanding all this assiduity, there still remains an important doubt, no conscientious judge will proceed to a sentence of guilty, all the more when there is question of an irremediable penalty like the the death penalty.

In the majority of crimes the external behavior manifests well enough, really, the internal sentiment from which it springs. Consequently, as a rule, one can—and besides at times one must —deduce from the external a substantially accurate conclusion, unless we want to make impossible juridical acts among mankind. On the other hand, one should not forget either that no human sentence decides definitively, in the last instance, the fate of a man, but only the judgment of God, whether for individual acts or for his entire life. Consequently, for every point in which human judges may fall short, the Supreme Judge will restore the balance, first, immediately after death, in the definitive judgment on a man's entire life, and then, later and more completely, in the presence of all in the last general judgment. Not that this dispenses the judge from exact and conscientious solicitude in the inquiry; but there is something of grandeur in the thought that there will be an ultimate balancing of guilt and punishment so perfect that it will leave nothing to be desired.[14]

MORAL RESPONSIBILITY BASIC FOR ALL

The imperfections of human justice are clear to everyone. One extreme of opinion is to ignore them, and to try to ignore the contributions which psychological science can make to our knowledge of human motivation, human responsibility, and human rehabilitation. This extreme devotion to the *status quo* would tend to hold all offenders responsible except raving maniacs, and would turn a deaf ear to reforms of almost any kind. Any attempt at improvement is attacked as a coddling of criminals. Probably the Holy

[14] *AAS*, 47 (1955), 60–85 at 65.

Father's suggestion (in the address to the jurists just quoted) that a religious institute be founded which would devote itself to the care and rehabilitation of criminal offenders would not escape this kind of destructive criticism; for he envisions a congregation whose members would be trained in modern sociological and psychological techniques.

But there is an opposite extreme which is still more dangerous because it promotes a conception of human nature which is basically false. This is the viewpoint that undermines all human responsibility by reducing man to a mechanism, or making his conduct the mere product of his instincts or of his unconscious drives. It is against such an extreme that the papal statements are principally directed. There is such a thing as freedom. There is such a thing as normality. Men do deliberately choose what is wrong and what is criminal. Criminality and mental illness are not just two faces of the same coin.

The philosophy of man which recognizes him as a free and responsible agent in his deliberate acts has been the common heritage of the canon law, the civil law, of ethics and of morals. These disciplines are in need of further knowledge about human responsibility, and those who profess them are eager to learn what science has to say about human responsibility. But they are looking to a needed reform of the criminal process. They are not interested in a philosophy which would abolish it.

Court officials complain that psychiatry cannot be really scientific because one can always get reputable experts on both sides whose testimony is diametrically opposed on the question of responsibility. It may be said that the really good, the truly scientific, psychiatrists would not so disagree.

The men who appear as experts sometimes do not deserve the reputation that they have with the uninitiated public. But the court cannot judge of this. An excellent psychiatrist like Gregory Zilboorg makes a devastating attack on the courts' criteria of criminal responsibility.[15] But then another competent man makes a still more devastating attack on Gregory Zilboorg.[16] The report of the Royal Commission, mentioned above (in note 9), puts it this way:

. . . The last hundred years have seen striking advances in scientific knowledge of insanity and mental abnormality; yet psychological medicine remains one of the youngest branches of science and it is often difficult to define the limits of recognized knowledge. There are many important questions on which psychiatrists of different schools are not agreed; there is no clear, precise or universally accepted terminology; and there is not infrequently a marked conflict of views on individual cases. . . . Psychiatrists express differing views about the kind and degree of mental abnormality which should entitle an offender to be absolved from responsibility for a criminal act. . . . Even if it were on other grounds desirable to do so, it would, in the present state of medical knowledge, be out of the question to remove the issue of criminal responsibility from the courts and entrust its determination to a panel of medical experts, as has sometimes been suggested. . . . Neither the law nor ethics can reasonably be expected to base itself on extreme and untried medical theories or to go beyond what appears to be the general consensus of moderate medical opinion. . . .

The lawyers seem to be saying: "First come to an agreement among yourselves as to the findings of your new

[15] Gregory Zilboorg, *The Psychology of the Criminal Act and Punishment*, New York: Harcourt, Brace, 1954.
[16] Frederic Wertham, review of Gregory Zilboorg, *op. cit.*, in *University of Chicago Law Review*, 22 (Winter, 1955), 569–81.

science—then we will be able to take judicial notice of established scientific facts of the psychological order."

And the judges in ecclesiastical courts will probably have the further reservation as to the psychiatrists' testimony on responsibility: "If you are a psychiatrist who does not believe in free will anyway, we cannot help being suspicious when you testify that someone is not responsible for something. Your denial of free will should lead you logically, in our opinion, to deny that anyone is ever responsible for anything."

Both in the lawyers' and canonists' camps, as well as in the mind of the man on the street, there is an unwillingness to concede that there is no practicable, workable distinction between mental sickness and mental health. When certain psychiatrists insist too strongly that there is no essential distinction between the two, they undermine their usefulness and the standing they should have in the courts, whether civil or ecclesiastical. Both canon and civil law are simply unwilling to entertain the idea that the ordinary man is so mentally sick that he cannot be criminally responsible for his acts, or, what amounts to the same thing, that everyone who actually does commit a crime must be on that account mentally sick and irresponsible. Catholic canonists and Catholic moralists react strenuously against this idea, especially if it is joined with the further notion that this sickness does away with moral responsibility in the ordinary individual, beset by the ordinary moral struggles which are a part of life itself.

The Royal Commission recognized in explicit terms that the question of moral responsibility is at the basis of the whole problem. But moral responsibility is meaningless unless a man is able to choose—unless he *could* have acted differently in the same circumstances. And so in the end we get back to our old friend, the mysterious workings of man's free will. This is definitely not a mere metaphysical problem. It is a practical matter for law, for morality, and for psychiatry. Moral responsibility is meaningless and criminal process is all an immense hoax, unless man is endowed with free will.

MATRIMONIAL CAPACITY OF THE PSYCHOPATH

It is difficult to find criminal cases involving mental illness in the records of ecclesiastical trials. Such trials are few in modern times, and when they occur the proceedings are not published. But it will be to the point to consider a case of matrimonial consent, tried before the Rota in 1941, in which the validity of the consent was attacked on the ground that the man was afflicted with "constitutional immorality." It may seem somewhat unchivalrous to imply that consent to marriage and consent to crime are comparable. But juridically and morally there is point to the analogy. In both cases the free and responsible consent of the parties is required. In both cases mental disturbance can destroy that freedom, invalidating the marriage in the one case, and excluding criminal imputability in the other.

The "constitutional immorality" described by the psychiatric experts in this case seems to be the anomaly which psychiatrists in this country now ascribe to the "psychopathic personality." Psychopaths are described as follows in a text on mental hygiene:

They are neither psychotic nor neurotic in the sense in which these adjectives are applicable to unambiguous cases of mental disorder. Nevertheless they exhibit a seeming pathological inability to be mindful of routine obligations and sensitive to the rights of others. It is as if they lacked the capacity to appreciate the ethical implications of conduct problems. The word *appreciate* is used advisedly in this context; for with them it is not a question of not *knowing* the "difference between right and wrong," but of not being able to evaluate such a difference emotionally. In a purely cognitive manner they "know" that it is "wrong" to stab a child, to pour acid on a puppy, or to steal money from a blind newspaper vendor. However, they fail to experience the emotional revulsion which crimes of this character arouse in the average man. . . .

The group of patients we have reference to are incapable of *feeling* any act to be wrong. In the older psychiatric literature they are sometimes referred to as victims of "moral insanity" or "moral imbecility". These terms are no longer employed as suitable for diagnostic purposes. Instead the modern psychiatrist calls these patients *psychopathic personalities*. What he means to convey by this designation is that some sort of inherent and presumably incurable character defect dooms the patient to a life of trouble with organized society. As a consequence a psychopath grows up to be an *amoral* adult. His misdemeanors and crimes—cheating, lying, embezzling, debauching, seducing—bring disgrace upon his family, but the disgrace has no influence on him. Neither has imprisonment, punishment, pleading or any other customary technique of dealing with the black sheep of the human flock. The psychopath is no more capable of sincere regret or genuine remorse than he is of experiencing righteous indignation. In despair his family often sends him to a psychiatric hospital or else he maneuvers himself there in order to dodge a prison sentence. In this way he and those like him come to be catalogued in official hospital statistics under the general caption "without psychosis" and the specific diagnosis of "psychopathic personality".[17]

[17] D. B. Klein, *Mental Hygiene: The Psychology of Personal Adjustment* (New York: Henry Holt, 1944), pp. 89–90.

The responsibility of the psychopath for his deeds is highly problematical. In *The Mask of Sanity*, Dr. Hervey Cleckley gives a fascinating account of these numerous, unfortunate, extremely trying and baffling personalities.[18] He considers psychopaths to be psychotic and largely irresponsible for their erratic behavior. Cavanagh and McGoldrick would probably endorse this view while recognizing the practical difficulties of having it acknowledged for juridical purposes at the present time.[19] Dr. Henry C. Schumacher is of the opinion that psychopaths are "semi-insane and semi-responsible."[20] At any rate this is the type of case on which expert psychiatric testimony is very likely to disagree. And nothing would be more likely to prejudice a case in the ecclesiastical courts than to appeal to a theory of "moral insanity."

EVALUATIVE COGNITION

It is very significant to note that, in the Rota case re-

[18] Hervey Cleckley, *The Mask of Sanity*, St. Louis: C. V. Mosby Co., 1950.

[19] John R. Cavanagh and James B. McGoldrick, S.J., *Fundamental Psychiatry* (Milwaukee: Bruce, 1953), p. 464.

[20] Henry C. Schumacher, "Psychopathic States," *Homiletic and Pastoral Review*, 40 (June, 1940), 964. Some enlightening comments on the pathologically lax conscience of the psychopath are offered by John R. Connery, S.J., "Notes on Moral Theology," *Theological Studies*, 17 (Dec., 1956), 549–83 at 553: "While moralists have always been aware of the peculiar problem of the scrupulous conscience, it is only recently that they have become aware of a pathology relating to the lax conscience. There is no doubt that the lax conscience may be for the most part the result of lax living. But it seems that a semi-pathological condition may also be responsible for such a conscience. Psychiatrists refer to the victims of such a conscience as psychopaths. Like scrupulous people, they are usually of normal intelligence and may be very well instructed. But just as scrupulous people are victims of uncontrolled guilt feelings, the psychopath is handicapped by a deficiency of such feelings. The psychopath seems to lack the minimum emotional response to moral obligations to make an efficacious and accurate judgment of moral responsibility. What he lacks is realization, or in the language of Cardinal Newman, a *real* assent to moral principles."

ferred to, some of these modern psychological views were given a hearing, and that the court was far from satisfied with a simple knowledge-of-right-and-wrong test as an adequate criterion of responsibility. In that case the psychiatric expert retained by the Rota itself held that Tito, the husband, although intelligent (he was a lawyer, but with a history of narcotic addiction), was incapable of valid matrimonial consent. Given his constitutional immorality, said the expert, "he could not evaluate sufficiently the ethical side of the act of marriage, much less the importance of the duties that derive from this act. He understood the act that he performed but he did not freely determine himself to it. Consequently, Signor Tito should be held irresponsible both from the moral and the juridical viewpoint."

There was much more expert testimony to the same effect, but in the end the Court refused to declare the marriage null. The factual evidence of mental incapacity at the time of the marriage itself and for the three years preceding it and the three years following it was very weak. Nevertheless, it is significant that the learned and influential judge, Monsignor Arthur Wynen, thought it necessary to examine at great length the psychological and psychiatric grounds alleged and, furthermore, that he admitted as a matter of principle, and as not inconsistent with scholastic philosophy and theology, that it is not enough, for freedom and imputability, that there be a mere conceptual cognition; there is required in addition the ability to weigh and evaluate the substantial elements of the proposed action. The following are excerpts from this interesting opinion:

In not a few judgments there is really a twofold cognitive function which can be and should be distinguished: the one merely

[271]

representative or *conceptual*, the other deliberative or *evaluative*; and this twofold function is principally in evidence in judgments which concern "practicable things" ["*agibilia*"], in other words in practical judgments. The merely conceptual cognition expresses *what* the object of cognition *is*, the evaluative cognition expresses what importance or worth it has, or *what value it has*. Generally, a man perceives both aspects together in the same act of cognition; especially an adult in those matters which pertain to ordinary, everyday experience. But neither factually nor conceptually do these two cognitions express the same thing; they express rather *diverse aspects* of the same object. Experience shows that the merely conceptual judgment is formed earlier and much more easily; an evaluative cognition is acquired later and with more difficulty. Furthermore it is to be noted, that the *use of reason* which is required for every human act, regards both conceptual cognition and evaluative cognition, and demands a capacity both for the *exercise* of reason and for the *dominion* of reason, that is, the capacity of a man to dispose of himself and of his action according to that twofold cognition of the object. . . .

Now it is one thing for a man to *lack* the requisite evaluative cognition, and another for him to *pay no attention* to it. A child of five years who sets fire to his father's hayloft, although he has conceptual cognition both of the hayloft and the fire, *does not have* evaluative cognition *of the crime*, that is of the *objectively very serious* violation of right order which he perpetrates; and consequently this violation cannot be imputed to him. He does have, however, both conceptual and evaluative cognition of his act inasmuch as it is *a wrongful childish deed*, and accordingly in this respect his action is imputed to him and is deserving of punishment. But an adult who posits the same external act, generally has not only conceptual cognition, but also evaluative cognition of the crime he commits, but he pays no attention to it; because notwithstanding it he proceeds to the commission of the crime, and therefore he should be fully accountable for it. And this essential difference between child and adult as regards the imputability of their own acts, obtains even more in civil law and especially in the law of contracts than it does in criminal law. A child of five years, who spends a thousand lire on sports and childish amusements, although he may perhaps understand very well conceptually what a thousand lire are, and what sports and amusements are, and what buying and selling are, nevertheless, because he lacks the necessary mental development and maturity, is not yet able to *evaluate and weigh*, not even as to substantials, what it is to spend a thousand lire on sports and amusements. Therefore, even from the viewpoint of natural law alone he must be said *to contract invalidly.*

Whenever a man, who because of his age is presumed to be endowed with the power of sufficiently evaluating something, is said nevertheless to have acted without sufficient evaluative cognition, that can arise either from the fact that he *did not want,* or from the fact that he *was unable,* to evaluate or weigh the proposed action sufficiently. One who *does not want* to acquire this knowledge will generally not escape either the subjective imputability or the objective obligatory force of his act, since he affects ignorance, and it is hardly ever possible to discern whether sufficient evaluative cognition was lacking—at least of a confused and implicit kind. But one who *is unable* to evaluate at least the substance of the proposed action, is obstructed in his natural power of appreciation, either by an impediment which is merely temporary and transitory (drunkenness, delirium, violent fever, etc.) or by an habitual defect (whether congenital or acquired during the course of his life); this type of habitual defect is present in not a few mental diseases and psychic anomalies, among which in recent times has been numbered so-called "constitutional immorality." [The italics are from the original.] [21]

21 Sacræ Romanæ Rotæ *decisiones,* vol. 33, decisio 15, Nullitas Matri-

This case has since been made the subject of a juridical monograph by the Italian Jesuit, G. M. Fazzari, which he calls "Ethical Evaluation and Matrimonial Consent." [22] In it he examines matrimonial consent from all sides, including its affective elements, and concludes that constitutional immorality can amount to a psychic incapacity to give valid consent. He is of the opinion that a person could have sufficient use of reason to be aware of the substantials of marriage within the meaning of canon 1082, namely, that marriage is a permanent society for the begetting of children, and still be incapable of giving a valid consent. For there is required in addition a maturity and normalcy of psychic elements which would permit the spontaneous transformation of the *knowledge* of marriage into a *rational appreciation*, at least confused and implicit, of all its essential aspects, particularly the ethical. However, the "appreciation" he insists on is rational. He does not stress emotional factors. A further study would be welcome, which would investigate these affective elements and determine in some degree the effect that emotional instability might have on valid consent.

To the moralist and the canonist and to many a diocesan official it is of more than usual interest that a judge of the standing of Monsignor Wynen could concede the possibility of deciding a case on the grounds of lack of evaluative consent, and the essay of Father Fazzari is further evidence that psychological findings are making some impression. But it will be some time before marriage will be successfully attacked on these grounds. After

monii coram Wynen, 25 Feb. 1941 (Rome: Vatican Polyglot Press, 1950), pp. 144–68.

[22] G. M. Fazzari, S.J., *Valutazione etica e consenso matrimoniale*, Naples: M. D. D'Auria, 1951.

all, the ecclesiastical courts demand moral certainty that a given consent was invalid by reason of mental incapacity. Constitutional immorality, as the Italian experts called it, and the psychopathic personality known to our psychiatrists, are among the more obscure chapters in psychiatric literature. If the courts hesitate to accept the concurring opinions of many experts, as they did in the case just described, it is clear that there would be little hope of an annulment in a case where the experts disagreed. Psychiatric experts will be very likely to disagree as to the moral and legal responsibility of psychopaths.

On the other hand, in a criminal case it should not be equally difficult to get an acquittal, because in criminal matters it is enough to establish with probability that one of the elements of the crime—internal culpability—is missing.

CONCLUSION

The foregoing considerations of a juridical kind have not solved our problems of subjective imputability. But they have illustrated vividly the fact that the same basic problems underlie juridical capacity as underlie capacity for moral activity. If there is one thing that stands out in the entire discussion of imputability it is this: In Catholic teaching, whether it comes from the mouth of the pope, or from the consensus of theologians and canonists, the normal man is considered a responsible individual, capable of controlling himself, of avoiding evil and of doing good. Furthermore, as we shall see more in detail in a later chapter, the concept of the normal man is not an illusion. And there is a presumption that men are normal until the opposite is shown. Nor is that presumption destroyed merely by the fact that man has indeed chosen evil, and a good deal of evil, rather than the good. For it is normal to man to be able to forsake the good, the *bonum honestum*, and of his own free will follow the evil, because of the pleasurable good that is in it. We cannot escape but must confront the *mysterium iniquitatis*.

13

Alcoholism and Subjective Imputability

IN THE PRESENT chapter we shall discuss a particular condition in which subjective imputability is affected. Alcoholism serves as a suitable illustration both because it is of such frequent occurrence in our society and because in it we can find examples of almost every degree of responsibility. We shall begin by describing in some detail what we mean by alcoholism (as distinct from mere drunkenness), then we shall discuss the moral responsibility of alcoholics for their condition, for their drinking, and their actions while drunk. We shall make some suggestions as to pastoral and professional practice in view of their modified responsibility and shall end with some brief remarks on the prevention of alcoholism.[1]

[1] For a general survey of the problems of alcohol and alcoholism, see: *Alcoholism, Science and Society*, Yale Center of Alcohol Studies: New Haven, Connecticut, 1945. This contains twenty-nine lectures on all phases of alcohol problems and alcoholism, delivered at the Yale Summer School of Alcohol Studies in 1945. Also, R. G. McCarthy and E. M. Douglass, *Alcohol and Social Responsibility*, New York: Thomas Y. Crowell Co. and Yale Plan Clinic, 1949. This is a general work on alcohol

WHAT IS ALCOHOLISM?

A few years ago the United States Public Health Service estimated that there were 400,000 cases of tuberculosis in the United States. At the same period it was estimated by scientific statisticians that there were 4,000,000 cases of alcoholism throughout the nation. This figure, which is now on the conservative side, is mentioned only to give some idea of the immense size of the problem of alcoholism: ten times as many cases of alcoholism as there are of tuberculosis. It pervades every walk of life, both sexes, and every condition of society. Five out of six alcoholics are between the ages of thirty and fifty-five. The picture of the alcoholic as a skid row character is entirely misleading. Less than ten percent of these four million are on skid row. The vast majority are still living at home, are still working more or less, and are still affecting the lives of the families with whom (or on whom) they live.

Alcoholism is not the same thing as drunkenness, nor even the same thing as excessive drinking over a long period of time. There seem to be certain people who are able to drink too much, getting drunk frequently over long periods of time, without becoming alcoholics. (However, proportionate to the amount and frequency of their excess and to other factors, they are in grave danger of becoming addicts.) If they are called on to give up drinking and are given strong enough reasons for doing so they can give it up by them-

problems in the United States, with special reference to academic instruction on these problems. Also, Marty Mann, *Primer on Alcoholism*, New York: Rinehart and Co., 1950. This contains fundamental information on alcoholism and practical advice for the family on what to do and what not to do in dealing with the alcoholic.

selves; not easily, perhaps, but with much less difficulty than the addict.

Alcoholism may be defined (descriptively) as the condition of those whose excessive drinking creates serious problems in the management of their lives, and yet who usually are unable to stop drinking permanently, even if they want to, without outside help.[2] This broad description includes almost all, if not all, those classified by scientific writers as alcoholics, chronic alcoholics, alcohol addicts, inebriates, etc. It would be recognized as applicable to the great majority of those persons who, because of problems connected with their drinking, seek help from priests, physicians, psychiatrists, clinics, and Alcoholics Anonymous, and to many more who need such help but do not seek it. And so alcoholism is not just plain drunkenness. It is drunkenness plus serious life-problems due to drink, plus addiction.

The alcoholic has these three traits: [3] (1) *Excess.* He has been drinking excessively over a period of years. (2) *Problems.* He has serious life-problems caused by or connected with his excessive drinking. (3) *Compulsion.* He does not stop drinking permanently even when he wants to and tries to, unless he gets outside help. When he tries to drink moderately he fails in spite of sincere efforts to stay within the bounds of moderation.

Excess is a matter of degree. Some alcoholics get completely drunk in the theological meaning of *ebrietas per-*

[2] John C. Ford, S.J., "Alcoholism," *Catholic Encyclopedia, Supplement II,* New York: The Gilmary Society, 1953. This is a general article on alcoholism, moral responsibility, rehabilitation and prevention.

[3] There are various practical guides for recognizing alcoholism and distinguishing it from mere drunkenness. See note 6, *infra.* What is said about the three traits of the alcoholic in the text is taken from John C. Ford, S.J., "The General Practitioner's Role in Alcoholism," *Linacre Quarterly,* 23 (Nov., 1956), 95–108 at 100 sq.

fecta only rarely, but they do get thoroughly and frequently under the influence. Some get drunk on rather small amounts, some on large quantities. The reason why the "period of years" is mentioned is that sometimes wild drinking over shorter periods turns out to be merely a passing phase, and such drinkers settle down and learn how to drink moderately. Hence it may be difficult to know whether one is dealing with a real case of alcoholism except on the basis of a rather extended drinking history. Naturally it is highly desirable that alcoholism be recognized as early as possible. But even if it could be recognized from the first drink (or before) it would probably be rather hard to convince a penitent that he had alcoholism except on the basis of his own continued, abnormal drinking behavior.

Problems are a matter of degree, too. They range all the way from a serious disruption of family harmony, through loss of job, or of health, loss of moral ideals, neglect of religious duties, loss of faith, loss of self-respect, hospitalization, commitment to institutions and jails, ending finally at times on skid row. It is very important for an adviser to realize that there are many, many alcoholics who have not yet seriously injured their health, or social position, or business standing, and who are very far indeed from skid row.

Compulsion, most of all, is a matter of degree. It operates with more or less frequency and more or less force. It is a kind of fascinated thinking about alcohol which takes possession of the alcoholic's mind on certain occasions, constrains him to drink even against his better judgment and his sincere determination not to. An alcoholic cannot safely take one drink. Not even of beer or of wine. It is even dangerous for him to take medicine, such as cough syrups or elixirs, which have an alcoholic content. It is often after a drink or two that his compulsion is touched off and he is overwhelmed by an addictive urge to drink more.

In saying that this fascinated thinking is compulsive we are far from implying that just because one alternative (drinking) is more attractive or alluring than the other (not drinking), one is compelled to choose it. Human emotion, passion, concupiscence, the attraction of the sense appetites, cause conflicts in all of us. That is not sickness, unless it is the sickness of original sin. But in the case of the alcoholic there is a type of compulsive thinking that has reached pathological proportions, a kind of fascination with one alternative which precludes a truly realistic appraisal of the other. This recurrent craving is often just as strong (at least from a psychological point of view and consequently from the viewpoint of moral imputability) as the craving of a drug addict for morphine or heroin.[4] When a person suffers from this sort of interference with normal powers of choice it is clear that his moral responsibility is affected.

It may be asked how addiction differs from compulsion and how both differ from habit. For purposes of estimating responsibility there seems to be no important difference between compulsive behavior and addictive behavior, though

[4] The problem of drug addiction is quite different in its social and medical aspects from that of alcoholism, but quite similar as far as moral responsibility is concerned. Alcoholics are prone to depend on any pain-relieving drug and become addicted to it. There are frequent cases of cross-addiction especially to barbiturates (sleeping pills), which are very dangerous to alcoholics. The new tranquillizers have been used in the treatment of chronic alcoholism with some success. It remains to be seen what precautions will have to be taken to avoid the dangers of habituation. When a drug is labelled "not habit-forming," this generally means that it is not physiologically habituating. Alcohol itself is not generally considered habit-forming in this pharmacological sense. But it is obviously a habit-forming drug in the common meaning of that phrase. Certain drugs labelled "not habit-forming" may be dangerously habit-forming for alcoholics.

the words may have very different connotations to the psychiatrist and the pharmacologist. Generally the word compulsion refers to psychological factors while the word addiction is used when there is a demonstrable physiological basis for a craving. It has not yet been shown that the alcoholic's craving for alcohol has a physiological basis comparable to that of the drug addict for his drug. But for the moralist the implications of compulsion and addiction are substantially the same. They both affect subjective responsibility and they both imply an abnormal, pathological condition. An addiction may be considered a habit which has reached pathological proportions. The compulsion we are talking about is also a habit which has reached pathological proportions. To speak of an alcoholic as a compulsive drinker and as an addictive drinker means the same thing as far as subjective moral imputability is concerned. Both addiction and compulsion admit of indefinite gradations of strength.[5]

The test of this compulsion is not the ability to stay away from alcohol completely for a week, or a month, or a year. So often the inexperienced will say: "He is not an alcoholic. He didn't touch a drop all during Lent, and there was plenty around." The test of alcoholism is not abstinence. Thousands of recovered alcoholics never touch a drop, but they are still alcoholics, because if they drank again they would soon be in trouble again. Once an alcoholic always an alcoholic. There are ex-drunks, but there are no ex-alcoholics. The test of compulsive drinking, of alcoholism, is the inability to drink regularly with true moderation. A person who can do that is not an alcoholic. If there is one

[5] See *supra* chapter 11 on compulsive urges.

thing on which all the experts are unanimously agreed it is this: an alcoholic can never learn to drink moderately. In fact, some would make this the definition of an alcoholic and the criterion of alcoholism: "a person who cannot learn to drink moderately no matter how hard he tries."

When these three are present together—excess, life-problems, and compulsion—the adviser need have little doubt that he is dealing with an alcoholic.[6]

THE SICKNESS OF ALCOHOLISM

It has been taken for granted in what was said above that alcoholism is a pathological condition. This point now requires further elucidation. The question is often asked whether alcoholism is a sickness or a moral problem, as if it must be one or the other. It is nearer the truth to say that it is both. The Massachusetts Commission on Alcoholism in its 1951 Report considers alcoholism to be "not only a medical and psychiatric problem, but also a behavior problem." Hence the formula, used with increasing frequency even by nonreligious agencies in the alcohol field, that alcoholism is a triple sickness, of body, of mind, and of spirit.[7]

[6] E. M. Jellinek, *Phases in the Drinking History of Alcoholics*, New Haven: Hillhouse Press, 1946, describes the characteristic behaviors of alcoholics in the progressive phases of their drinking. A list of these behaviors, useful for helping the alcoholic to diagnose himself as an alcoholic can be found in J. C. Ford, S.J., *Man Takes a Drink* (New York: P. J. Kenedy & Sons, 1955), pp. 92–96.

[7] Treating alcoholics as sick persons may give a few of them an excuse to go on drinking, but to ask the question "Alcoholism—Vice or Disease?" and to answer without qualification that it is a vice, oversimplifies the problems and really distorts the facts. See an article with that title by Milton Lomask in the *Sign*, 32 (Jan., 1953), 22–24. On alcoholism as an illness, Richard J. Murphy, S.J., "A Plea for the Alcoholic," *Australasian Catholic Record*, 28 (Jan., 1951), 23–30. Regarding alcoholism as a mental illness, see Edward A. Strecker, M.D., "Psychotherapy in Pathological

That alcoholism is a medical problem, at least in part, is now generally recognized. The educational work of the National Council on Alcoholism, the Yale Center of Alcohol Studies, and of other agencies has made a considerable impression. The general public has heard over and over again: (1) that the alcoholic is a sick person; (2) that the alcoholic can be helped; (3) that he is worth helping; (4) that this is a medical and public health responsibility. The medical profession itself now stands committed to the concept of alcoholism as a sickness. For instance the World Health Organization and the American Medical Association, to name but two influential groups, both accept the concept.

The idea has encountered some resistance, however. One reason is that it is impossible at present to identify a definite disease entity which all alcoholics have in common. Alcoholism is not like diabetes or tuberculosis or the various heart diseases in this respect. Exaggerated claims of this kind merely put obstacles in the way of acceptance of alcoholism as the sort of illness it is.

Another objection to the illness concept is raised by those who feel that this gives the alcoholic a good reason to go on drinking, and to say: "I can't help it; I'm a sick man." There are a few cases of this kind, but very few. It is not an excuse made by the vast majority of alcoholics who are still drinking. For the vast majority of these do not believe they are alcoholics themselves. When they read or hear about

Drinking," *Journal of the American Medical Association*, 147 (Oct. 27, 1951), 813–15. Dr. Strecker says that pathological drinking is a psychoneurosis and he advocates psychotherapy as the best treatment. Others besides doctors might meditate on this concluding paragraph: "I have indicated that the attitude of the therapist should be mature, nonemotional, and objective, but much understanding and humility are needed. As he deals with alcoholic patients, in all sincerity the therapist should be able to say to himself, 'There, but for the grace of God, go I.' "

alcoholism as a sickness they invariably think it is somebody else who has the sickness. But when they finally learn that they themselves have it, they learn at the same time that it is a sickness they can do something about, a sickness that can be arrested if they will take the necessary steps to arrest it.

At all events the primary question is not whether the alcoholic will abuse the sickness concept or whether it is good tactics to tell him that he is sick. The primary question is whether he is sick. The truth of the matter comes first; tactics afterwards. Actually, the sickness concept has worked better than anything else in getting alcoholics to do something about their drinking.

The medical profession in general and psychiatry in particular are the proper judges of what the label "sickness" means, and they are the proper judges whether the condition, alcoholism, deserves that label. At present the overwhelming majority of physicians concede that alcoholism is a medical problem, and it would be difficult, if not impossible, to find a single medical expert in the alcohol field who is not convinced that the alcoholic is a sick person who deserves to be treated as a patient. Medical associations and medical schools are now following the lead of the American Medical Association in this respect.

Perhaps the most telling reason for looking at alcoholism as a sickness is the simple fact that an alcoholic can never learn to drink normally, no matter how hard he tries. On this point the experts are unanimous, and it is absolutely agreed that the practical goal of treatment must be complete abstinence. After years of sobriety an alcoholic will react abnormally if he starts drinking again. Why is this so unless there is something wrong with him? Unless there is

[285]

something inside him, physiological or psychological or both, that makes him react that way. That something, whatever it is, is rightly called pathological.[8]

The explanation why this is so, and the whole question of etiology, leave much to be desired. Researchers in physiology have not been able to agree so far on a clear, definite, organic or functional pathology which afflicts all or most alcoholics. But some of them believe that the abnormal drinking of some alcoholics results partly from a bodily pathology. Still more believe that in many or most alcoholics, once they have become addicts, physiological changes have occurred which prevent them from ever becoming normal drinkers. On the psychological side the causation is also obscure, although psychological explanations are in the ascendancy at the present time. It is much easier, at least, to point to some psychological trait, for instance a neurotic trait, as a contributing factor to the abnormal drinking, than it is to identify a bodily pathology.

But whatever the causes, it seems clear that the psychological and/or physiological mechanisms involved in addiction deserve to be called pathological. The alcoholic, once he has become an addict, that is, a compulsive drinker, has acquired a dependence on alcohol which is beyond his power to control, unaided. We have already seen that this dependence is often as strong and sometimes stronger than drug addiction. He is the victim of a habit so severe and so strong that it has assumed pathological proportions.

[8] The practical goal of therapy, total abstinence for life, is much more important than trying to ferret out the elusive and little known causes of alcoholism. Even if these causes are discovered the drinking itself remains as a problem to be solved. Cf. Harry M. Tiebout, M.D., "Address to National States Conference on Alcoholism," given in October, 1955, reprinted in *The A.A. Grapevine*, 13 (Sept., 1956), 5–10.

It is precisely at this point that the most persistent resistance to the sickness concept occurs. Alcoholism involves, as a general rule, conduct and misconduct, including the excessive drinking itself, which at first sight looks to the ordinary person as though it were within the power of the drinker to control. Even the alcoholic himself goes on believing for years that he "can take it or leave it," when it is obvious to everyone else that he is incapable of drinking moderately and has lost control. And since the compulsion to drink is not absolute and uninterrupted, but takes over with more or less frequency and more or less force, the question of the alcoholic's control on a particular occasion, and the consequent degree of his moral responsibility, is never an easy one.

But no one who has a wide acquaintance with these problems in the concrete believes the alcoholic merely has to use his will power in order to stop drinking. No one believes that he inflicts the agonies of a long drinking career on himself out of sheer obduracy and wilfulness. There is something wrong with him which cannot be explained in merely moral terms.

Perhaps self-indulgence has degenerated into addiction. But once the addiction has set in there is a new problem. It is no longer the comparatively simple moral problem of deliberate drunkenness. It is the complex problem of alcoholism, which includes moral problems but cannot be reduced to them. It is because the pathology is so complex that we take refuge in the formula: a triple sickness, of body, mind and soul.

A great many alcoholics begin their drinking by way of harmless self-indulgence. But this indulgence soon becomes so attractive that it leads to sinful excess. Sins of deliberate

[287]

drunkenness become habitual. The fibers of character gradually become weakened. The alcoholic regresses in his emotional attitudes and his moral outlook. Little by little one moral ideal after another is allowed to grow dim. Honesty goes. Humility goes. Purity goes.

There ensue: increasing selfishness and egocentricity; increasing self-deception; increasing neglect of family, business and friends; increasing resentments and cynicism; neglect of the sacraments; neglect of Mass; finally, in some cases, a despairing rejection of Almighty God Himself. The lessons learned in childhood are disdained. What began as harmless self-indulgence has degenerated into addiction. The alcoholic finds himself morally and spiritually bankrupt, at odds with God, at odds with his own conscience, and finally deprived of his own self-respect.

This is not true of all alcoholics by any means. But the gradual process of deterioration, for which they are in varying degrees responsible, is true of so many that it must be considered characteristic of the condition. This position has been confirmed by the experience of Alcoholics Anonymous, which has been more successful than any other agency in this country in the large-scale rehabilitation of alcoholics. Their central program, the "Twelve Suggested Steps of Recovery," is a program of moral and spiritual rejuvenation. If this medicine of the soul is so successful in arresting alcoholism, it is fair to conclude that the alcoholic's sickness is also a sickness of the soul.

MORAL IMPUTABILITY

We are not speaking here of the morality of drinking, and we take it for granted that the virtue of sobriety can be practiced, *suppositis supponendis*, by one who uses alcoholic beverages with true moderation. Nor are we interested in determining the degrees of sinfulness in various stages of intoxication.[9] Our principal concern is the special question of the subjective imputability of the drinking itself in the case of a person who has alcoholism. But incidentally to this we will also say something about his responsibility for becoming an alcoholic, his responsibility for acts performed while drunk, and his responsibility for doing something about his condition. All these questions are to be discussed in the light of the fundamental supposition that alcoholism is a pathological condition of varying degrees of seriousness.[10]

Is alcoholism a condition for which the alcoholic is responsible? Some alcoholics may be but little responsible for their condition, either because their addiction has a physiological basis over which they never had control, or because they were compulsive drinkers almost from the beginning. There seem to be some individuals, most of them neurotics, perhaps, who become addicted to alcohol almost as soon as they start using it. They are "addictive personalities." When they look back at their drinking history after recovery they are convinced that they were alcoholics from the moment they took their first drink. Their condition is not the result of long overindulgence and they are not more responsible for it than a neurotic is responsible for his neurosis.

[9] The problem of alcoholism should be sharply distinguished from other related problems, for instance the question of drinking or not drinking (moderation or total abstinence), and the question of drinking too much (drunkenness). For an explanation of the moral implications of these questions and the practice of the virtue of sobriety, see *Man Takes a Drink*, New York: P. J. Kenedy & Sons, 1955.

[10] For a bibliography on alcoholism with special reference to the moral aspects of the problem, see, John C. Ford, S.J., *Depth Psychology, Morality and Alcoholism*, Weston, Mass.: Weston College Press, 1951.

On the other hand, some alcoholics are responsible for their condition in the sense that it is the result of long-continued excessive drinking for which they were responsible. To the extent that they foresaw addiction as the end-result or the probable end-result of their excess they are responsible for not having prevented it.

But subjectively, it seems that not many alcoholics are mortally guilty as far as the addiction itself is concerned. Very few believe that they will ever become addicts. There is nothing more insidious and blinding than alcoholic excess. Men and women who are beginning to drink too much are warned by their friends what will happen to them. But they do not believe it. They are convinced that they are going to be different from the horrible examples that are pointed out to them. They succeed in deceiving themselves.

Add to this the general ignorance about the nature of alcoholism and the moral confusion with which the majority of them consider the question of excessive drinking itself. Many do not believe that drunkenness is a sin "as long as it doesn't hurt anyone but myself." Others, misled by loose theological ideas, do not believe that excess is mortally sinful unless they come close to losing consciousness. Few would ever be in this frame of mind: "Unless I do something about my drinking I may become an addict; it is seriously sinful for me to run that risk, but I don't care." What the potential alcoholic says to himself at that moment is: "I *will* do something about it; I'll change to beer," or "I'll go on the wagon for Lent," etc. etc. As a result, it seems to be a rare case where the future alcoholic sees and recognizes the danger he is in with sufficient clarity to be mortally guilty *in causa* of the addiction when it finally sets in.

Alcoholism and Subjective Imputability

Certain religious persons who believe that total abstinence is obligatory for all Christians, use as an argument the danger of future addiction involved in any use of beverage alcohol. They quote statistics to show that of 80,000,000 users in the United States more than 4,000,000 become alcoholics. Therefore, they conclude, to drink means running a risk of one chance in twenty of becoming an alcoholic, and no one can reasonably run such a risk. In our terminology their position would be that drinking at all is an occasion of sin because it involves the danger of future addiction and all the sins that go with addiction.

It is not reasonable, however, to impose moral obligations on the entire community, and on each individual of a community, on the basis of general statistics of danger. It is true that for certain individuals the danger may be so great that it creates an obligation to forego alcohol entirely. But mere statistical dangers, even if they are true of the population *en masse*, cannot take the place of the virtue of prudence as a guide to the individual conscience. The statistics lose all meaning, for instance, in the case of a person who has already been drinking moderately for thirty years. The circumstances of individuals make the statistics inapplicable to them. The moral law does not oblige us always to forego an action because we foresee in it the remote possibility of future evil. Is it wrong to go driving on Sunday just for pleasure, foreseeing that pleasure driving adds to the tremendous toll of week-end deaths on our highways? If we had to follow such a rule we would eventually arrive at a state of rigid immobility (like a paralyzed scrupulant), because almost everything can result in evil consequences. The dangers of evil consequences, when significant, have to be weighed in view of all the individual's circumstances against the advantages of action. This is the function of the virtue of prudence.

With regard to the addictive drinking itself, it is impossible to lay down a rule of thumb by which we can judge the subjective imputability of an alcoholic's drinking episodes. There are so many kinds of alcoholics, and in each alcoholic there are so many stages of compulsion, and in each stage there are so many different circumstances in which the act of drinking takes place, that any exact, mechanical rule is impossible. But the following considerations justify the assertion that the responsibility of the average alcoholic for his drinking is notably diminished, especially after he has had a few drinks; that our judgment of his sins of drinking should incline toward leniency; and that there are a great many cases where he is not mortally guilty of becoming drunk.

The first of these considerations has already been explained: the compulsive character of the drinking. The alcoholic suffers from a pathological condition. Where drinking is concerned he is a definitely abnormal individual, whose freedom not to drink has been affected in an abnormal way. The alcoholic experiences at times an attraction for alcohol which is well-nigh irresistible when he is left to himself. But in saying that the alcoholic drinks compulsively it is not meant that he always does so, or that when he does the compulsion is always complete. Very often after having had one or two drinks the alcoholic finds himself in the grip of this compelling addiction. But at times even after weeks or months of sobriety he appears to start drinking without being responsible or being only partly responsible for what he is doing.

[292]

Secondly, many authors think that alcoholism is a psychoneurosis. Without offering any opinion on this technical point, we can usefully compare the alcoholic to the psychoneurotic where subjective responsibility is concerned, and the comparison is a *fortiori*. Theologians and psychiatrists are agreed in attributing to many neurotics a diminished amount of responsibility.[11]

Thirdly, the usual impediments of human acts bear upon the average alcoholic in an exaggerated way where his drinking is concerned. *Ignorance* as to the immorality of drunkenness or at least of its serious immorality is present in very many cases. The mental confusion of the alcoholic who is still drinking, even though not drunk, nor even under the influence, is appalling. It usually takes months of sobriety to bring him back to clear thinking and good judgment. *Concupiscence*, that is, the desire for the sensitive pleasure that comes from drink, is complicated by a pathological craving which some believe to have a physiological basis. This craving after a few drinks are taken seems to become definitely physiological. And even if it is only the result of psychological factors it is recognized to be pathologically strong. *Habit* in the alcoholic is complicated by a pathological process of dependence and habituation which may be partly physiological as well as psychological. In a report based on

[11] James C. Royce, S.J., confirms this conclusion in an excellent paper: "The Moral Responsibility of the Neurotic," *Manuscript*, Alma College, Alma, California, 1947. Cf. also Pierre C. Simonart, "The Imputability of the Mental Patient," *Linacre Quarterly*, 15 (Oct., 1947), p. 8–15; John R. Cavanagh, "Nervous Mental Diseases II," *American Ecclesiastical Review*, 109 (Oct., 1943) 257–71; Robert E. Britt, "Alcoholism and Some Moral Issues," *Linacre Quarterly*, 13 (Jan.-Apr., 1945) 15–24; Rudolf Allers, "Abnormality: A Chapter in Moral Psychology. VI. Moral Responsibility of the Neurotic," *Homiletic and Pastoral Review*, 42 (May, 1942) 727–33; Rudolf Allers, "Irresistible Impulses," *American Ecclesiastical Review*, 100 (Mar., 1939) 208–19; Henry C. Schumacher, "Psychopathic States," *Homiletic and Pastoral Review*, 40 (June, 1940) 964-71.

the observation of 2275 cases it is stated that "basically, there is no difference between the opium addicts and the alcohol addict. The mechanism of addiction is the same and the abrupt withdrawal symptoms may be very stormy in both types." [12]

From all these considerations the least we can conclude is that the alcoholic's responsibility for the drinking itself is generally diminished to a considerable extent, frequently beyond the point of mortal sin, and that it is sometimes eliminated. This substantial diminution of imputability occurs especially after he has begun drinking, but each alcoholic, each drinking episode, and even each act of drinking must be judged on its own merits.

We must usually have recourse to the conscience of the individual alcoholic to discover whether he has sinned grievously or not. While he is still drinking and for some time thereafter he is a poor judge, or at least an untrustworthy witness on this point. Even without meaning to, he may be rationalizing his conduct and trying to excuse it. Or he may err in the other direction because he has no information about alcoholism, and in his confusion does not recognize the compulsive character of his drinking. Many alcoholics are overburdened with false feelings of neurotic guilt which make them very poor judges of the state of their own conscience at the time the drinking took place. But a great many alcoholics who have come back to normal

[12] R. C. Young, "Clinical Observations on the Treatment of the Alcoholic," *Medical Surgical Journal*, 100 (1948), 539–46. Robert H. Felix, "Some Comments on the Psychopathology of Drug Addiction," *Mental Hygiene*, 23 (Oct., 1939), 567–82, says that nearly all workers in the field are agreed today that drug addiction is a disease of a psychiatric kind. Cf. also, Pullar-Strecker, "A Review of the Literature on Addiction," *British Journal of Addiction*, 45 (1948), 125–76, which reviews the literature from 1945 to April, 1948.

and have been properly instructed about themselves and their alcoholism have learned to look at themselves honestly and objectively. The honest and enlightened testimony of their own consciences is often the best criterion we have of the degree of their responsibility. Since their condition and their craving are pathological we should tend to be lenient in assessing the subjective moral responsibility. In the final analysis the judgment must be left to a merciful God.

Although the alcoholic may be powerless over alcohol, and unable at times directly to resist the craving for drink, yet it is within his power, generally speaking, to do something about his drinking. He is therefore responsible for taking the necessary means to get over his addiction. Some need psychiatric help; many need medical help; almost all need spiritual help. But the same elements of confusion, ignorance, hopelessness, and despair may modify considerably the subjective responsibility in this matter, too. Today there is new hope for the alcoholic because the kind of help he needs is more and more easily available to him.

RESPONSIBILITY FOR ACTS WHILE DRINKING

The rule which canon law sets down to estimate responsibility for ecclesiastical crimes committed under the influence of liquor is an excellent general norm of the moral imputability of acts performed while drinking. Canon 2201, § 3 reads as follows:

A crime committed during deliberate drunkenness is not without some imputability, but it is less than when the same crime is committed by one who is fully in possession of himself, unless, however, the drunkenness was sought for on purpose to commit the crime or excuse it; but when the law is violated during indeliberate drunkenness imputability is banished entirely if the drunkenness destroys completely the use of reason; it is diminished if the use of reason is only partly destroyed. The same is to be said of other similar mental disturbances.

Accordingly, with regard to sins of fighting, impurity, automobile accidents etc., if a person (alcoholic or not) foresees that any of these are likely to happen and deliberately goes on drinking regardless of consequences, he is guilty. The general rule is that a person is not guilty of the acts committed while completely drunk unless he foresaw the likelihood that they would happen, and was deliberately willing to go ahead and take a chance that they would happen. In such a case he is guilty of them in the sight of God, whether or not they actually happen. Subjectively the alcoholic, or other drinker, frequently does not contract this guilt because he says to himself, very foolishly but very sincerely: "This time it will not happen; because this time I will take just a few drinks and go home."

But if the person is not completely drunk and does not foresee the evil consequences, then his guilt depends on how much control he has left when he causes them. Merely because a man is drinking, and even on an extended bout, one should not conclude that he is without the use of reason and entirely without responsibility for what he does. This is true both of alcoholics and of nonalcoholics. Some alcoholics go on drinking for days or weeks or months without ever being "theologically" drunk, except perhaps at the end of the day. The rest of the time they are under the influence of liquor, but they know what they are doing. Their misconduct and sins are imputable to them, not merely *in causa* but *in se* with a variation in the responsibility according to the degree that alcohol has clouded their faculties.

The alcohol may even sharpen the drinker's faculties in some circumstances, for instance when he is very nervous and shaky and the alcohol quiets him down so that he is able to pay attention to what he is doing. The average alcoholic feels himself more or less guilty for the things that happen while he is in this state, although his general confusion of mind is an attenuating circumstance. He may feel that if he had not been drinking he never would have done these things; but he realizes that even though drinking he did not have to do them. Sometimes he feels that the reason he was drinking was in order to be bold enough to do these very things. At other times, for instance after a blackout, he is generally convinced that he was so under the influence of alcohol that he was not responsible, even though he was not entirely drunk.

The remarkable thing about some of these cases is that the alcoholic, though he feels responsible for the sins committed while on a spree, does not consider himself responsible for the drinking itself. That was something he *had* to do, or at least had to continue once he got started. The drinking itself was presented to his mind with an inevitability that in nowise attaches to the other sins committed while drinking. As one alcoholic (not in the late stages of alcoholism) put it: "The need of drinking once you start is like the need of attending to the wants of nature; you do not argue about it; you have to attend to it and you do." This is a further indication of the compulsive character of the drinking.

THE BLACKOUT

A blackout here does not mean a loss of consciousness or a fainting spell. It means a loss of memory with regard to a

[297]

certain period of time caused by excessive drinking. In other words, it is a type of amnesia. Sometimes it happens when a person is obviously under the influence of alcohol and those about him can see that his conduct is irrational or hilarious or otherwise abnormal. At other times it happens when a man seems to be behaving quite rationally. Those about him do not suspect that he is drinking heavily, and he carries on rather complicated affairs with the appearance of rationality. In one case, for instance, a surgeon who had been drinking heavily performed a delicate emergency operation and prescribed all the proper medication and procedures on the patient's chart, but remembered nothing of it the next morning. Sometimes blackouts last for days or even weeks. The great majority of alcoholics have experienced blackouts. Most begin to have them towards the beginning of their alcoholic careers, though some have them later and a few never. When blackouts occur with increasing frequency in proportion to the number of drinking episodes it is a serious warning sign of oncoming alcoholism.[13]

Alcoholic blackouts raise interesting problems about moral imputability, but the problems are not entirely different from, although more frequent than, cases of amnesia arising from other causes. A person who is knocked unconscious by a blow on the head often has no recollection of the events that occurred for some time preceding the blow. There is no reason to suspect that his acts during that preliminary period were not rational human acts. The mere fact that he now has no recollection of them does not render them suspect. Mere lack of memory is not a proof

[13] On the blackout in the drinking careers of a large group of recovered alcoholics, see E. M. Jellinek, *Phases in the Drinking History of Alcoholics*, New Haven: Hillhouse Press, 1946.

that reason was not operating and in control. On the other hand when a person receives a blow on the head without becoming unconscious and continues to behave with apparent rationality, but afterwards remembers nothing of the events that took place, the lack of memory along with the blow on the head are strong reasons for suspecting that he was not a fully responsible human being during that period —especially, of course, if his decisions are unusual, if he is "not like himself."

A person who is hypnotized may talk rationally and afterwards remember nothing. No one would hold him accountable *in actu* for what he says or does while hypnotized.[14] A man may make excellent syllogisms under hypnosis, but this does not prove that he is capable of a human act. Sleepwalkers sometimes talk sense, too. Even acts performed under post-hypnotic suggestion are at least suspect as to freedom and imputability.

The first question about the alcoholic blackout is a rather academic one, not discussed by moralists. Would it be gravely sinful to drink to excess foreseeing a blackout in which one's conduct would be apparently rational, but after which there would be no recollection of the conduct? It seems that *per se* this would be gravely sinful like deliberate complete drunkenness, because it amounts to a serious mutilation of the higher faculties, which could be justified only by serious reasons.

The second, more practical question, concerns the black-

---

[14] Reliable psychiatrists say however that people in these states retain their fundamental deepseated moral convictions. An attempt to get them to go counter to these convictions will often bring them out of hypnosis. Because of this we might say that they have a certain negative sense of responsibility, i.e., they will not act contrary to these deepseated convictions. This is not true of those whose moral standards are superficial, based on fear or human respect.

out where the person acts with apparent rationality (like the surgeon above) perhaps over a long period of time, making contracts, committing sins, receiving or administering the sacraments, entering marriage, etc. In the present state of our knowledge, we have grave doubts that such acts are really responsible acts. The person is in such an abnormal condition, in such a deeply altered state of consciousness, that he should not be held then and there fully responsible for acts performed in this state—whether good ones or bad ones. However, he may be responsible *in causa* for some of them. The mere fact that he does not remember them afterwards is not the thing that evidences their lack of freedom, but the fact that the loss of memory was due to the violent disturbing effect of continued excess in the use of alcohol. He is like the person who suffers a blow on the head and then continues to act with apparent rationality, but remembers nothing afterwards.

In making a practical decision as to whether acts with juridical or sacramental implications should be repeated, perhaps the advice of a neurological or psychiatric expert would be needed, because there are degrees of severity in blackouts. Furthermore, professional examination of the person *during* the blackout period, if that were ever feasible, might reveal that the apparently rational conduct was only superficially such, and was really proceeding from a profoundly disturbed individual, whose personality was radically altered, who literally was not himself.

PASTORAL AND PROFESSIONAL PRACTICE

When the adviser is satisfied that he is dealing with an alcoholic he should be lenient rather than severe in judging his subjective guilt as to the drinking, but he should not make blanket appraisals. Each case must be decided on its merits; it is very difficult to generalize about alcoholics. They differ very widely.

Should the confessor forbid an alcoholic under pain of mortal sin to take even one drink, on the ground that for the alcoholic one drink is a proximate occasion of grave excess? It is true that even one sizeable drink is so dangerous for the average alcoholic that they are generally obliged objectively *sub gravi* not to drink at all. But usually it is unwise and improper for the confessor or counselor to impose this grave obligation on excessive drinkers. First, because the judgment whether a person is a real alcoholic, or is one who can learn to handle drink, is sometimes a difficult judgment for the confessor to make. The penitent may be firmly convinced he is not an alcoholic, and may have medical advice to that effect. Secondly, because in the case of the true alcoholic it is often better to leave him in good faith on this point. Telling him that one drink is mortally sinful for him will not be very likely to prevent him from taking the drink. He will not be able to believe that one drink is so sinful for him. Then, too, there are certain exceptional cases in which the sudden withdrawal of all alcohol without any substituted medication could be dangerous. General statements about mortal sin would have to make allowance for a great variety of circumstances.

The alcoholic drinker is often in a state of despair and frustration when he finds himself powerless to do what he wants to do. One such drinker said: "At first I drank because I *wanted* to; then I drank because I *needed* to; finally I drank because I *had* to." Such a drinker is often the victim of pathological feelings of guilt and remorse. One of the reasons he drinks is to relieve the unbearable tension engendered by these feelings. To put him under the additional strain of fearing that one drink means mortal sin and the loss of the friendship of God may be just the touch needed to drive him to drink. Our general theological principles permit leaving him in good faith in these circumstances, especially when we remember that in the case of the truly compulsive drinker even his first drink may be taken at times compulsively and so, *de facto*, will not be mortally sinful for him.

For these reasons it is not generally advisable to tell the alcoholic that for him one drink means mortal sin; and much worse to refuse absolution unless he makes a promise never to take a drink again. The alcoholic's conduct where alcohol is concerned is unpredictable even to himself, and the confessor will be realistic if he recognizes that his alcoholic penitent is often literally incapable of making and keeping such a promise.

With regard to the pledge, the confessor should remember that although the pledge has been a wonderfully effective instrument in the *prevention* of alcoholism, it is not by itself of much use in the *rehabilitation* of alcoholics. And the further the alcoholic has progressed along the stages of increasing addiction the less likely it is that by itself it will do him any good. If the pledge is used, for instance by way of trial and for a short time, at the request of the alcoholic, it should be made plain to him that it does not impose any new obligation under pain of sin. It is a sacred resolution, made for supernatural motives, to do something that is pleasing to God.

The confessional is the place for absolution of the alcoholic's sins, and for some brief advice about his drinking problems. Effective counseling must be carried on outside the confessional. The alcoholic is suffering from a complicated triple sickness of body, mind, and soul. The priest or any other adviser will make a great mistake if he imagines that he is competent to handle this whole problem by himself. The priest can handle the spiritual side of it, if he has learned well the fundamentals about alcoholism and alcoholics. He can help the alcoholic with the hardest problem of all: really to recognize himself and diagnose himself as an alcoholic. But it generally requires a continued, co-operative effort to restore an alcoholic to permanent sobriety. The adviser should consider himself part of this cooperative effort and not hesitate to put his consultant in touch with other agencies for medical, psychiatric, or social help.

The best of all the allies which the priest has in this work is Alcoholics Anonymous.[15] The program of this organization has been more successful in the permanent, contented recovery of large numbers of alcoholics than anything else we know. It offers help to alcoholics that they cannot get anywhere else. It is almost universally available. It does not cost anything, and it works. It is a mistake for any counselor to give his consultant the impression that his long range recovery is up to himself, as though he can remain sober merely by deciding to, by exercising his will power and making regular use of the sacraments and the other means

[15] The national and international headquarters of Alcoholics Anonymous is located in New York. Address: Alcoholics Anonymous, P.O. Box 459, Grand Central Annex, New York, 17, N.Y. Their principal publications are: *Alcoholics Anonymous* (revised edition), New York: The Alcoholic Foundation, 1955; and *The Twelve Steps and Twelve Traditions*, New York: Harper and Bros., 1953. For the families of alcoholics, especially the wives, there is an organization known as "The Al-Anon Family Groups Inc." This is an offshoot of A.A. but not directly connected with it. There are hundreds of these groups throughout the country. Their headquarters are at P.O. Box 1475, Grand Central Annex, New York, 17, N. Y.

of grace. He should help the alcoholic to realize that he is suffering from a progressive and insidious disease, and that he needs continued outside help.

The best resource available for this help in the majority of cases is A. A. Anyone who hopes to work with alcoholics should know this program thoroughly, not merely from the literature but by attendance at their meetings. He should be personally acquainted with some successful members of A. A. so that when an alcoholic is willing to accept help from them, the counselor will not merely "send him to A. A.," but will contact the right people in A. A. to help this particular individual.

Although in its beginnings A. A. had a connection with the Oxford Groups, and received some ideas and terminology from them, it was never integrated into that movement. At a very early date of its twenty-one year history A. A. severed all connection with Buchmanism, retaining none of the elements which would be objectionable to Catholics. It has no connection whatever with M.R.A. (which is a further development of Buchmanism) and is not a religion or a religious movement. It is part of the fixed tradition of A.A. to prescind from all theological involvements, contenting itself with the simple fundamental principle that the alcoholic needs the help of God to recover. Catholics need have no fear that in joining A.A. they will be taking part in a non-Catholic religious program. The Twelve Steps of A.A. are in thorough harmony with Catholic theology and asceticism.

In the beginning it was feared that A.A. might foment religious indifferentism and lead Catholics away from their faith. It is now clear from more than twenty years of experience that this fear is unfounded. Just the opposite is true.

Thousands of Catholics have returned to the active practice of their faith and many non-Catholics have been converted. The faith and religious practice of Catholic A.A.'s should be protected by participation in Catholic activities. Membership in Catholic organizations, old and new, whether specifically directed towards helping alcoholics or not, can achieve this purpose. Above all, the frequent reception of the sacraments should be inculcated.[16]

PREVENTION OF ALCOHOLISM

The absolute legal prohibition of alcoholic beverages is favored by very few Catholics in the United States. They generally consider that even if this would reduce the amount of alcoholism and other evils connected with the use of alcohol, the price paid, in restricting the liberty of large numbers of temperate users of alcohol, and in the inevitable lawlessness which would accompany attempted enforce-

[16] In an address to the National Clergy Conference on Alcoholism, reprinted in the *Priest*, 10 (Aug., 1954), 683–90, Archbishop Richard J. Cushing, D.D., of Boston, made some notable comments on the priest's pastoral duties with regard to alcoholics. "The priest who aspires to be a complete confessor and effective spiritual director will make it his business to keep informed on the new techniques both of psychiatrists and non-professional therapy in the cure or at least control of alcoholism. Such a priest will have at his fingertips information concerning clinics on alcoholism in nearby hospitals. He will try to know which doctors have taken a special interest in these cases. Far from having a negative attitude toward psychiatry, he will be eager to know and to work with trustworthy psychiatrists whose techniques are approved and whose moral principles are straight. He will especially make it his business to know which of his devout parishioners may be in a position to introduce individuals to Alcoholics Anonymous, the work of which no priest can possibly ignore. He will acquaint sufferers from alcoholism with the heroic story of Matt Talbot and will preach devotion to him. He will decide in the light of local circumstances whether a Temperance Movement is needed in his region and the form it should take."

The National Clergy Conference on Alcoholism (P.O. Box 1194, Indianapolis, 6, Indiana) holds an annual conference in a different city of the United States each year. This meeting is for the Catholic clergy, to whom the group offers assistance in their pastoral problems.

ment, would be too high. It is recognized by everyone, however, that some legal controls are necessary, and all the states have legal machinery to regulate the hours and conditions under which alcoholic beverages can be procured or dispensed. To the extent that legal regulation makes it more difficult and more expensive to drink, the number of drinkers and the amount drunk are diminished. Fewer drinkers and less drinking, especially of hard liquor, presumably result, in the course of time, in decreasing the number of alcoholics.

A growing dissatisfaction with the amount of advertising of alcoholic beverages, especially the wine and beer advertising on radio and television, is likely to lead to further legal restrictions in this regard. Such curtailment of advertising would hardly be reflected in an immediate or measurable decrease in alcoholism. But it is the opinion of many that much of this advertising engenders, especially in young people, false and exaggerated ideas as to the place and prestige of social drinking in our society, and thus reinforces dangerous drinking customs prevalent in the United States. Like others who appeal to sense appetites, the beverage alcohol advertisers have the advantage, in their pursuit of profits, of being able to cater to the lower, pleasure-seeking instincts of human beings. Human nature being what it is, these instincts are easily and frequently abused. The advertisers of such products, therefore, have a special social responsibility. When they fail to fulfill it, and when the abuses become intolerable, the industry becomes an easy and inevitable mark for further legal restrictions.

Education must play an important role in the prevention of alcoholism, as in any other public health problem. The dramatic success of Alcoholics Anonymous in rehabilitating alcoholics has roused public interest and focussed attention on alcohol problems. This in itself has had immense educational impact. The National Council on Alcoholism (formerly the National Committee on Alcoholism) conducts a nationwide campaign of popular education, with branches in fifty or sixty cities of the United States.[17] The Yale Center of Alcohol Studies, including the Laboratory of Applied Physiology, the Yale Plan Clinic, and the Yale Summer School of Alcohol Studies, has done pioneer work in research and publications, both scientific and popular. Other scientific centers are doing similar research, for instance, the Alcoholism Research Foundation, in Seattle, and the National Research Council, in New York.

The Association for the Advancement of Instruction about Alcohol and Narcotics has as its object to assist private and public school educators to discharge effectively their responsibility to inform students concerning alcohol and narcotics. As a rule, states require alcohol education by law, but the teaching has often been haphazard and ineffective. The upper high school grades are in peculiar need of this instruction and orientation, but it is also appropriate at the college level. There are available now text materials for schoolroom use which present the facts and the problems in

[17] The National Council on Alcoholism, Suite 454, New York Academy of Medicine Building, 2 East 103 St., New York, 29, N. Y., is the national clearinghouse for information on developments and activities in the field of alcoholism. It disseminates the latest findings in this field, and also guides and stimulates the establishment of community programs on alcoholism. Literature is available from the national headquarters. The local affiliates operate programs of information, organization, education and guidance. Some of them are in a position to guide the individual alcoholic, through experienced counselors, to the help best suited to him. They can also inform the priest of all the local treatment facilities for handling alcoholics.

a scientific, unemotional, and unprejudiced way.[18] In seminaries, students for the priesthood should receive more
thorough and realistic information and training about
alcohol and alcoholism and about the practical methods of
dealing pastorally with alcohol problems.[19]

Education can help to prevent alcoholism, not merely by
giving the scientific facts, by pointing out the dangers of
excess and the warning signs of oncoming addiction, but

[18] The Association for the Advancement of Instruction about Alcohol
and Narcotics has its headquarters at 52 Hillhouse Ave., New Haven, Conn.
They include narcotics in their title and in their interest because most of
the state laws requiring instruction about alcohol in the public schools (all
states have such laws) also require instruction about narcotics. W. B.
Spalding and J. R. Montague, *Alcohol and Human Affairs*, Yonkers, New
York: World Book Co., 1949, is a high school text which contains a brief
and informative appendix about narcotics. For a good treatment of basic
alcohol information suitable to high school and college students see R. G.
McCarthy, *Facts About Alcohol*, Chicago: Science Research Associates,
1951. This is one of the pamphlets of the Life Adjustment Series. Robert
Straus and Selden D. Bacon, *Drinking in College*, New Haven: Yale University Press, 1953, is a valuable statistical and sociological study of the
drinking habits of American college men and women. The most complete
and indispensable vade mecum for the educator at high school and college
level is R. G. McCarthy, *Teen-Agers and Alcohol: A Handbook for the
Educator*, New Haven: Yale Center of Alcohol Studies, 1956.

[19] See, J. C. Ford, S.J., "Alcohol Education in the Seminary," *Bulletin
of the National Catholic Educational Association*, 50 (Aug., 1953), 98–106.
This article concludes: "Alcohol problems are so extensive and so pervasive in the lives of the Catholic faithful and clergy that the seminary has
an educational responsibility to prepare the seminarian to meet these problems. Although something is being done to discharge this responsibility, it
is not nearly enough, considering the extent of the problems. The seminary
can and should provide for the personal education of the seminarian where
alcohol is concerned, and for his professional education in the pastoral care
of excessive drinkers and alcoholics. This can be done without the institution of new courses of study, by the use of materials now or soon to be
available, and by the exercise of commensurate ingenuity within the
academic and spiritual programs already in existence." The Yale School of
Alcohol Studies which is in session every summer during the month of
July provides an excellent opportunity for priests and seminarians who
desire to make a more thorough study of the modern scientific approach to
alcohol problems. The headquarters of the school are at Yale University
in New Haven. The medical schools are now beginning to provide education on the medical care of alcoholics as part of the regular curriculum.
See *Journal of the American Medical Association*, 53 (Nov. 7, 1953), 931.

especially by influencing the social attitudes toward drinking. There are social pressures which almost force people (especially young people) to drink. There are drinking customs which tend to condone and even to promote excessive drinking, especially of hard liquors. Scientific education can help to modify these pressures and customs. Further studies of the causes of alcoholism from the sociological and psychiatric points of view should be welcomed, since such information can give intelligent direction to a movement aimed at eliminating excess and abuse. Since one of the causes of alcoholism is often found in the maladjusted personality of the victim, it is hoped that practical principles of mental hygiene can be developed and applied which will enable such personalities to come to terms with life without resorting to the delusive solution which alcohol appears to offer for their problems. Nor should there be any conflict between the principles of true Christian asceticism and sane mental hygiene. Both recognize self-discipline as fundamental. Consequently education in the virtue of temperance, which inculcates self-denial and self-discipline in drinking as in other sense pleasures, should be part of any educational program which deals with a problem of human behavior.

The practice of total abstinence for supernatural motives (self-denial, penance, good example, reparation to our Lord for sins of intemperance, etc.) has the highest approval of the Church and its theologians. The idea is current, however, that there is something Jansenistic or puritanical about it, or that it is a Protestant, or at least an un-Catholic, ideal. This is far from the truth. This mistaken idea has been engendered by the fact that some Protestant denominations take the false position that total abstinence is obligatory on all Christians, and many of them have been active crusaders for absolute prohibition. Besides, such organizations as the Women's Christian Temperance Union, the Anti-Saloon League (now known as the Temperance League of America), Allied Youth, and others, are of Protestant origin or inspiration. However, Catholic total abstinence societies both in Europe and America have received papal approval and strong encouragement, and their members have been granted special indulgences by the Holy See.

The Pioneer Total Abstinence Association of the Sacred Heart has been extremely successful in Ireland.[20] In the United States the Catholic Total Abstinence Union of America was formerly very large and influential and continues to do good work on a lesser scale today. In Canada and in parts of New England the Cercle Lacordaire and the Cercle Jeanne d'Arc are successful total abstinence organizations. Given the size of the alcohol problem in this country (not merely of alcoholism but of excess and abuse that falls short of alcoholism), a strong and vigorous total abstinence movement should be welcomed as an important ally and significant factor in the prevention of alcoholism. The voluntary pledge for years or for life, based on solid motives like the supernatural ones mentioned above, or even based on a reasonable fear of excess and addiction, and supported by a program of social activities as the Father Matthew Societies were in this country, could become again as it was in

[20] In September, 1956, Pius XII spoke on intemperance to a group of members of Ireland's police force who belonged to the Pioneer Total Abstinence Association of the Sacred Heart. His Holiness made a distinction between intemperance and alcoholism, saying, "In more than one country of the world intemperance in drink, so often leading to alcoholism, has become a harrowing menace and an actual spiritual tragedy for thousands of souls. . . . It is a social evil and a spiritual deterioration calling for enlightened study and self-sacrificing zeal for every apostle, lay and cleric" (Quoted in the Brooklyn *Tablet*, Sept. 22, 1956).

the past a potent preventive of alcoholism. And for those segments of the population in which excess is more prevalent, or where the incidence of alcoholism is disproportionately high, total abstinence is a peculiarly appropriate and effective means of prevention. The total abstainer who remains a total abstainer will never become an alcoholic.

This does not exclude virtuous moderation as a preventive measure. For it is equally true that the moderate drinker who remains a moderate drinker will never become an alcoholic. And since the call to a voluntary work of supererogation based on supernatural motives is not likely to reach the mass of our population, and the fear of excess and addiction in the remote future is not a very effective deterrent for the average young person, reliance on the total abstinence movement alone as a preventive of alcoholism does not seem to be sufficient. In addition there is required a strong temperance movement in the literal sense of the word temperance: virtuous moderation. An effective movement for such moderation would include the educational program referred to above, and would attempt to change the dangerous drinking customs and attitudes of our society, thus diminishing the social pressures which lead people to drink in an immoderate way. There is no intrinsic reason why two social movements, one for total abstinence, and one for virtuous moderation, should not work side by side as friendly allies in a common cause. There are no contradictory principles involved which would make the two movements natural enemies.

It will only be by the constant, wholehearted cooperation of many diverse elements in our society that alcoholism can be prevented to a significant degree. Sane legal controls, scientific education, mental hygiene, total abstinence, wholesome moderation, and the other factors mentioned, all must be brought to work together and to contribute their share to the prevention of alcoholism. But in the last analysis it must not be forgotten that the excessive drinking of alcohol is a problem of human behavior. Like every such problem it has theological implications, illustrating vividly the mysterious interplay of free will and divine grace within the human soul. The grace of God is all-important in the rehabilitation of the alcoholic. It is not less important in the more general problem of the prevention of alcoholic excess and alcoholism.[21]

[21] This material on prevention of alcoholism is taken from the article "Alcoholism" in the *Catholic Encyclopedia, Supplement II.* This article is published as a separate pamphlet by the Gilmary Society, New York, 1953.

14

Psychiatry and Catholicism

I N MAY, 1955, the *Woman's Home Companion* carried an article entitled: "What Does Your Church Think of Psychiatry?" In the course of this article it was noted that readers who were interested in the attitude of the Catholic Church could write to Msgr. John J. Hayes at 566 Elm St., Stamford, Connecticut. Msgr. Hayes is the chaplain of the Guild of Catholic Psychiatrists. As a result of that reference he received 1431 letters in two months and of these 812 expressed varying degrees of surprise that Catholics could have anything to do with psychiatry.[1]

Perhaps this surprisingly widespread misconception is not so surprising if we recall certain ill-considered but widely publicized statements about psychiatry and psychoanalysis that have been made by ecclesiastics. In 1952, Msgr. Pericle Felici, a judge of the Sacred Roman Rota and a consultor of the Sacred Congregation of the Sacraments, wrote an article

[1] John J. Hayes, "Chaplain's Letter," *Bulletin of the Guild of Catholic Psychiatrists*, 3 (Dec., 1955), 2.

[313]

in which, though not speaking officially for the Church in any sense, he said some very severe things about psychoanalysis. For instance, a newspaper quoted one of his statements as follows: "It is therefore, difficult, to excuse from mortal sin anyone who knowing all this, adopts this method of cure [psychoanalysis] and voluntarily subjects himself to this form of treatment." [2] He clarified this later by saying that he referred only to a certain kind of Freudian psychoanalysis, not to psychoanalysis in general.

It was probably because of the discussion and confusion aroused by this article that the Holy Father, six months later, took up the question of psychoanalysis and made an important statement concerning one aspect of it. The pope was addressing an international congress of physicians and spoke to them about various limitations which the moral law puts on scientific research and medical practice. In his remarks on this occasion the Holy Father found fault with a certain attitude and technique ("pansexualism") of a certain school of psychiatry, but both the text of his remarks and a subsequent "inspired" comment in the pages of *L'Osservatore Romano* made it very clear that he had not intended to condemn psychiatry in general or psychoanalysis in particular.[3]

NO FUNDAMENTAL CONFLICT

On April 13 of the following year, 1953, the Holy Father received in special audience delegates to the Fifth International Congress of Psychotherapy and Clinical Psychology

[2] Boston *Globe*, April 9, 1952. Msgr. Felici's article originally appeared in a monthly bulletin published for the professional use of the clergy of the diocese of Rome, "La psicanalise," *Bollettino del clero Romano* (Apr., 1952), p. 114.
[3] *AAS*, 44 (1952), 779–89 at 783–84. See also *L'Osservatore Romano*, An. 92, n. 222 (Sept. 21, 1952), 1.

and delivered an important address to them. He insisted on some fundamental principles on the relationship between psychiatry, morality and religion, but his cordial reception of the psychiatrists and psychoanalysts and the friendly words which he closed his address showed a spirit far removed from hostility to this modern branch of science. He said:

Be assured that the Church follows your research and your medical practice with warm interest and best wishes. You work on a terrain that is very difficult. Your activity, however, is capable of achieving precious results for medicine, for the knowledge of the soul in general, for the religious dispositions of man and for their development. May Providence and divine grace light your path! In pledge thereof We impart to you with fatherly good will Our Apostolic Blessing.[4]

The following facts also demonstrate that there is no fundamental opposition or necessary hostility between Catholicism and psychiatry. First, the ecclesiastical courts from the highest to the lowest regularly make use of the services and testimony of psychiatric experts in marriage cases and other cases. Some courts use certain psychiatrists with such regularity that they acquire a quasi-official status as psychiatrists of the tribunal. Secondly, the diocesan Catholic Charities offices throughout the United States regularly make use of the services of psychiatrists and refer cases to them. Thirdly, the Catholic hospitals regularly have on their staffs psychiatrists whose services they use and recommend. Fourthly, a brief statement of the policy followed in Catholic hospitals of both Canada and United States—a statement which is based on the papal address

[4] AAS, 45 (1953), 278–83 at 283.

to the Psychotherapists and Clinical Psychologists— runs as follows:

There is no objection on principle and in general to psychoanalysis or any other form of psychotherapy. The psychiatrists and psychotherapists, however, must observe the cautions dictated by sound morality, such as: avoiding the error of pansexualism; never counselling even material sin; respecting the secrets that the patient is not permitted to reveal; avoiding the disproportionate risk of moral dangers.[5]

If all this represents the "official" attitude of the Catholic Church (so far as there is any such thing) toward psychiatry, how does it come about that so many Catholics and not a few priests have such unfavorable opinions of it? Why is it so often stated or implied that there is definite opposition between psychiatry and religion? Fifty years ago this was not the case. The "alienist" who treated mental patients (or arranged for their custody) and his method of treating them, caused no particular concern to the clergy. After all why should psychiatry, the healer of sick minds, be at odds with religion, the healer of sick souls? Is it not in accord with true religious principles and the charity of Christ to do everything we can to heal the sick mind and cure the troubled soul?

One reason may be that Catholic writers who condemn vigorously the materialism, atheism, and determinism of Freud and of certain of his followers, although they distinguish between such psychiatrists and others, do not really drive the distinction home, and leave their readers with

[5] Quoted from *Ethical and Religious Directives for Catholic Hospitals* (St. Louis: The Catholic Hospital Association, 1955), n. 46. This booklet is the basis for the official moral code used in all Catholic Hospitals in Canada and for the code that is now official in many of the dioceses in the United States.

false impressions. A common denominator of such books and writings is that the authors profess to condemn only a small group of materialistic psychiatrists; and a common effect is that the total development of the books greatly blurs this important distinction, so that the good name of psychiatry itself is jeopardized in the minds of the readers. Francis J. Braceland, M.D., has said, when commenting on objections of this kind raised against certain psychiatrists:

Psychiatrists and most analysts would agree with . . . these objections, but it is an unfortunate fact that most of the listening and reading audience fails to discriminate so nicely and consequently the psychiatrist has little peace of soul when he is being belabored with a stick. The blows fall upon the just and the unjust, even though the group which is the object of the attack is a limited one.[6]

OVERLAPPING FIELDS

But there is a more fundamental reason than this why there is apparent opposition and sometimes real opposition between religion and certain schools of psychiatry. It is this: Both the theologian and the psychiatrist are concerned with human nature and human behavior. And some psychiatrists have very different notions from those of Catholic teaching as to the nature of man, his purpose in life, what morality means, and what in the concrete is morally good and morally evil behavior. Where you have two authorities both dealing with the same field—human beings and their human conduct—and these two authorities differ radically in their philosophy of human nature and human behavior,

[6] See Francis J. Braceland, M.D., reviewing *Peace of Soul*, by Fulton J. Sheen, D.D., in *America*, 81 (May 7, 1949), 192–3; and reviewing *Psychiatry and Asceticism*, by Felix D. Duffey, C.S.C., in *Books on Trial*, 8 (Mar., 1950), 255.

it is not strange that at times they come into conflict. And it is not strange, either, that they misunderstand each other, thus giving rise to seeming conflicts, which closer observation and more accurate understanding will dispel. Some psychiatrists, and in particular some psychoanalysts, do differ radically from Catholic teaching on fundamental points about man and his destiny. When other medical men, for instance, internists or surgeons, differ thus it is frequently of no particular importance, because they are going to treat only the body anyway. But the psychiatrist deals with the mind and the motives and the behavior of his patient.

Psychiatry is the science and the art of healing sick minds. It is a more general term than psychoanalysis, and includes all the different theories and methods of healing sick minds. Psychoanalysis is one type or method of psychiatry. There are various psychoanalytic schools, but all these schools derive originally from Freud and his followers, and all have this in common: they attribute to man's unconscious a large, active, and dynamic role in his behavior, both normal and abnormal; they use a method of analysis to get at the unconscious; and by means of this analysis try to heal the sick mind, especially in the less severe mental disorders called neuroses. This method of therapy has become increasingly popular during the last few decades, and even among psychiatrists who would not call themselves psychoanalysts the concepts and some of the techniques of psychoanalysis have been found useful and put to work.

The sharper conflicts of modern times have not been between religion and psychiatry in general, but between religion and psychoanalysis in some of its manifestations. The reason is not far to seek. Freud, the founder of psychoanalysis, could refer to religion (and morality, too, for that matter) as a "compulsive neurosis," and could name a book on religion *The Future of an Illusion.* He had a peculiar genius for rubbing people the wrong way and for getting himself misunderstood. But apart from the misunderstandings, it remains incontrovertibly true that Freud had views of religion, morality, human nature, and human behavior, which are radically opposed to the teachings of religion— not just the Catholic religion, but to Christianity in general, and to all the theistic religions of the world. Add to this the extreme emphasis on sex with which his name and that of psychoanalysis have been associated and it is not hard to understand the hostility. Sex is so sacred, so personal, and so touchy that disagreements about it are usually on a very emotional plane. Psychoanalysis was born and nurtured in an atmosphere of hostility to religion and traditional sexual morality; and though much of it nowadays has been purged of what is false and objectionable, it should cause no surprise that men of God and believers in God are still somewhat suspicious.

However, the heated tone which formerly characterized discussions about psychoanalysis and religion is now becoming a thing of the past, and there are many evidences on both sides of a sincere desire for *rapprochement*.[7] Many Catholic scholars have made appraisals of psychoanalysis, some being very favorable, some being quite reserved, others

[7] William C. Bier. S.J., "Sigmund Freud and the Faith," *America*, 96 (Nov. 17, 1956), 192–96 at 195–96, mentions the Gallahue Seminar at the Menninger Foundation, Topeka, Kansas; Workshops on Pastoral Care and Psychiatry conducted at St. John's University, Collegeville, Minnesota; and the new National Academy of Religion and Mental Health, New York, and others. There have also been summer institutes on similar topics at Detroit University, Fordham University and elsewhere in the United States.

taking a middle ground.[8] Usually when Catholics discuss the matter they distinguish, with Dr. Ch.-H. Nodet,[9] between Freud's metaphysics (his philosophical tenets), his psychology (which embraces the structure of the personality: id, ego, superego; the role of the dynamic unconscious; the instincts, etc.), and his therapeutic technique (the uncovering of hidden conflicts through free association in the psychoanalytical interview, etc.). Following this plan we shall make some brief comments on the philosophy of Freud, the psychology of psychoanalysis, and about the therapy, the method of treatment itself. We speak of the philosophy of Freud, and not that of psychoanalysis, because Freud's materialistic philosophy, though shared by many of his followers, is repudiated by many others and should not be considered essential to psychoanalysis.

THE PHILOSOPHY OF FREUD

Freud was a materialist. Not a materialist in the sense that he was a person of no ideals or of low ideals. But a philosophical materialist, that is, one who believes that there is only one thing in the universe and that one thing is

[8] Rudolf Allers, *The Successful Error*, New York: Sheed and Ward, 1940; and A. Blanchette, "The Philosophy of Psychoanalysis," *Review of the University of Ottawa*, 16 (1946), 28*–57*, reject the Freudian system almost completely. The writers in *Cahiers Laënnec*, 8 (May, 1948), generally take a very favorable view of Freudian theory and therapy inasfar as that is compatible with Catholic principles, e.g.,: I. Caruso, Louis Beirnaert, S.J., Ch.-H. Nodet, F. Pasche, etc. Cf. *New Problems in Medical Ethics*, edited by Peter Flood, O.S.B., III (Westminster, Md.: The Newman Press, 1957), 81–143. Among those who have taken a more moderate and critical view of psychoanalysis are: Joseph Donceel, S.J., "Second Thoughts on Freud," *Thought*, 24 (Sept., 1949), 466–84; Roland Dalbiez, *Psychoanalytical Method and the Doctrine of Freud*, 2 vols. transl. by T. F. Lindsay, London and New York: Longmans Green, 1941 and 1948; Joseph Nuttin, *Psychoanalysis and Personality: A Dynamic Theory of Normal Personality*, New York: Sheed and Ward, 1953.

[9] Ch.-H. Nodet, M.D., "Psychanalyse et Morale," *Cahiers Laënnec*, 8 (May, 1948), 22–36; *New Problems in Medical Ethics*, loc. cit., 103–17.

matter. Religion teaches that there are two things in the universe, matter and spirit. God is a spirit. The soul of man is a spirit. For Freud, man is not essentially different from the other animals; he has no soul or spirit distinct from the matter of which he is composed; he is merely a more highly organized type of brute matter. Roland Dalbiez, an outstanding Catholic critic and admirer of Freud's genius, says of him: "He almost comes not to regard anything as natural to man but the characteristics he shares with the other animals." [10]

Obviously there is a definite and irreconcilable conflict between this philosophy of human nature and the Catholic philosophy. If Freud was a genius, he exercised his genius in exploring those instincts, feelings, and emotions which man shares with the lower animals. The critic just referred to put it this way: "The specific nature of the spiritual values eludes the instrument of investigation which Freud's genius created. . . . Freud's work is the most profound analysis that history has ever known of the less human elements in human nature." [11]

It is in direct contradiction of this materialistic view of man's nature that the Holy Father in his address to the psychotherapists makes the following impressive statement:

Medicine has learned to look upon the human body as a mechanism of great precision, whose parts fit into one another. The place and the characteristics of these parts are dependent on the whole, they serve its existence and its functions. This, however, is all the more true of the soul, whose delicate wheels have been assembled with much more care. The various psychic

[10] Roland Dalbiez, *op. cit.*, II, 306.
[11] *Ibid.*, p. 325 and p. 327.

faculties and functions form part of the whole spiritual being, and are at the service of its final purpose.

It is useless to develop this point further. But you, psychologists and psychic healers, must bear this fact in mind: the existence of each psychic faculty and function is explained by the purpose of the whole man. What constitutes man is principally his soul, the substantial form of his nature. From it, ultimately, flows all the life activity of man; in it are rooted all the psychic forces, with their own proper structure and their organic law; it is the soul which nature charges with the government of all man's energies, insofar as these have not yet acquired their final determination.[12]

Freud was an atheist. Obviously a materialist must be an atheist if he is logical, because the personal God who created the world and governs it by His providence is a pure spirit. To Freud this God whom we worship is a mere myth and a delusion, the product of the unconscious. Again the Holy Father contradicts: "We know, on the contrary, that religion, the natural and supernatural knowledge of God and worship of Him, do not proceed from the unconscious or the subconscious, nor from an impulse of the affections, but from the clear and certain knowledge of God by means of His natural and positive revelation." [13]

Freud was a determinist. He denied that man has a free will. For him man has no more power of free choice than the brute animals have, and all his actions from the cradle to the grave are determined by forces over which he has no freely chosen control. Determinism is also a natural corollary of materialism. It is only a spiritual being that can be endowed with the power of free choice. For Freud the

[12] *AAS,* 45 (1953), 278–86 at 279.
[13] *Ibid.,* p. 284.

choices we call free are often the product of unconscious dynamic factors which determine them this way or that, though we may imagine they are free. Here again there is an absolute conflict with Catholic doctrine, according to which man is really free in some of his choices, in the sense we have explained in an earlier chapter. And once again the Holy Father insists:

Given this ontological and psychological fact [that it is the soul which is charged with the government of all man's energies] it follows that it would be quite unreal to attempt, in theory or in practice, to entrust the determining role of the whole to one particular factor, for example, to one of the elementary psychic dynamisms, and thus install a secondary power at the helm. Those psychic dynamisms may be *in* the soul, *in* man; they are not, however, *the* soul nor *the* man. They are energies of considerable intensity, perhaps, but nature has entrusted their direction to what is at the center, namely, the spiritual soul endowed with intellect and will, which is normally capable of governing these energies. That these energies may exercise pressure upon an activity, does not necessarily signify that they compel it. To deprive the soul of its central place would be to deny an ontological and psychic reality.[14]

Materialism, atheism, determinism do not constitute all of Freud's philosophy of man, but they are a very important part of it, and they naturally result in giving him a view of human nature, human destiny, and human behavior which is fundamentally at variance with religious teachings. It is silly and futile to try, as some have done, to reconcile these ideas of Freud, considered at the philosophical level, with Catholic teaching. Similar ideas permeate much psychoanalytical writing, and some of Freud's contemporary

[14] *Ibid.*, p. 279.

followers share his philosophy. But others do not. It is possible to subscribe to much of the psychological theory of psychoanalysis, and to make use of many psychoanalytical techniques without adhering to materialism, atheism, or determinism at all.

THE PSYCHOLOGY OF PSYCHOANALYSIS

At the psychological level psychoanalysis deals with the unconscious, its dynamic character, the structure of the personality, the nature of emotional drives and of instincts, especially the sex instinct. If we leave aside the question of free will there is not much in all this which comes into clear and direct conflict with Catholic teaching. Much of it has found acceptance among competent Catholic critics; much of it has no bearing on questions of faith and morals. If the theologian were to make a general criticism he would probably say that psychoanalytical psychology seems to him to overemphasize the instinctive, emotional, and irrational elements in human nature, not paying sufficient attention to the role of the intellect and the will. This overemphasis is most marked where sex is concerned. The critics who call attention to these and other defects are by no means exclusively Catholic.

But it is not the part of the moralist or the theologian to pass judgment on psychological theories, whether of the school of psychoanalysis or of other schools. This is the work of positive science and of rational psychology. One of the tasks that confront the Catholic psychologist is to separate the chaff from the wheat in depth psychology by careful and objective study. The scholarly conclusion of Father Joseph Donceel, S.J., commends itself by its measured language and thoughtful tone:

The system as a whole, in its pure Freudian form, must be rejected. But as it is nowadays presented by some of Freud's successors or disciples it gradually becomes more acceptable. Lifted out of their materialistic context, pruned of their exaggerations, quite a number of the Freudian discoveries can be reinterpreted in a sense that fits them neatly into a Christian conception of man, not only as confirmations of what was known before, but also as new and deeper insights into some aspects of human nature.[15]

PSYCHOANALYTIC THERAPY

The third level at which we look at psychoanalysis is the therapeutic level. This is the treatment of the patient as it takes place in the doctor's office. The most important question to ask about any medical treatment is whether it works or not. If it works, if it cures the patient it is a good treatment, provided always it does not make use of immoral means to do so. The moral law does transcend every other value, and as the Holy Father pointed out, the moral law does at times set limits to medical research and medical practice.[16]

The question whether psychoanalytical treatment works well or not is a question for medical science to settle. Some medical scientists have a rather poor opinion of it, especially considering how expensive a long analysis is. But others are enthusiastic in the claims they make for successful cures through analytical methods. Psychoanalysis is in its infancy. Time and the scientific method should eventually settle this question about its practical therapeutic value.

[15] Joseph Donceel, S.J., *art. cit.*, p. 484.
[16] Pius XII, "The Moral Limits of Medical Research and Treatment" (Address to the Histopathologists), *AAS*, 44 (1952), 779–89.

Meantime the other question does concern the theologian and moralist. Does psychoanalytical treatment offend against the moral law? Does it make use of immoral means to cure the patient? The best general answer to this question is given in *Ethical and Religious Directives for Catholic Hospitals*. We quote this directive on psychotherapy again:

There is no objection on principle and in general to psychoanalysis or any other form of psychotherapy. The psychiatrists and psychotherapists however, must observe the cautions dictated by sound morality, such as: avoiding the error of pansexualism; never counselling even material sin; respecting the secrets that the patient is not permitted to reveal,[17] avoiding the disproportionate risk of moral dangers.[18]

[17] In his address to the psychotherapists, *AAS*, 45 (1953), 283, Pius XII was at pains to safeguard the secret of confession (in case a priest were being psychoanalyzed), and the professional secret in general. Difficult problems of professional secrecy also arise when religious superiors send their subjects to the psychiatrist for treatment. If the psychiatrist is to report back to the superior and tell him what he has learned from the patient's self-revelation, this may involve a violation of canon 530, § 1, which strictly forbids superiors to demand an account of conscience from their subjects. Furthermore, if the information is going to be used for the external government of the religious (or of the religious community) contrary to his wishes or intent, there may be a violation of the secret of manifestation or at least of the secrecy of the paternal forum, as well as a violation of the doctor's obligation of professional secrecy to the patient. An analogous problem arises in court procedure in criminal cases where mental abnormality is alleged as a defense. See Gerard O'Brien, "Psychiatry and the Defence of Insanity," *Bulletin of the Guild of Catholic Psychiatrists*, 4 (April, 1956), 3–20 at 10–11; and John C. Ford, S.J., "Criminal Responsibility in Canon Law and Catholic Thought," *ibid.*, 3 (Dec., 1955), 3–22 at 18. As a practical way of avoiding some of the difficulties that can occur in religious life it should be understood beforehand by all concerned what use is to be made of the information, and if possible the explicit permission of the subject should be obtained for such use. For an excellent treatment of the obligations of secrecy of the master of novices, with principles that apply to religious life generally, see John R. Post, S.J., "The Novice Master and Secrecy," *Review for Religious*, 15 (Jan., 1956), 11–20.
[18] Cf. *supra*, footnote 5.

PRECAUTIONS IN PSYCHOTHERAPY

We shall now call attention to some of these moral dangers and the precautions against them, basing our remarks largely on the two papal statements already referred to. It is not to be thought that all the dangers referred to exist whenever psychiatry or psychoanalysis is used. Frequently none of them is present. But experience seems to indicate that these dangers are not imaginary. Hence they regularly need to be kept in mind, and sometimes need to be emphasized.

First, some psychiatrists and psychoanalysts give advice which is contrary to the moral law. For instance, they advise a patient to masturbate or fornicate, or to get a divorce and remarry, for therapeutic reasons. It is a libel on the profession, however, to say that reputable psychoanalysts advise sexual promiscuity. Psychoanalysts have been much maligned in this regard. One should remember also that psychoanalysts are not the only ones who sometimes advise immoral conduct. Lawyers have been known to do it. Physicians and nonanalytical psychiatrists have been known to do it. Priests have been known to do it.

But the danger needs to be specifically pointed out in the case of psychotherapy because of the character of the sexual theories and materialistic views embraced by some psychotherapists, and also because of the infiltration of existentialist morality into psychological circles. Pius XII, addressing himself to the psychotherapists, warns them against a morality which fastens its attention almost exclusively on "existential" man, *homo ut hic*, to the disparagement of those universal, objective standards which are based on "essential" man, *homo ut sic*. He denied that between these two conceptions there lies a chasm which cannot be crossed except at the expense of traditional psychology and ethics. "Consequently," he said, "it would be erroneous to establish for real life standards which would move away from natural and Christian morality, and which, for want of a better word, could be called 'personalist ethics.'" [19]

Even among some Catholic authors it was suggested that it might be permissible for therapeutic purposes to counsel an act which, though objectively sinful in itself, would be posited without guilt, either because the person acted in good faith, or because he acted through compulsion. His Holiness excludes this theory in clear terms:

Respect for God and His holiness must always be reflected in man's conscious acts. When, even without subjective fault on the part of the person involved, these acts are in contrast to the Divine Model, they still run counter to the ultimate purpose of his being. That is why what is called "material sin" is something which should not exist, and which constitutes in the moral order a reality not to be discounted.

From this, a conclusion follows for psychotherapy. In the presence of material sin it cannot remain neutral. It can, for the moment, tolerate what remains inevitable. Yet it must know that God cannot justify such an action. With still less reason, can psychotherapy counsel a patient to commit material sin, on the ground that it will be without subjective guilt. Such counsel would also be wrong if this action were regarded as necessary for the psychic easing of the patient, and thus as being part of the treatment. One may never counsel a conscious action which would be a deformation, and not an image, of the divine perfection.[20]

[19] *AAS*, 45 (1953), 280.
[20] Loc. cit., pp. 285–86. See Joseph J. Farraher, S.J., "Notes on Moral

Secondly, psychoanalytic treatment sometimes involves the patient emotionally to a dangerous degree with the analyst. The phenomenon of "transference" as it is called, is not something necessarily immoral, but it can be dangerous. It is said that Breuer, Freud's first colleague in psychoanalytical method, parted company with Freud, because, among other things, he considered the method improper on this account. But here again we should be careful not to misjudge the psychoanalyst or his motives. Occasional lurid newspaper stories of misconduct by psychiatrists should no more prejudice us against the professional conduct of psychiatrists in general, than canon 904 and the Constitution *Sacramentum Pœnitentiæ* of Benedict XIV should prejudice us against the behavior of confessors. Psychiatrists and psychoanalysts deserve the same presumption of good intent and good character that we owe to other professional men.

Thirdly, in some cases moral crises may result from revealing to the patient (or helping him to discover) the unconscious sources of his conduct. His moral world may be turned upside down.[21] The analyst helps him to take his mind apart, but who is to put it together again? The analyst? According to what principles? Ideally the Freudian analyst is almost a passive bystander. But in practice he is often unable to, or does not, maintain a neutral attitude toward the moral values involved in the patient's behavior, past, present, and future. His very neutrality can be mislead-

Theology," *Theological Studies*, 16 (June, 1955), 233–69 at 237, citing Fernando Azcárate, S.J., "Pio XII y la psiquiatría," *Razón y Fe*, 150 (Jul.–Aug., 1954), 43–58, and *ibid.*, (Sept.–Oct., 1954), 219–34.

[21] Cf. R. P. Tesson, S.J., "Description de la conscience morale et incidences psychiatriques," *Cahiers Laënnec*, 8 (May, 1948), 3–21 at 20; Cf. *New Problems in Medical Ethics*, *loc. cit.*, 85–102 at 101.

ing to the patient. Despite the theory, the obvious fact is that one cannot spend endless hours in discussing the most intimate problems of one's life and conduct with another human being who, whether he wants to or not, must stand as a guide and mentor, without being influenced by that other's fundamental beliefs about human behavior and conduct. The danger will vary with the characters of the persons concerned, and the nature of the illness being treated; but in general, if the analyst's philosophy of human nature and human conduct is false, there is danger to a greater or lesser degree that some of it will rub off on the patient.

Psychoanalysts themselves are not in agreement as to whether the treatment does or could or should prescind entirely from moral values. Gregory Zilboorg believes that social and moral philosophy is beyond the scope of psychoanalytic treatment, but because of the borderline areas insists that the analyst needs a philosophy of values.[22] Dr. Ch.-H. Nodet, on the other hand, believes that in all psychoanalytic treatment the patient is constantly confronted with a system of values involving certain moral truths. One of the most important of these is that others should be loved for themselves. Dr. Nodet considers the desire to be loved and approved an infantile trait: the adult should be altruistic. But on the question of altruism Dr. Nodet finds himself immediately in theological hot water. It is the old question of the limits of *amor benevolentiæ* and *amor concupiscentiæ*, and the pitfall of exaggerated altruism.[23]

[22] Gregory Zilboorg, "Psychoanalytic Borderlines," *American Journal of Psychiatry*, 112 (Mar., 1956), 706–10.

[23] John R. Connery, S.J., gives a résumé of this discussion in "Notes on Moral Theology," *Theological Studies*, 17 (Dec., 1956), 549–83 at 550, 551, citing: Ch.–H. Nodet, "Psychiatrie et vie religieuse," *Encyclopédie médico-chirurgicale*, 3, pp. 10, 11. Nodet's article is discussed by Louis

Whether or not Dr. Nodet's opinion is extreme, and deserves to be rejected on theological grounds, as L. Beirnaert, S.J., contends, it is clear that in Catholic teaching well-ordered self-love is fundamental to a life of virtue. Pius XII rejects the extreme position of some psychoanalysts on this point:

Beginning with certain psychological explanations, the thesis is formulated that the unconditioned extroversion of the ego is the fundamental law of congenital altruism and of its dynamic tendencies. This is a logical, psychological, and ethical error. There exists, in fact, a defence, an esteem, a love and a service of one's personal self, which is not only justified but demanded by psychology and morality. Nature makes this plain, and it is also a lesson of the Christian faith (cf. St. Thomas, *Summa Theol.* II ª, II ᵃᵉ, q, 26, a.4, in c.)! Our Lord taught: "Thou shalt love thy neighbor as thyself" (Mark, XII, 31). Christ, then, proposes as the rule of love of neighbor, charity towards oneself, not the contrary. Applied psychology would misapprehend this reality, if it were to describe all consideration of the ego as psychic inhibition, error, a return to a former state of development, under the pretext that it is contrary to the natural altruism of the psychism.[24]

FREE ASSOCIATION

Fourthly, the technique of free association itself, the most characteristic thing about analytical treatment, is not free from danger in certain cases. In free association the patient is encouraged to talk freely to the analyst, expressing whatever comes into his mind, letting the thoughts run from one thing to another, letting one thought freely lead

---

Beirnaert, S.J., "Psychanalyse et foi chrétienne," *Études*, 288 (Feb., 1956), 219–30.

[24] Pius XII to the Psychotherapists, *AAS*, 45 (1953), 282–83.

to or associate with another thought. The purpose is to get at the unconscious source of the neurotic trouble, to expose it to the light of day, on the theory that mere exposure, if achieved in the proper emotional setting, will eliminate the trouble, or at least will set the stage for further treatment and emotional re-education. The technique of free association and the emotional "abreaction" which results from it involve "re-living the emotional experiences of the past." [25] It is also a sort of "daydreaming aloud." Nothing is to be held back: "No modesty, no shame, no duty of charity, can justify the omission of a fact of consciousness." [26] Apart from the question of safeguarding secrets, especially that of the confessional when the patient is a priest, this method of free association may involve considerable danger of consent to unchaste desires. It sometimes involves bodily excitement of a sexual kind.

It seems likely that the Holy Father was speaking of certain abuses of the method of free association, and possibly, too, the phenomenon of abreaction where sexual emotions are involved, in a much-quoted passage of his address to the histopathologists. We give the passage in full:

Here is another example [of a limitation placed on medical practice by the moral law]: to get rid of psychic repressions, inhibitions, complexes, man is not free to excite within himself, for therapeutic purposes, each and every one of those appetites of the sexual sphere which stir or are stirred within his being, and roll their impure waves in his unconscious or in his subconscious. He cannot make them the object of his fully conscious imaginings or desires, with all the disturbances and repercussions which such a procedure entails. For a man and for a

[25] Ch.-H. Nodet, "Psychanalyse et Morale," *Cahiers Laënnec,* 8 (May, 1948), 22–36; cf. *New Problems in Medical Ethics, loc. cit.,* 103–117.
[26] Donceel, *art. cit.,* p. 470.

Christian there exists a law of integrity and purity, of personal self-respect, which forbids plunging oneself so completely into the world of sexual images and inclinations. At this point "the medical and psychotherapeutic interest" of the patient finds a moral limitation. It is not established, indeed it is inaccurate to say that the pansexual method of a certain school of psychoanalysis is an indispensable, integral part of all serious psychotherapy worthy of the name; that the fact of having neglected this method in the past has caused serious psychic injuries, mistakes in the theory and practice of education, of psychotherapy, and still more of pastoral care; that it is imperative to fill this gap and to initiate all who are concerned with psychological questions in the leading ideas, and even if necessary in the practical application of this technique of sexuality.

We speak thus because these assertions are too often made with apodictic assurance. It would be better, in the field of instinctive life, to pay more attention to indirect treatments, and the action of the conscious psychism on the totality of imaginative and affective activity. This technique avoids the above-mentioned deviations. It tends to clarify, to heal, to direct; it influences also the dynamics of sexuality on which so much insistence is made, and which is supposed to be present, or in fact is actually present in the unconscious or the subconscious.[27]

UNCHANGING MORAL PRINCIPLES

We can take it for granted that the Holy Father is not enunciating any new moral principles in his discourse. He is simply applying old principles to a new set of facts. What are the principles? There are at least these three. It is immoral deliberately to re-approve unchaste actions that have been performed in the past. It is immoral deliberately to indulge the desire of unchaste acts. It is immoral delib-

[27] *AAS*, 44 (1952), 779–89 at 783.

erately to excite within oneself, or to acquiesce in, unchaste feelings and emotions. To do any of these things even for therapeutic purposes is forbidden by moral law. It is not permitted to do evil that good may come of it.

This does not mean, however, that sex must not be mentioned in the psychiatric interview, or that the patient, especially one whose troubles are sexual, cannot reveal what is going through his mind to the analyst. It is the *deliberate indulgence* of unchaste desires and emotions, and the *deliberate exploitation* of them which is forbidden by moral law. A patient with a bodily ailment might find the doctor's examination a source of troublesome sexual thoughts or of sexual excitement. But he is not forbidden on that account to undergo the examination. These manifestations are not desired; they are not directly intended. His attitude toward them is reluctantly permissive. Likewise the neurotic patient may find the psychoanalytic interview, the process of free association, and the necessity of expressing the sexual content of consciousness a source of temptation and excitement. When this is merely incidental to the treatment it is not necessarily immoral. Even when it is foreseen that this will occur it can be excused by the necessity which occasions it and the hoped for restoration to sound mental health.

Somewhere, here, a delicate line needs to be drawn. It is not drawn by the papal statement, which clearly was not intended to rule out all use of free association, but condemned only "pansexual" techniques.

PSYCHIATRIC ABREACTION

The difficulty of drawing the line is more pronounced in the case of abreaction than it is with regard to free association in general. Abreaction is a sort of emotional discharge or release which takes place when, in the course of the analytic treatment, traumatic experiences, hitherto buried in the unconscious, are integrated into consciousness. It is difficult to find out exactly what happens in abreaction. Probably it differs a great deal in different patients, and in the hands of different analysts. The matter has not been discussed adequately as yet by moralists.

Most Reverend Michael J. Browne has very serious doubts about the morality of abreaction which is concerned with sexual or aggressive feelings. If the emotional catharsis of a sexual or aggressive kind is an essential part of the treatment, it seems to him that one would be intending at least material sin in order that good might come of it.[28] André Snoeck, S.J., some years ago, was ready to make rather wide concessions to the psychotherapists in the matter of abreaction.[29] John R. Connery, S.J., remains doubtful:

If the actual execution of the sinful desire or repetition of the sinful experience were necessary, the analyst would not be justified in encouraging it or promoting it, even though the present state of the patient might make it only a material sin. But I doubt that reputable psychoanalysts today would maintain the need of such expression. Everyone will admit that sexual expression relieves sexual desire, but everyone knows as well that yielding to the sex appetite also strengthens it. So I doubt that sexual expression would, or even could, be considered a genuine therapy in these cases. But let us suppose that the original sex desire or experience was repressed by a fear of castration. The treatment might consist in conscious recall of this desire or experience (not carrying it out again) for the purpose of dismissing

[28] Michael J. Browne, "The Morality of Abreaction," *Irish Theological Quarterly*, 23 (Jan., 1956), 1–11.

[29] André Snoeck, S.J., "Moral Reflections on Psychiatric Abreaction," *Theological Studies*, 13 (June, 1952), 173–89.

the desire or repudiating the experience on rational grounds rather than through repression by fear. This would not involve either formal or material sin. It might include some risk in the recall of temptation or sin, but I am inclined to think that the risk would be slight. Presumably one is dealing with repressions which took place in childhood. I should think that recalling even in some detail sinful desires or experiences of childhood would hardly be a source of temptation for the ordinary adult, especially when he is relating them in the presence of someone else.[30]

Until we have more definite evidence as to what actually occurs in abreaction, and as to what happens to the individual who experiences it, and why, it is impossible to pass a general judgment on its morality. Perhaps from the moral viewpoint it is not one thing but many. Meantime the best we can do is to rely on the application of our general principles to the individual cases as they occur. It is the deliberate indulgence of what theologians call technically *delectatio venerea, gaudium, desiderium,* or *delectatio morosa* which is forbidden by moral law. It is not clear that abreaction of itself, or necessarily, involves any of these.[31]

[30] John R. Connery, S.J., "Notes on Moral Theology," *Theological Studies,* 17 (Dec., 1956), 549–83 at 551–2.

[31] Prudence requires that in the choice of a psychiatrist, as in the choice of any professional consultant where religious or moral issues may be involved, care should be taken that his principles and practices are acceptable. To find a psychiatrist who is both competent in his field and trustworthy from this point of view is not always easy. We are in grave need of more Catholics who will take up this branch of psychological medicine. One way of finding a suitable psychiatrist is to contact the superintendent of a Catholic hospital, explain briefly the nature of the problem, and ask for the names of men on the staff or other reliable men. Another way is to contact the local office of the Catholic Charities of the diocese. The physician need not be a Catholic, but he should be one whose principles and practices do not offend against Catholic morality.

COOPERATION OF PRIEST AND PSYCHIATRIST

Toward the end of his discourse to the psychotherapists the pope mentioned the fact that nowadays it is not uncommon for the priest to refer pathological cases to the doctor. But in cases of real sin, he said, it should be rather the doctor who directs the patient to God, and refers him to those who have the power to remit sin in the name of God.[32] It is laboring the obvious, perhaps, to emphasize the need of cooperation between priests and psychiatrists. The fact that there is such a discipline as pastoral psychiatry, while from the press are pouring numberless books and articles dealing with this topic, is enough in itself to demonstrate the need.[33]

Every priest is baffled at times by problems, in the lives of his penitents and consultants, which refuse to be solved by the supernatural means at his disposal. Psychiatrists, too, frequently encounter cases where they feel at a loss without professional help from a spiritual guide. Usually it is not a question of deciding whether this person is a neurotic or a sinner but of recognizing the fact that he is both and proceeding accordingly.[34] The difficulty often is that neither the priest nor the psychiatrist dares to send his penitent or his patient to the other, because he does not know what kind of reception the person will get or what kind of treatment and advice he will receive. The need of cooperation arises, for example, in cases of scrupulosity (an obsessive fear

[32] *AAS*, 45 (1953), 285.
[33] It is impossible to list even a small proportion of such books and articles. For some useful titles, see Joseph J. Farraher, S.J., "Notes on Moral Theology," *Theological Studies*, 16 (June, 1955), 233–69 at 235–36. See also *Theological Studies*, 15 (Mar., 1954), 63.
[34] Cf. John C. Ford, S.J., *Depth Psychology, Morality and Alcoholism* (Weston, Mass.: Weston College Press, 1951), p. 62.

of sin), of alcohol and drug addiction, of compulsive masturbation, and of homosexuality.[35] Religious superiors, too, feel
the need of psychiatric help in screening candidates for the
seminary or novitiate, and when their subjects suffer mental
breakdowns. A desideratum of the first importance at
present is to provide confessors and religious superiors with
the kind of practical criteria they need in order to decide
whether a penitent or a subject needs professional psychiatric help.

But there can be no successful cooperation without
mutual respect. There can be no real respect without mutual
understanding. Given mutual respect and understanding
the cooperation which is so badly needed can result in
precious benefits to the minds and souls of men. In what
follows we will develop a little further the ideas of mutual
respect and mutual understanding.

MUTUAL RESPECT

Unless the priest has a fundamental respect for the person and the profession of the psychiatrist there can be little
hope of fruitful collaboration. Respect for his person means

---

[35] It is not within the scope of the present chapter to deal with the im-
portant problem of pastoral help for homosexuals. Some useful references:
John F. Harvey, O.S.F.S., "Homosexuality as a Pastoral Problem," *Theo-
logical Studies*, 16 (Mar., 1955), 86–108; Robert Odenwald, "Counseling
the Homosexual," *The Priest*, 9 (Dec., 1953), 940–44; James J. Fischer,
S.J., "Counseling the Adolescent Invert," *The Theologian* (manuscript,
Woodstock College, Woodstock, Md.), 11 (Winter, 1955), 15–26;
Thomas Verner Moore, O.S.B., "The Pathogenesis and Treatment of
Homosexual Disorders," *Journal of Personality*, 14 (Sept., 1945). Among
the most useful books on the subject for priest and penitent alike is *The
Invert and His Social Adjustment*, by Anomaly, London: Baillière, Tindall
and Cox, 1929; second revised edition, 1948, published in the United States
by Williams and Wilkins, Baltimore, 1949. See also the papers and discussions on homosexuality in *Proceedings of the Second Institute for the
Clergy on Problems in Pastoral Psychology*, New York: Fordham University, 1957.

that he is presumed to be an upright and competent practitioner, at least until there is good reason in the individual case to judge the opposite. Such respect does not admit continual ill-natured jokes at the expense of the psychiatrist, or an attitude of superiority over him in dealing with people's troubles, or a habit of harsh criticism of his foibles and mistakes. It is childish to judge the whole profession in the light of one individual's shortcomings. It is illogical to condemn the whole profession day in and day out, but then expect it to work miracles when a desperate case requires immediate psychiatric care. After all, psychiatry is still in its infancy.

Respect for the psychiatrist's profession means that the priest has a high regard for that branch of medical science which deals with mental and emotional ills. He does not dismiss the whole business (as so many uninformed persons do) as modern foolishness. He recognizes that there is such a thing as emotional illness and there are sick people who fall far short of anything that can be described by the words "insane" and "mentally unbalanced"; that this constitutes real pathology; and that psychiatry has its proper role and *raison d'être* in treating such pathology and in preventing it through sound mental hygiene.[36]

As for the psychiatrist, he too can hope for little success in working with a priest unless he has this basic respect for the person and the profession of the priest. If his attitude is one of not quite hidden hostility and disparagement; if he believes everyone who says to him: "The priest told me so and so"; if he judges all priests on the basis of some un-

[36] Robert P. Odenwald, "Mental Hygiene and the Priest," *Homiletic and Pastoral Review*, 51 (Dec., 1950), 235-42. In this excellent article the author covers various aspects of parish life in which the priest can help individuals to achieve emotional stability.

pleasant experience with one or two of them; if at heart he thinks religion is an illusion and conventional morality a neurosis, how can he hope to get cooperation? It is not essential to this fundamental respect that the psychiatrist accept the teachings of the Catholic Church, or of any organized form of religion, although in the case of psychoanalysis there are special difficulties, as we have seen, in undergoing analysis with a nonbeliever. But it is essential that the psychiatrist recognize the spiritual and religious side of human nature and respect it, and that he acknowledge the professional competence of the priesthood to deal with religious, spiritual and moral problems.

A Catholic believer has a great advantage here. But just as one need not be a "believer" in Freudian theory in order to have respect for the person and profession of the psychiatrist, so one need not be a believer in Catholicism in order to have respect for the person and profession of the priest. However, both priest and psychiatrist should stay in their own fields. Each is a specialist and should stick to his specialty. It is a mistake to play the psychiatrist in the confessional. It is a mistake to play spiritual father in the doctor's office. Not that the priest can ever prescind entirely from or be indifferent to the possible emotional illness of his penitent. Not that the psychiatrist can ever prescind entirely from or be indifferent to the moral and spiritual values in his patient's conduct. And admittedly it is difficult to draw the line as to where the resources of psychological medicine end and the resources of professional religious help begin. Note that we are talking about professional help. Every good, sensible man, professional or lay, who loves his neighbor in the spirit of the Gospel, can give common-sense psychological help, and common-sense spiritual help to his troubled neighbor. No one may ever abdicate the fundamental office of charity. But the majority of Catholics who comment on this matter seem to be firmly convinced that priest and psychiatrist should each stick to his own speciality as far as possible. There are certainly too many amateur psychiatrists in the world, and perhaps there are too many amateur father confessors, too.[37]

MUTUAL UNDERSTANDING

There can be no real respect without mutual understanding. This means an understanding of points of difference where they really exist, as well as points of agreement; the elimination of misunderstandings where the differences are only apparent, and a sympathetic insight into one another's aims and ideals. Both priest and psychiatrist should be *willing to learn* from each other.

The priest for his part, should know what modern psychiatry is, what it aims at, what is meant by the dynamic approach to psychiatric problems. He should be acquainted in a general way with the various kinds of therapy used by psychiatrists, and with practical criteria, not for diagnosing, but for recognizing, or at least suspecting, common forms of psychiatric illness. There are many cases in which it is not easy for the priest to determine whether the difficulties of his penitent, consultant or religious subject, are such as to require professional psychiatric care. And yet it is often the priest who is in a position to be the first to recognize the need, because he receives the confidences of people. So often a mentally disturbed person will tell his inmost, troublesome thoughts to a priest and ask rather wistfully

[37] J. S. Cammack, S.J., "Confessor and/or Psychiatrist," *Clergy Review*, 18 (Apr., 1940), 290–303.

whether the priest thinks he is losing his mind. If the priest could be supplied with workable criteria for distinguishing the passing, superficial disorders from deeper disturbances requiring immediate care, he would be in a strong position to direct his consultant to such help. What he needs is the kind of criteria which would provide him with at least a well-founded, well-informed suspicion of serious psychiatric illness. For instance, it is obviously unrealistic to send all the numberless scrupulants to the psychiatrist for help. Which ones really need that help, and which ones can be safely dealt with by the priest himself?

It is because of this kind of problem that more and more seminaries are introducing lectures on psychiatry, and are giving their students psychiatric orientation. Some provide for hospital experience in mental institutions where regular courses are established to orient clerics in pastoral psychology. This kind of training is invaluable in giving the future priest the kind of understanding he needs, if he is to co-operate effectively with psychiatrists later on in his priestly work.

The psychiatrist on his side is also frequently in need of more information about what revealed religion is, about what the Catholic faith is and what the Catholic Church claims to be. There are some Catholic psychiatrists, too, who need to learn more about these matters. Their formal religious instruction may have ended with the Number Three Catechism, and since that time their religious knowledge has been overlaid with all sorts of accretions and distortions. They may labor under the impression that because they were "born and brought up Catholics" they understand well enough the Catholic faith. A psychiatrist who is going to work intimately with a Catholic patient should know what Catholics believe about confession and the essential difference (with only superficial similarities) between the work of the priest in the confessional and the work of the psychiatrist in therapy. He should know what Catholics mean by the "dangers" of psychoanalysis. He also needs to understand the transcendent character of the moral order, the absolute immorality of intrinsically evil acts, the fundamentals of Catholic sex morality, what Catholics mean by free will, and the Catholic doctrine of original sin. This last is particularly important because so frequently misunderstood. It is confused with the Protestant doctrine according to which original sin essentially vitiated man's nature and freedom. In Catholic theology original sin leaves man's nature essentially intact—stripped of supernatural gifts, damaged in his natural endowments, but not essentially damaged, not intrinsically vitiated. The psychiatrist is not expected to be a theologian, but he would profit by an understanding of a doctrine which has such a fundamental bearing on our conception of human nature and of the emotional ills and conflicts which beset it.[38] Without some

[38] See Cyril Vollert, S.J., "Original Sin and Education," *Review for Religious*, 5 (1946), 217–28; reprinted in *The Linacre Quarterly*, 16 (Aug., 1950), 13–22. This article was written primarily for religious educators, but everything in it should be of interest to Catholic physicians and of special profit to psychiatrists. The careful reading of Father Vollert's article should lead to these conclusions: 1. Since original sin took away only our supernatural endowment and left our human nature intact, it is not necessary, generally speaking, for a psychiatrist to know about original sin in order to *diagnose* a mental illness. 2. On the other hand, since the psychiatrist aims at the integration of the human personality, it would benefit him immeasurably to know the revealed doctrines pertinent to the Fall of man and to his restoration in Christ. The psychiatrist who knows and accepts these doctrines will realize that, though his therapeutic helps are valuable for emotional integration, they do not suffice in themselves for the adequate rebuilding of the human personality.

understanding of matters such as these it will be difficult to cooperate with a priest in helping the mentally ill.

REAL GUILT AND NEUROTIC GUILT

Both priest and psychiatrist should be aware of the fundamental distinction between real guilt and neurotic guilt. The priest is concerned with real guilt. In the confessional he applies to souls who are sick with the sickness of sin the healing power of Christ's grace, administered through absolution. It washes away real guilt from those who have really sinned and who are now really repentant. The psychiatrist is often concerned not with real guilt, contracted through the deliberate choice of sin, but with neurotic guilt in its various manifestations. The priest may tend to overlook the existence of neurotic guilt. The psychiatrist may fail to give real guilt its due.

Dr. Karl Stern gives in a single paragraph four criteria of neurotic guilt which are useful to both priest and psychiatrist, but especially to the priest. The first three of these are practical criteria which he can use to recognize pathological guilt feelings:

What then is the difference between guilt and neurotic guilt? The concept of guilt is closely associated with the concept of justice. Guilt has the quality of proportion. The greater your wrong, the guiltier you are. There is something about this proportion which can almost be quantified. If you find and keep a hundred dollars which belongs to your neighbor, common sense would say that you are much guiltier than if you took a couple of postage stamps from him without returning them. A compulsive-obsessive ("scrupulous") person may feel guiltier for not having returned a couple of postage stamps than a man convicted of theft of one hundred dollars. Secondly, objective guilt can be assuaged. Like debt, to which it is related, it can be paid. Neurotic guilt is insatiable. You cannot appease it. You cannot pay it off. Thirdly, objective guilt does not necessarily depend on emotion. A man may regard himself as guilty and be perfectly relaxed about it. Neurotic guilt is so inextricably interwoven with anxiety, that that which is experienced subjectively is at times only the anxiety without conscious feelings of guilt. Finally, (and this is related to point number one) neurotic guilt is related to repressed drives just as much as to realized acts. Objective guilt refers to realized acts only.[39]

As to real guilt, it will be instructive to cite, especially for the benefit of the psychiatrist, the passage from Pius XII's discourse to the psychotherapists which insists on the reality of guilt and speaks of the cooperation between priest and physician where real guilt is concerned:

To the transcendent relations of the psychism, there belongs also the sense of guilt, the awareness of having violated a higher law, by which nevertheless, one recognizes himself as being bound, an awareness which can find expression in suffering and in psychic disorder.

Psychotherapy, here, approaches a phenomenon which is not within its own exclusive field of competence, for this phenomenon is also, if not principally, of a religious nature. No one will deny that there can exist—and not infrequently—an irrational and even morbid sense of guilt. Yet a person may also be aware of a real guilt which has not been wiped away. Neither psychology nor ethics possesses an infallible criterion for cases of this kind, since the workings of conscience which beget this sense of guilt have too personal and subtle a structure. In any case, it is certain that no purely psychological treatment will cure a genuine sense of guilt. Even if psychotherapists, perhaps

[39] Karl Stern, *The Third Revolution* (New York: Harcourt Brace, 1954), pp. 202–03.

even in good faith, question its existence, it still abides. Even if the sense of guilt be eliminated by medical intervention, auto-suggestion, or outside persuasion, the fault remains, and psychotherapy would deceive both itself and others, if, in order to do away with the sense of guilt, it pretended that the fault no longer exists.

The means of eliminating the fault does not belong to the purely psychological order. As every Christian knows, it consists in contrition and sacramental absolution by the priest. Here, it is the root of the evil, it is the fault itself, which is extirpated, even though remorse may continue to make itself felt. Nowadays, in certain pathological cases, it is not rare for the priest to send his penitent to a doctor. In the present case, the doctor should rather direct his patient toward God, and to those who have the power to remit the fault itself in the name of God.[40]

THE NORMAL MAN

Finally, let us close our discussion of psychiatry and Catholicism with some reflections on the meaning of the "normal man," to whom, following the lead of His Holiness, we have referred so frequently. It is the normal man whose fundamental human responsibility we have been defending throughout these chapters. It is hoped that these brief considerations may eliminate some misunderstandings on the part of both priest and psychiatrist, while leaving the task of actually defining mental illness and mental health to those who are competent in these fields.

In Catholic teaching, whether it comes from the mouth of the pope, or from the consensus of theologians or of canonists, the normal man is considered a responsible individual, capable of controlling himself, of avoiding evil

40 *AAS*, 45 (1953), 285.

and of doing good. And there is a presumption that men are normal until the opposite is shown. Nor is that presumption destroyed merely by the fact that a man has indeed chosen the evil, and a good deal of the evil, rather than the good. For it is normal to man to be able to forsake the good, the *bonum honestum*, and of his own free will follow the evil, because of the pleasurable good that is in it.

But the word "normal," which we use so frequently and so fluently, has become suspect in some circles. Some psychiatrists seem to object to using it at all—as if it had no meaning, as if there were no such thing as a normal person. Perhaps the reason is that the word is equivocal. It is used in different senses by different persons.

Sometimes normal means conformed to some ideal standard. If an ideal standard of human personality is imagined, it is easy to see that everyone will be in some respect abnormal, because no matter what the standard is everyone will fall short of it in some respect.

Sometimes normal means average, and where measurable quantities are involved people can be classified as average or more or less average, while those who are too far away from the average can be called abnormal in that particular respect. If the average weight of adult men is 175 pounds, then a weight of 300 pounds would be abnormal. If average intelligence can be represented by the figure 100 then a person whose intelligence rating is 200 would be abnormal. But such abnormality does not necessarily involve pathology. A genius is abnormal from this point of view; but he is not mentally ill because he is mentally egregious.

Sometimes conduct is called normal when it conforms to the conduct which is usual in a given group. Adjustment to the group becomes a standard of normality. But conduct can be right or wrong, and it is not what the group uniformly does that makes it right. It would be a misleading use of language, in a group where most of the members told lies at times, to call those few who did not tell lies abnormal;—statistically abnormal, if you like, but not humanly, or morally, or even psychologically abnormal.[41]

It would seem that those who object to the word normal, as having little or no meaning, fasten their attention too exclusively on one or another of these meanings. They are impressed also by the fact that so-called "normality" shades off into so-called "abnormality" by imperceptible degrees, and by the fact that certain pathological psychic traits or symptoms can be identified as exaggerated versions of the same traits in so-called "normal" persons. It is natural enough, but fallacious nevertheless, to conclude that because one cannot draw a definite line separating normal from abnormal, therefore there is no real distinction between them; or to conclude from the continuity of a certain trait through various degrees from normal to abnormal, that everyone is a little bit abnormal, while pathological individuals are very much so. And it is natural, too, that those who deal so continually with mental illness would be tempted to make the abnormal the norm of the normal. Modern dynamic psychological theory in its origins and in

---

[41] The ability to adjust to things as they are may be some sort of criterion of psychological normality, but the measure of good morality is adjustment to things as they ought to be. See John R. Connery, S.J., "Notes on Moral Theology," *Theological Studies*, 15 (Dec., 1954), 594–626 at 626, on drawing moral conclusions from statistics. On the Kinsey report as a statistical basis for morality, see W. E. Garrison, "Morals and Majorities," *Christian Century*, 70 (Sept. 16, 1953), 1053, commented on in *Theological Studies*, 15 (Mar., 1954), 92–93.

its development has relied very heavily on the clinical observation of people who are so sick that they have to see the doctor and be put into a hospital.

The fact that desirable, or at least tolerable, traits may shade off into undesirable ones when exaggerated is not a new idea nor an unacceptable one in scholastic thought. The medium virtutis is a commonplace; one sins against a virtue not only by defect but by excess. But even from the viewpoint of scientific psychology it is by no means agreed upon by all that any perfect continuity from normal to abnormal exists. Gordon Allport expresses his position as follows:

Is the normal personality simply an undistinguished edition of the mentally diseased? We do not hold this view in reference to organic conditions. There is no continuum of states from cancer to no-cancer. The patient either has a malignant growth or else he hasn't; there are no intermediate conditions. Similarly a diseased mind is in many respects functionally quite different from (and not merely an exaggeration of) the normal mind.

The belief in the perfect continuity of the normal and the abnormal . . . has resulted in the rapid multiplication of studies of disordered people, partly because, confined as they are to institutions, they are easily accessible, and partly because the extreme nature of their disorders makes them more interesting and more spectacular. Actually the number of studies of neurotic and psychotic personalities far exceeds the number devoted to normal personality, although, of course, the ratio in the world at large is precisely the opposite. The uncritical carrying over of the point of view of the mental hospital into the world outside has made . . . for serious one-sidedness in the psychological study of the normal personality. This charge is justified, even though occasionally the discoveries of psychopathology may be of indirect aid to the psychology of normality.[42]

Perhaps the idea that everyone is abnormal merely means that human nature is a very imperfect thing after all. Man's passions are actually not subject to his reason as they should be. His instincts continually try to escape the control of his higher nature. That is a fact of everyday experience. Perhaps it is not impossible to describe some of the effects of original sin in terms of dynamic psychology. The theologian's concept of the struggle between the law of the members and the law of the mind does not exclude the idea that there may be unconscious elements in that struggle, or that some of man's conflicts are due to a too-dominant unconscious. Sometimes one gets the impression that the emotional maturity envisioned as ideal would be pretty much like Adam's gift of integrity before the Fall, and that our Lord and His Blessed Mother are our only examples of complete emotional maturity. If abnormal means lacking the gift of integrity, then indeed we are all abnormal—with the abnormality induced by original sin. But such abnormality in its effects on human freedom and human responsibility, with or without the help of divine grace, would be explained in completely different ways in Catholic theology and in the theology of the Protestant Reformation.

None of these considerations should make us despair of giving some real meaning to the terms normal and abnormal. Common sense tells us that there must be a significant difference and distinction between mental illness and mental health. In fact it is obvious to everyone that even

[42] Gordon W. Allport, *Personality: A Psychological Interpretation* (New York: Henry Holt, 1937; rev. ed., 1945), p. 76.

if there is a broad borderland of cases which are hard to classify, so that one would hesitate to say that they were sane or insane, mentally well or mentally ill, yet the vast majority of persons are definitely outside that borderland, in one direction or the other.

Just as in the spectrum the colors fade into one another, and yet one part is definitely red and another part definitely orange; and just as philosophers cannot draw the line between what nature can do and what is beyond the powers of nature, and yet some events are clearly miraculous and others not; and just as we moralists cannot always draw the line between what is certainly a grave sum and what is not, and yet some sums are indubitably grave, others indubitably not; so in the case of human beings, some are definitely mentally ill, while many more are definitely not. Perhaps neither the moralist nor the psychiatrist nor the man on the street has a scientific criterion of normality—one that classifies all cases. The layman may have only a crude one— like the amount of deviation in conduct and thinking from that of the general run of men—or the need of getting medical help because of mental difficulties. Or perhaps both layman and expert could achieve a measure of agreement by saying that the normal person, that is the mentally well person, is the one in whom elements of balance definitely outweigh elements of imbalance.[43]

[43] John R. Cavanagh, "Criminal Responsibility and Free Will," *Bulletin of the Guild of Catholic Psychiatrists*, 3 (Dec., 1955), 24–33 at 24–25, gives the following definition of the normal and of mental illness: "The *normal person* may be defined as one who conforms to the average human being in his methods of thinking, feeling, willing and acting, is reasonably happy, emotionally balanced, and adjusted and oriented toward future goals. *Mental illness* may, therefore, be defined as that condition in which an individual for a more or less prolonged period of time, to a greater or lesser degree, deviates from the average human being in ways of thinking, feeling, willing and acting, or is unreasonably unhappy, or emotionally unstable and

The Catholic theologian feels that he is on fairly secure ground when he insists that there is a real and significant difference between mental illness and mental health, between psychological normality and psychological abnormality. Besides psychological authority for that proposition, he has the common sense of mankind on his side. The central theme of the present volume is bound up with the concept of normality and the recognition of the existence of normality. We have been concerned with at least these three general propositions: first, that there exists an objective moral order of values; secondly, that the Church established by Christ is the authoritative teacher of what that moral order is; and thirdly, that *the normal man is a free and responsible individual*, capable of rejecting that moral order and offending God, but capable also, with the help of God's grace, of observing it, and achieving his final destiny, which is the eternal love of God.

---

unadjustable, or poorly oriented toward future goals. It must be understood that this is a very general definition designed to cover *all* forms of emotional and mental illness."

Bibliography

Alcoholics Anonymous. Rev. ed. New York: The Alcoholic Foundation, 1955.

Alcoholism, Science and Society. New Haven, Conn.: Yale Center of Alcohol Studies, 1945.

ALLERS, Rudolf. "Abnormality: A Chapter in Moral Psychology. VI. Moral Responsibility of the Neurotic," *Homiletic and Pastoral Review*, 42 (1942), 727–33.

————. "Annulment of Marriage by Lack of Consent because of Insanity," *American Ecclesiastical Review*, 101 (1939), 325–43.

————. "Irresistible Impulses: A Question of Moral Psychology," *American Ecclesiastical Review*, 100 (1939), 208–19.

————. *The Successful Error.* New York: Sheed & Ward, 1940.

ALLPORT, Gordon W. *Personality: A Psychological Interpretation.* Rev. ed. New York: Henry Holt & Co., 1945.

"ANOMALY." *The Invert and His Social Adjustment.* 2nd rev. ed. Baltimore: Williams and Wilkins, 1949.

AZCARATE, Fernando, S.J. "Pio XII y la psiquiatría," *Razón y Fe*, 150 (1954), 43–58; 219–34.

BEIRNAERT, Louis, S.J. "Psychanalyse et foi chrétienne," *études*, 288 (1956), 219–30.

BENARD, Edmond D. "The Doctrinal Value of the Ordinary Teaching of the Holy Father in View of *Humani Generis*," *Proceedings of the Sixth Annual Convention of The Catholic Theological Society of America* (1951), 78–107.

BERAZA, Blasius, S.J. *Tractatus de gratia Christi.* Bilbao: Elexpuru Hermanos, 1916.

BERTKE, Stanley. *The Possibility of Invincible Ignorance of the Natural Law.* Washington, D.C.: Catholic University of America Press, 1941.

BIER, William C., S.J. "Sigmund Freud and the Faith," *America*, 96 (Nov. 17, 1956), 192–96.

BIHLER, Hugh, S.J. "Psychology of Instinct." Manuscript. Woodstock College, Woodstock, Md., 1950.

[353]

Bibliography

BLANCHETTE, A. "The Philosophy of Psychoanalysis," Review of the University of Ottawa, 16 (1946), 28 *–57 *.

BONNAR, Alphonsus, O.F.M. "Criminal Responsibility," Catholic Medical Quarterly, 9 (July, 1956), 67–73.

BORTOLASO, G., S.J. "Etica dell' amore ed etica dell' obbligazione," La Civiltà Cattolica, 103 (1952), 368–79.

BOSCHI, A., S.J. "La Cosi detta 'Morale Nuova'," La Scuola Cattolica, 34 (Sept.–Oct., 1956), 336–50.

BRACELAND, Francis J. Review of Felix D. DUFFEY's Psychiatry and Asceticism, in Books on Trial, 8 (1955), 255.

———. Review of Fulton J. SHEEN's Peace of Soul, in America, 81 (May 7, 1949), 192–93.

BRITT, Robert E. "Alcoholism and Some Moral Issues," Linacre Quarterly, 13 (Jan.–Apr., 1945), 15–24.

BURKE, Eugene M., C.S.P. "The Scientific Teaching of Theology in the Seminary," Proceedings of the Fourth Annual Convention of The Catholic Theological Society of America (1949), 129–73.

CAMMACK, J. S., S.J. "Confessor and/or Psychiatrist," Clergy Review, 18 (Apr., 1940), 290–303.

———. Moral Problems of Mental Defect. New York: Benziger Bros., 1939.

CARPENTIER, René, S.J. "Vers une morale de la charité," Gregorianum, 34 (1953), 32–55.

CAVANAGH, John R. "Criminal Responsibility and Free Will," Bulletin of the Guild of Catholic Psychiatrists, 3 (Dec., 1955), 24–33.

———. "Nervous Mental Diseases II," American Ecclesiastical Review, 109 (1943), 257–71.

———. "A Psychiatrist Looks at the Durham Decision," Catholic University of America Law Review, 5 (1955), 25–54.

CAVANAGH, John R. and McGOLDRICK, James B., S.J. Fundamental Psychiatry. Milwaukee: Bruce Publishing Co., 1953.

CLARK, Francis, S.J. "The Challenge to Moral Theology," Clergy Review, 38 (Apr., 1953), 214–23.

CLECKLEY, Hervey. The Mask of Sanity. St. Louis: C. V. Mosby Co., 1950.

CONNELL, Francis J., C.SS.R. "Juvenile Courtships," American Ecclesiastical Review, 132 (1955), 181–90.

CONNERY, John R., S.J. "Notes on Moral Theology," Theological Studies, 15 (1954), 594–626.

———. "Notes on Moral Theology," Theological Studies, 17 (1956), 549–83.

———. "Prudence and Morality," Theological Studies, 13 (1952), 564–82.

COOGAN, John E., S.J. "The Religious Ultimates of Justice Holmes," American Ecclesiastical Review, 132 (1955), 73–83.

COPLESTON, Frederick, S.J. Contemporary Philosophy. Westminster, Md.: The Newman Press, 1956.

COTTER, A. C., S.J. The Encyclical "Humani Generis." Weston, Mass.: Weston College Press, 1951.

COTTER, James T. "Teaching Moral Theology," American Ecclesiastical Review, 70 (1924), 413–15.

Bibliography

CREUSEN, Joseph, S.J. *Problemi di vita coniugale*. Rome: S.A.L.E.S., 1955,
————. "Le 'Voeu d'Abnégation' du R. P. Vermeersch, S.J. (1858–1936),"
Gregorianum 21 (1940), 607.
CUSHING, Richard J. "Address to the National Clergy Conference on Alco-
holism," *Priest*, 10 (1954), 683–90.
DALBIEZ, Roland. *Psychoanalytical Method and the Doctrine of Freud.*
Translated by T. F. LINDSAY. 2 vols. London and New York: Long-
mans Green, 1941–1948.
DE LETTER, P., S.J. "In Defence of Christian Conscience," *The Clergy
Monthly*, 17 (1953), 81–88.
DELHAYE, Ph. "Le théologie morale d'hier et d'aujourd'hui," *Revue des
sciences religieuses*, 27 (1953), 112–30.
DONCEEL, Joseph, S.J. "Second Thoughts on Freud," *Thought*, 24 (Sept.,
1949), 466–84.
DUFF, Edward, S.J. *The Social Thought of the World Council of
Churches*. New York: Association Press, 1956.
DUHAMEL, Joseph S., S.J. and HAYDEN, Jerome, O.S.B. "Theological and
Psychiatric Aspects of Habitual Sin." I. "Theological Aspects" by Jo-
seph S. DUHAMEL, S.J. II. "Psychiatric Aspects" by Jerome HAYDEN,
O.S.B. *Proceedings of the Eleventh Annual Convention of The Cath-
olic Theological Society of America* (1956), 130–63.
"EPISCOPUS." "Disinfecting Moral Theology," *American Ecclesiastical Re-
view*, 70 (1924), 187–89.
ERMECKE, Gustav. "Die katholische Moraltheologie heute," *Theologie
und Glaube*, 41 (1951), 127–42.
FABREGAS, M., S.J. "De obligatione vitandi probabile periculum peccandi,"
Periodica de re morali, canonica, liturgica, 30 (1941), 20–45.
FARRAHER, Joseph J., S.J. "Notes on Moral Theology," *Theological Studies*,
16 (1955), 233–69.
FAZZARI, G. M., S.J. *Valutazione etica e consenso matrimoniale*. Naples:
Editore M. D. D'Auria, 1951.
FELIX, Robert H. "Some Comments on the Psychopathology of Drug Ad-
diction," *Mental Hygiene*, 23 (Oct., 1939), 567–82.
FERM, Vergilius (ed.). *Encyclopedia of Morals*. New York: Philosophical
Library, Inc., 1956.
FISCHER, James J., S.J. "Counseling the Adolescent Invert," *The Theo-
logian* (Manuscript, Woodstock College, Woodstock, Md.), 11 (Win-
ter, 1955), 15–26.
FLOOD, Peter, O.S.B. (ed.). *New Problems in Medical Ethics*. 3 vols. West-
minster, Md.: The Newman Press, 1953–1957.
FORD, John C., S.J. "Alcohol Education in the Seminary," *Bulletin of the
National Catholic Educational Association*, 50 (Aug., 1953), 98–106.
————. "Alcoholism," *Catholic Encyclopedia*. Supplement *II*. New York:
The Gilmary Society, 1953.
————. "Criminal Responsibility in Canon Law and Catholic Thought,"
Bulletin of the Guild of Catholic Psychiatrists, 3 (Dec., 1955), 3–22.
————. *Depth Psychology, Morality and Alcoholism*. Weston, Mass.:
Weston College Press, 1951.
————. "The Fundamentals of Holmes' Juristic Philosophy," *Proceedings*

Bibliography

of the Jesuit Philosophical Association (18th convention, 1941), Weston, Mass.: Weston College Press.

———. "The General Practitioner's Role in Alcoholism," Linacre Quarterly, 23 (1956), 95–108.

———. Man Takes a Drink. New York: P. J. Kenedy & Sons, 1955.

———. "Reply to Father Vann," Homiletic and Pastoral Review, 57 (Nov., 1956), 124–27.

FRANZELIN, Johann Baptist. Tractatus de divina traditione et scriptura. 2nd ed. Rome, 1875.

FUCHS, Joseph, S.J. "éthique objective et éthique de situation. A propos de l'Instruction du Saint-Office du 2 février 1956," Nouvelle revue théologique, 78 (1956), 798–819.

———. "Die Liebe als Aufbauprinzip der Moraltheologie," Scholastik, 29 (1954), 79–87.

———. "Morale théologique et morale de situation," Nouvelle revue théologique, 76 (1954), 1073–85.

———. "Situationsethik in theologischer Sicht," Scholastik, 27 (1952), 161–82.

———. Situation und Entscheidung, Grundfragen christlicher Situationsethik. Frankfort on the Main, 1952.

GAGERN, Baron Frederick von. The Problem of Onanism. Translated by Meyrick BOOTH. Westminster, Md.: The Newman Press, 1955.

GARRIGOU-LAGRANGE, Reginald, O.P. Beatitude: A Commentary on St. Thomas' Theological Summa, Iᵃ IIᵃᵉ, qq. 1–54. Translated by Patrick CUMMINS, O.S.B. St. Louis: B. Herder Book Co., 1956.

GARRISON, W. E. "Morals and Majorities," Christian Century, 70 (Sept. 16, 1953), 1053.

GÉRAUD, Joseph. "Procédés actuels d'investigation de la conscience," L'Ami du clergé, 58 (1948), 518.

GILLEMAN, Gérard, S.J. Le primat de la charité en théologie morale. Paris: Desclée, de Brouwer, 1952.

GRAZIA, Edward di. "The Distinction of Being Mad," University of Chicago Law Review, 22 (1955), 339–55.

GUERRERO, E., S.J. Review of Jacques LECLERCQ's L'enseignement de la morale chrétienne, in Razón y Fe, 148 (July–Aug., 1953), 84.

GUTTMACHER, Manfred S. "The Psychiatrist as an Expert Witness," University of Chicago Law Review, 22 (1955), 325–30.

HAERING, Bernhard, C.SS.R. Das Gesetz Christi. Freiburg-im-Breisgau: Wewel, 1954.

HAMEL, édouard, S.J. "L'erreur sur la personne dans la damnification. étude de théologie positive," Sciences ecclésiastiques, 8 (1956), 335–84.

HARVEY, John F., O.S.F.S. "Homosexuality as a Pastoral Problem," Theological Studies, 16 (1955), 86–108.

HAYES, John J. "Chaplain's Letter," Bulletin of the Guild of Catholic Psychiatrists, 3 (Dec., 1955), 2.

HILDEBRAND, Dietrich von and JOURDAIN, Alice. True Morality and Its Counterfeits. New York: David McKay Inc., 1955.

Bibliography

HILL, Warren P. "The Psychological Realism of Thurman Arnold," *University of Chicago Law Review*, 22 (1955), 377–96.

HIRSCHER, John Baptist. *Die Christliche Moral als Lehre von der Verwirklichung des göttlichen Reiches in der Menschheit.* Tübingen, 1835–1836.

JELLINEK, E. M. *Phases in the Drinking History of Alcoholics.* New Haven, Conn.: Hillhouse Press, 1946.

JOURNET, Charles. *The Church of the Word Incarnate. I. The Apostolic Hierarchy.* New York: Sheed & Ward, 1955.

JURGENMEIER, F. *Der mystische Leib Christi als Grundprinzip der Aszetik.* 7th ed. Paderborn, 1938.

KALVEN, Harry, Jr. "Introduction," to a symposium on "Insanity and the Criminal Law: A Critique of Durham vs. United States," *University of Chicago Law Review*, 22 (1955), 317–19.

KATZ, Wilbur G. "Law, Psychiatry and Free Will," *University of Chicago Law Review*, 22 (1955), 397–404.

KELLY, Gerald, S.J. *The Good Confessor.* New York: The Sentinel Press, 1951.

KELLY, Gerald, S.J. in collaboration with B. R. FULKERSON, S.J., and C. F. WHITFORD, S.J. *Modern Youth and Chastity.* St. Louis: The Queen's Work, 1943.

KLEIN, D. B. *Mental Hygiene: The Psychology of Personal Adjustment.* New York: Henry Holt & Co., 1944.

KREILKAMP, Karl. "Dean Pound and the End of Law," *Fordham Law Review*, 9 (1940), 196–232.

LINDWORSKY, Johann, S.J. *The Training of the Will.* Milwaukee: Bruce Publishing Co., 1929.

LOMASK, Milton. "Alcoholism—Vice or Disease," *The Sign*, 32 (1953), 22–24.

LYNCH, John J., S.J. "Notes on Moral Theology," *Theological Studies*, 17 (1956), 167–96.

McCARTHY, R. G. *Facts About Alcohol.* Chicago: Science Research Associates, 1951.

———. *Teen-Agers and Alcohol: A Handbook for the Educator.* New Haven, Conn.: Yale Center for Alcohol Studies, 1956.

McCARTHY, R. G. and DOUGLASS, E. M. *Alcohol and Social Responsibility.* New York: Thomas Y. Crowell Co. and Yale Plan Clinic, 1949.

MANN, Marty. *Primer on Alcoholism.* New York: Rinehart and Co., 1950.

MERSCH, Émile, S.J. *Morale et Corps Mystique.* 3rd ed. Paris: Desclée, de Brouwer, 1949. English translation from the 2nd ed. by Daniel F. RYAN, S.J. New York: P. J. Kenedy & Sons, 1939.

MONTCHEUIL, Yves de, S.J. *Mélanges théologiques.* Paris, 1946.

MOORE, Thomas Verner, O.S.B. *The Driving Forces of Human Nature and Their Adjustment.* New York: Grune and Stratton, 1950.

———. "The Pathogenesis and Treatment of Homosexual Disorders," *Journal of Personality*, 14 (Sept., 1945).

MURPHY, Richard J., S.J. "A Plea for the Alcoholic," *Australasian Catholic Record*, 28 (1951), 23–30.

[357]

Bibliography

NAPHOLC, P., S.J. "De vera proximæ occasionis peccati notione," *Periodica de re morali, canonica, liturgica,* 21 (1932), 1*–34*; 129*–57*.

NOLAN, Paul. "Freedom of Will and Irresistible Impulse," *Catholic University of America Law Review,* 5 (1955), 55–62.

NOORT, Gerardus van. *Dogmatic Theology. II. Christ's Church.* Translated and revised by John J. CASTELOT, S.S. and William R. MURPHY, S.S. Westminster, Md.: The Newman Press, 1957.

NOPPEL, Constantin, S.J. *Ædificatio Corporis Christi. Aufriss der Pastoral.* 2nd ed. Freiburg-im-Breisgau: Herder, 1949.

NUTTIN, Joseph. *Psychoanalysis and Personality: A Dynamic Theory of Normal Personality.* New York: Sheed & Ward, 1953.

O'BRIEN, Gerard. "Psychiatry and the Defense of Insanity," *Bulletin of the Guild of Catholic Psychiatrists,* 4 (Apr., 1956), 3–20.

ODENWALD, Robert B. "Counseling the Homosexual," *Priest,* 9 (Mar., 1955), 86–108.

——. "Mental Hygiene and the Priest," *Homiletic and Pastoral Review,* 51 (1950), 235–42.

ODIER, Charles. *Les deux sources, consciente et inconsciente de la vie morale.* (Cahiers de Philosophie: "Etre et Penser"). Neuchâtel, Switz.: Éditions de la Bacconière, 1943–1947.

ORCHARD, Dom Bernard, et al. (ed.). *A Catholic Commentary on Holy Scripture.* New York: Thomas Nelson & Sons, 1953.

PERKINS, John F. "Defect of the Youth Correction Authority Act," *Journal of Criminal Law and Criminology,* 32 (1942), 111–18.

——. "Indeterminate Control of Offenders: Arbitrary and Discriminatory," *Law and Contemporary Problems* (Duke University Law School), (Autumn, 1942).

PINCKAERS, Servais, O.P. "The Revival of Moral Theology," *Cross Currents,* 7 (Winter, 1957), 56–67.

PLÉ, Albert, O.P. "Thou Shalt Love," *Cross and Crown,* 4 (Dec., 1952), 466–72.

POST, John R., S.J. "The Novice Master and Secrecy," *Review for Religious,* 15 (1956), 11–20.

Proceedings of the Second Institute of the Clergy on Problems in Pastoral Psychology. New York: Fordham University, 1957.

RAHNER, Karl, S.J. "Situationsethik und Sündenmystik," *Stimmen der Zeit,* 145 (1949–50), 330–42.

RANWEZ, E. "Pour ou contre une spiritualité du devoir," *Revue diocésaine de Namur,* 8 (Jan.–June, 1953), 43–58.

REGAN, A., C.SS.R. "The Proximate Occasion of Sin according to St. Alphonsus," *Australasian Catholic Record,* 26 (1949), 97–109.

REGATILLO, Eduardo F., S.J. and ZALBA, Marcelino, S.J. *Theologiæ moralis summa. I. Theologia moralis fundamentalis. Tractatus de virtutibus theologicis* by Marcelino ZALBA, S.J. 2nd ed. Madrid: Biblioteca de Autores Cristianos, 1957.

RIMAUD, Jean, S.J. "Les psychologues contre la morale," *Études,* 263 (1949), 3–22.

ROBERTI, Franciscus. *De delictis et pœnis.* Rome: Catholic Book Agency, n.d.

Bibliography

ROCHE, Philip Q. "Criminality and Mental Illness—Two Faces of the Same Coin," *University of Chicago Law Review*, 22 (1955), 320–24.

ROYCE, James C., S.J. "The Moral Responsibility of the Neurotic," Manuscript. Alma College, Alma, Calif., 1947.

RUBINSTEIN, H. S., SHAPIRO, H. D. and FREEMAN, Walter. "The Treatment of Morbid Sex Craving with Testosterone Propionate," *American Journal of Psychiatry*, 97 (1940), 703.

RYAN, Gerald A. *Principles of Episcopal Jurisdiction*. Washington, D.C.: Catholic University of America Press, 1939.

SCHILLING, O. *Handbuch der Moraltheologie*. Stuttgart, 1952.

SCHMIDT, John Rogg. "Attendance of Priests at Dances," *The Jurist*, 11 (1951), 77–99; 251–85.

SCHUMACHER, Henry C. "Psychopathic States," *Homiletic and Pastoral Review*, 40 (1940), 964.

SEILER, Johann Michael. *Handbuch der Christlichen Moral*. Munich, 1817.

SIMONART, Pierre C. "The Imputability of the Mental Patient," *Linacre Quarterly*, 15 (Oct., 1947), 8–15.

SLATER, Eliot. "The M'Naughton Rules and Modern Concepts of Responsibility," *British Medical Journal* (Sept. 25, 1954), pp. 713–18.

SLATER, T., S.J. "The Confessor's Standard of Morality," *American Ecclesiastical Review*, 68 (1923), 38–43.

SNOECK, André, S.J. "Moral Reflections on Psychiatric Abreactions," *Theological Studies*, 13 (1952), 173–89.

SPALDING, W. B. and MONTAGUE, J. R. *Alcohol and Human Affairs*. Yonkers, N.Y.: World Book Co., 1949.

SPIRER, Jess. "The Psychology of Irresistible Impulse," *Journal of Criminal Law and Criminology*, 33 (1943), 457–62.

STERN, Karl. *The Third Revolution*. New York: Harcourt, Brace & Co., 1954.

STEVAUX, Albert: "L'église et la morale," *Revue diocésaine de Tournai*, 8 (1953), 305–19.

STRAUS, Robert and BACON, Selden D. *Drinking in College*. New Haven, Conn.: Yale University Press, 1953.

STRECKER, Edward A. "Psychotherapy in Pathological Drinking," *Journal of the American Medical Association*, 147 (Oct. 27, 1951), 813–15.

TER HAAR, Francis, C.SS.R. *Casus Conscientiæ de præcipuus hujus ætatis peccandi occasionibus*. 2nd ed. Turin: Marietti, 1939.

———. *De occasionariis et recidivis*. Turin: Marietti, 1927.

"THEOLOGUS." Review of Arthur VERMEERSCH's *Theologiæ moralis principia, responsa, consilia*, in *American Ecclesiastical Review*, 70 (1924), 327–28.

THILS, G. *Tendances Actuelles en théologie morale*. Gembloux, 1940.

TIBERGHIEN, P. "Vice et maladie," *Mélanges de science religieuse*, 5 (1948), 197–216.

TIEBOUT, Harry M. "Address to National States Conference on Alcoholism," *The A. A. Grapevine*, 13 (Sept., 1956), 5–10.

TILLMANN, Fritz. *Handbuch der katholischen Sittenlehre*. With the collaboration of Th. MUENCKER and Th. STEINBUECHEL. Vol. III. *Die*

Bibliography

Idee der Nachfolge Christi. 2nd ed. Düsseldorf, 1940. Vol. IV, 1 and 2. *Die Verwirklichung der Nachfolge Christi.* 3rd ed. Düsseldorf, 1947.

————. *Der Meister ruft. Eine Laienmoral für gläubige Christen.* Düsseldorf, 1937.

Twelve Steps and Twelve Traditions, The. New York: Harper & Bros., 1953.

VANN, Gerald, O.P. "Unconscious Motivation and Pseudo-Virtue," *Homiletic and Pastoral Review,* 57 (1956), 115–23.

VERMEERSCH, Arthur, S.J. "Soixante ans de théologie morale," *Nouvelle revue théologique,* 56 (1929), 880.

————. *Theologiæ moralis principia, responsa, consilia.* 4 vols. 3rd ed. Rome: Gregorian University, 1947.

VOLLERT, Cyril, S.J. "Original Sin and Education," *Review for Religious,* 5 (1946), 217–28.

WECHSLER, Henry. "The Criteria of Criminal Responsibility," *University Chicago Law Review,* 22 (1955), 367–76.

WEIHOFEN, Henry. "The Flowering of New Hampshire," *University of Chicago Law Review,* 22 (1955), 356–66.

WERNZ, Franz Xavier, S.J. *Ius canonicum.* 6 vols. Revised by J. VIDAL, S.J. Rome: Gregorian University, 1935.

WERTHAM, Frederic. "Psychoauthoritarianism and the Law," *University of Chicago Law Review,* 22 (1955), 336–38.

————. Review of Gregory ZILBOORG's *The Psychology of the Criminal Act and Punishment,* in *University of Chicago Law Review,* 22 (1955), 569–81.

YEAGER, Natalie R. and CONSALVO, Gennaro J. "A Proposal for a Fountainhead of Rationality in the Jurisprudence of Insanity," *Catholic University of America Law Review,* 5 (1955), 63–87.

YOUNG, R. C. "Clinical Observation on the Treatment of the Alcoholic," *Medical Surgical Journal,* 100 (1948), 539–46.

ZALBA, Marcelino, S.J. "Exposición de la moral cristiana," *Estudios eclesiasticos,* 29 (1955), 65–80.

————. "Inquietudes metodológicos en teologia moral," *Arbor* (Madrid), 3 (Mar., 1955), 1–19.

ZEIGER, Ivo, S.J. "De conditione theologiæ moralis moderna," *Periodica de re morali, canonica, liturgica,* 28 (1939), 177–89.

ZILBOORG, Gregory. "Psychoanalytic Borderlines," *American Journal of Psychiatry,* 112 (Mar., 1956), 706–10.

————. *The Psychology of the Criminal Act and Punishment.* New York: Harcourt, Brace & Co., 1954.

————. "A Step Toward Enlightened Justice," *University of Chicago Law Review,* 22 (1955), 331–35.

Index

Index

[362]

Index

Dalbiez, Roland, quoted on free will, 186, 195–96
Dancing, 166–72
Decision, personal, 135–36
De jure et justitia, 45
Delhaye, Ph., critic of moral theology, 47–49
Deliberation in sin, 219–28
De synodo diœcesana, 39
Deux sources, consciente et inconsciente de la vie morale, Les, 192–93
District of Columbia. Court of Appeals, on right-wrong test, 251
Donceel, Joseph, S.J., on Freudian psychology, 324–25
Drinking
pathological, 284n
question of, 289n
Drug addiction, 281n
Duff, Edward, S.J., "ethic of inspiration," 134–35
Duhamel, Joseph S., S.J., on St. Thomas and free actions, 221n–222n
Durham case, 248–53

Enseignement de la morale chrétienne L', 51
Episcopal teaching, 33–41
"Episcopus," on moral theology, 62–64
Ermecke, Gustav, and moral theology, 73–75
Ethical Evaluation and Matrimonial Consent, 274
Ethics, definition, 3. See also "Sin mysticism"; Situation ethics
Existentialism, 130, 135–36
Pius XII on, 104–23 passim

Fabregas, Michael, S.J., on occasions of sin, 154–55
Father Matthew Societies, 310–11
Fazzari, G. M., S.J., Ethical Evaluation and Matrimonial Consent, 274
Felici, Pericle, on psychoanalysis, 313–14

Free association
Pius XII on, 332–33
technique of, 331–33
Free choice, 94–96 passim.
Freedom
degrees of, 207–9
imputability and, 201–47
philosophical, 211–14
psychological, 211–14
Free will, 185–91 passim, 199–200, 203–5
Freudian psychology, Donceel on, 324–25
Freud, Sigmund
and religion, 318–19
philosophy of, 320–24
Fuchs, Joseph, S.J.
on love as basis of morality, 83
on situation ethics, 128–29, 132–33

Gagern, F. von, on self-abuse, 234–35
Garrigou-Lagrange, R., O.P., and moral theology, 49–51
Gilleman, Gérard, S.J.
and moral theology, 76–79
on theology courses, 101–2
Gospel, law of, 92
Grace
and freedom of the will, 198–99
doctrine of, 217–19
Guideposts in judgments of imputability, theological, 214–19
Guild of Catholic Psychiatrists, 313
Guilt
and mental illness, 239–47 passim
neurotic, 344–46
philosophy of, Pius XII on, 263–64
real, Pius XII on, 345–46

Handbook of Christian Morality, 60
Hayes, John J., 313
Hirscher, J. B., Christian Morality as the Doctrine of the Realization of the Kingdom of God in Mankind, 60
Hogan, Abbé, on moral theology, 63

[363]

Index

Index

Index

autonomy of the will, 260–62
conscience, 139–40, 177–78
courtship, 159–60
doctrinal value of teaching, 22–28
existentialism, 104–23 *passim*
film classification, 145
free association, 332–33
frequent confession, 98–99
guilt and punishment, 263–64, 345–46
Humani generis, 31–32
human responsibility, 259–60
intemperance, 310n
magisterium, 23
Magnificate Dominum, 33, 119
medical morality, 17–18
moral teaching of, 20–22
motivation, 196–97
Munificentissimus Deus, 22
new morality, 109–23 *passim*
power of moralists, 89
psychic dynamisms, 323
psychic faculty of man, 321–22
psychoanalysis, 314
psychotherapy, 327–28
rights of the Church, 12–17
Sacramentum ordinis, 22
seal of confession and psychoanalysis, 326n
sin, 217, 226–27
Solennità della Pentecoste, La, 16n–17n
teaching authority of the Church, 33–34
truths of religion, 6–7
Pledge, in alcoholism, 302
Plenary Council. U.S. Second, Baltimore, on money-raising for the Church, 166
Plenary Council. U.S. Third, Baltimore, on money-raising for the Church, 166–67
Pope Speaks, The, on public messages of Pope Pius XII, 20n–21n
Pound, Roscoe, and law, 8
Precept and counsel, 86–87
Priest, cooperation with psychiatrist, 337–44

Primacy of Charity in Moral Theology, The, 76
Prudence, and mortal sin, 150–51
Pseudo-virtues of the unconscious, 191–94
Psychiatrist
   choice of, 336n
   cooperation with priest, 337–44
Psychiatry
   Catholicism and, 313–52
   courses in seminaries, 342
   definition, 318
   "official" attitude of Church toward, 316
   use in Catholic hospitals, 315–16
   use in courts, 315
Psychic determinism, 186–87
Psychic dynamisms, Pius XII on, 323
Psychoanalysis
   definition, 318
   moral law and, 326
   seal of confession and, 326n
   Pius XII on, 314
   psychology of, 324–25
   therapeutic, 325–26
Psychopathic personalities, 268–69
Psychopaths, matrimonial capacity of, 268–75
Psychotherapy, and moral dangers, 327–31
Psychotics and responsibility, 256–57
Public life, and the new morality, 110
Punishment, papal statements on, 259–64

Questions, controverted, 39–40
Quietism, 84n

Rahner, Karl, S.J., and situation ethics, 124–25
Ranwez, E., on love and obligation, 92–93
Raymond of Peñafort, *Summa*, 45
Reason, St. Thomas on, 221
Regan, A., C.SS.R., on occasion of sin, 148–51

[366]

Index

Religion, Pius XII on, 322
Religious education of children, 108–9
Responsibility
 degrees of, 207–9
 for acts while drinking, 295–97
 human, 174–203
  Pius XII on, 259–60
 moral, 249n–250n, 264–68
Restitution, St. Alphonsus on, 155–56
Revelation, necessity of, 4–7
"Right-wrong test," 220n, 251
Royal Commission on Capital Punishment, 252–53
 on psychological medicine, 266
Rule of M'Naghten's Case, cited, 250–51, 262

Sacramentum ordinis (apostolic constitution), 22
Sacred Consistorial Congregation, on dances for pious purposes, 167–68
St. John's University, Collegeville, Minn., noted, 319n
Sanctity, and obligation, 92–96
Schilling, O., and moral theology, 66–67
Schizophrenia, 222–23
Schmidt, John Rogg, on dances for pious purposes, 168–69
Schumacher, Henry C., on psychopaths, 270
Schweitzer, Albert, philosophy of, 8–9
Seiler, J. M., Handbook of Christian Morality, 60
Self-abuse, imputability of, 233–39
Self-assertion, 136–40
Self-love, Beirnaert on, 331
Seminary
 alcohol education in, 308n
 theology in, criticism of, 96–102
Si diligis (allocution), on teaching authority of the Church, 33
Sin
 conditions for responsibility, 205–7

definition of, 254
deliberation of, 219–28
mortal, 216–17
 danger of, 151
 degrees of freedom for, 209–11
 gravity of, 152, 155–57
 proximate occasion, 147–55
 subjective guilt of, 241n
occasions of. See Occasions of sin
original, 343n
Pius XII on, 226–27
venial, 147
Singulari quadam (encyclical), 14–15
"Sin mysticism," 125n
Situation ethics, 124–40
 and the Holy See, 104–23
Situationism, 90, 132, 136–40
Slater, Thomas, S.J., on Vermeersch's moral theology, 62
Snoeck, André, S.J., on masturbation, 237–38
Social question, and the Church, 16n–17n
Solennità della Pentecoste, La (radio message), 16n–17n
State, authority of, 15–16
Sterilization, 29–30
Stern, Karl, criteria of neurotic guilt, 344–45
Stevaux, Albert, and interpretation of Church law, 131
Stress and imputability, 201–47
Supreme Sacred Congregation of the Holy Office, on "situation ethics," 121–23

Teaching
 episcopal, 33–41
 papal, doctrinal and interpretative, 19–32
Teen-age company-keeping, 160–66
Temperance League of America, 310
Ter Haar, Francis, C.SS.R., on occasions of sin, 154–55
Theologiæ moralis principia, responsa, consilia, 61–66
Theologian and papal teaching, 29–32

[367]

Index

A NOTE ON THE TYPE

IN WHICH THIS BOOK WAS SET

This book has been set in Electra, a type face created in 1935 by W. A. Dwiggins, the well-known Boston artist. This type falls within the "modern" family of type styles, but was drawn to avoid the extreme contrast between "thick and thin" elements that marks most "modern" type faces. The design is not based upon any traditional model, and is not an attempt to revive or to reconstruct any historic type. Since its birth, Electra has met with success because of its easy-to-read quality. This book was composed and printed by the York Composition Company, Inc., of York, Pa., and bound by Moore and Company of Baltimore, Md. The design and typography of this book are by Howard N. King